D0929935

# HANDBOOK ON THE MAINTENANCE OF REPTILES IN CAPTIVITY

K.R.G. WELCH

ROBERT E. KRIEGER PUBLISHING COMPANY
MALABAR, FLORIDA
1987

Original Edition 1987

Printed and Published by
ROBERT E. KRIEGER PUBLISHING COMPANY, INC.
KRIEGER DRIVE
MALABAR, FL 32950

Printed in the United States of America

Library of Congress Cataloging-in-Publication Data

Welch, Kenneth R. G.
  Handbook on the maintenance of reptiles in captivity.

  Bibliography: p.
  Includes index.
  1. Reptiles.    2. Wild animals, Captive.
3. Reptiles as pets.    I. Title.
QL665.W45   1987         639.3'9         86-15325
ISBN 0-89874-830-5

10   9   8   7   6   5   4   3   2

# CONTENTS

# PREFACE

Over the years, many conversations with fellow reptile keepers have helped to develop the idea of a Handbook, and to all those who gave their time and thoughts go my thanks. I would like to extend special thanks to all the contributors to this volume: Professor J. L. Cloudsley-Thompson, P. S. Cooke, D. G. Garthwaite, C. J. Howard, Dr. O. F. Jackson, J. W. Verkerk, A. B. van Woerkom, A. S. Wright, and D. Wright. My personal appreciation is extended to A. S. Wright and to my wife, Elizabeth, for help with an early draft.

My intention is to continue the idea presented here over the years to come, and to such an end, all comments on present and future inclusions, as well as references for inclusion, will be appreciated.

# 1

# Maintenance of Reptiles in Captivity

**Introduction.** The aim of this text is not to tell the reader how to keep reptiles but to act as a guide, a base for the beginner to start from, and at least in part, a handbook for the more experienced reptile keeper. The text is divided into four parts. The first is an introduction to the successful maintenance of reptiles in captivity; the second supplies supplementary notes to the introduction; the third gives specific accounts on the keeping of a selection of reptiles in captivity; and finally, the list of species includes references on their maintenance in captivity, breeding results, behaviour, ecology, and other necessary knowledge for keeping those species in captivity. Three appendices are included: the first lists venomous colubrids; the second gives known incubation times (in days) and temperatures (° C) for a variety of species; and the third lists herpetological societies.

The reader now should note the following: hybrids (as compared to natural intergrades, Dunn 1937) are not acknowledged in this book, and no article on crossbreeding is knowingly included within these pages. Hybridization weakens the gene pool, so that resulting young could not and should not be considered for reintroduction of a species to the wild—a consideration, for some reptiles, that may in the not-too-distant future become a reality. Also, the hybrid should not be used in any further breeding program; thus, the breeding of any hybrid is a pointless exercise.

Reptile keepers are under an obligation to study and learn from the animals in their care and should keep all necessary records (p. 22), both to relate that information to their colleagues and, further, to maintain those animals with the highest standards of husbandry, without which the keeper has no right to possess them.

Today there are many reptile breeders whose actions should not be encouraged. It is known that in wild populations of many species, albinos and other freak colour phases occasionally appear but, due to their unnatural colouring, do not survive long. Recent trading has shown that, with care, some breeders can now regularly offer these unnatural forms at an inflated price. Such a weakness in an animal's bloodline (which surely this is) should be avoided in all healthy breeding stock; then, maybe in the not too distant future, this distasteful practice will return to the laboratory—even there the use of unnatural colours is undoubtedly limited.

**First things first.** The initial questions for the would-be reptile keeper are: what species is going to be kept? what is known about that species? how are the animals going to be housed? from where will they be obtained?

The first question is a personal choice. A photograph may catch the eye; a friend may already have that species or may have bred a species and is wanting to find homes for the young. You may find and catch something unusual. Quite often reptile keepers find they have an unexplainable feel for a species.

The second question is of utmost importance and should be fully researched. All details and information collected should be written down and filed with the records you will keep (p. 22). The information collected will be essential in determining how you will keep and care for the animals; it may even determine which species you keep. An important point with many reptiles is identification, and you should record in full the reference used to identify your species. If the species name was confirmed for you, that person's name should also be recorded.

Having decided what species will be kept and having equipped yourself with all available knowledge, you must then decide how they are to be housed. Are they going to be kept inside or outside? A phrase that appears all too often in articles on breeding reptiles is "stimulus used for reproduction." The only stimulus that should be necessary is good husbandry, which calls for consideration of the following points for all reptiles, kept inside or out:

1. **The animals.** How many can be kept together? Are the males territorial? Fighting can result in serious injuries or death. It has been found to be beneficial for many species of snakes to keep the sexes separate except during the mating season.

2. **Space and habitat.** Behaviour will determine how much space is to be given and how it is to be arranged. You should consider whether vegetation is to be included, how much water is needed, and how much shelter is available.

3. **Light.** What length of photoperiod is needed? Do the animals need ultraviolet light? Tonge (1985) showed that the presence of ultraviolet reduced and even eliminated the occurrence of deformities in the lizard *Leiolopisma telfairii*. For reptiles indoors, any form of light decided on will have to be provided; whilst outside, any enclosure built must ensure availability, for at least part of the day, of direct sunlight onto the floor of the enclosure.

4. **Temperature.** What is the preferred temperature of your species? Too high a temperature kills, even in the desert (p. 34). Too low a temperature can result in poor health, inability to digest food properly, and eventual death. Obviously, with reptiles kept outside, there should be plenty of opportunity available for the animals to hide from the rays of the sun. One subject that is rarely discussed is thermoregulation, an understanding of which is essential for all reptile keepers. It is important for all chelonians (Brattstrom and Collins 1972) and lizards (Avery 1979, 1985). Avery (1985) "demonstrated that a knowledge of the diversity of reptilian thermoregulation may help those who want to keep a particular species successfully in captivity. In particular, it may help in devising accommodation which will enable the animals to respond to their environment in similar ways to those in which they do in the field." Thought must also go to the coincidence of light and temperature:

Example: *Epicrates striatus striatus*. Young *Epicrates s. striatus* kept by the author spent most of the day in hiding, becoming active at dusk when the temperature was between 20 ° and 24 °C. If the temperature was too low at dusk, they would be found the following day hiding in a much warmer part of the vivarium. The night of the following day would be accompanied with a much longer period of activity for the snakes.

It is now being realised that hibernation is an essential process for many reptiles, especially now that the benefits of this cooling period on captive reproduction are becoming more obvious (Tryon 1985). Bruyndonck (1984) suggests the use of a fridge, while Finnegan (1984) shows construction of an hibernaculum. One immediate benefit to most keepers is that winter is often a time of food supply problems. If the animal is asleep for three or four months, this problem is removed. An important point for consideration is whether the annimals are ready to enter hibernation. Chelonian keepers have an ideal guide in the weight-against-length graph of Jackson (1980), while other keepers must judge for themselves whether the animals are healthy and have been feeding well up to two weeks prior to commencement of the hibernation period. With reptiles kept outside, the keeper must decide early in the year whether to allow the animals to hibernate freely, a point which must be taken into consideration when constructing any outside enclosure. Alternatively, the animals can be collected and put into a controlled artificial hibernaculum.

5. **Moisture.** How will water be made available? Will the animal need humidity in the air, moisture on or in the ground, or a bowl of drinking water? The animal and its surroundings may need to be sprayed, as many reptiles are known to drink by lapping rain or dew. In all reptiles, including desert species, a bowl of clean water should be available. This should not be taken from the tap, as this can contain chlorine and other harmful substances. In the case of desert reptiles, water need only be available a few days a week. In an outside enclosure, open to the elements, good drainage must be included in its construction, as well as a permanent water supply that will not turn stagnant. What should be remembered in all cases is that too much moisture causes many health problems, such as skin blisters on the venter of snakes, and too little moisture can very quickly lead to death by dehydration.

Example: *Micrurus lemniscatus diutius*. A specimen of this attractive coral snake collected in the wild by this writer was brought home to study. The snake was transported in a tin full of moist leaf litter and arrived home in good condition. It was immediately put into an aquarium with 10 mm of gravel on the floor. A water bowl and a pile of moist moss, the latter covered with a clean piece of bark, completed the vivarium. A young *Natrix natrix helvetica* was available and was put into the vivarium overnight. The following morning the *Natrix* had been eaten, but the *Micrurus* appeared unwell. On close examination, it was found to be dehydrating. The cage was liberally sprayed and the moss sodden with water. The snake temporarily recovered but then again appeared to be dehydrating. Eventually the gravel was deepened to 25 mm and water poured onto the gravel until only the very top of the layer of gravel was actually above water. This proved successful and supported the opinion of J. Boos (personal communication) on *Amphisbaena fuliginosus*.

6. **Food.** What is the required prey-species of your reptile? What size of food is required? How secure is your supply? When keeping reptiles with a restricted diet, it is essential to ensure that a regular supply of food can be guaranteed prior to obtaining the animal. Remember that food requirements can alter with age and size of the reptile. Mineral and vitamin supplements may be needed (p. 19). Care has to be taken when feeding reptiles in an outside enclosure. Insectivorous lizards will be able to catch some of their own food, but this will have to be regularly supplemented. Feeding snakes in an outside enclosure could present many problems. Due to the undoubtedly limited size of any enclosure, a breeding colony of frogs or mice within the enclosure would not be feasible, so food will have to be supplied at regular intervals. Another problem with snakes kept outside is that of being sure all the animals are eating. For this reason, snakes should be examined at regular intervals and, if necessary, fed individually before being returned to the enclosure.

Mice are the commonest source of food used by the majority of snake keepers, and their breeding requires organisation to ensure availability of the right sizes as needed. Frogs are usually collected as required, which, though saving the bother of having to maintain them, does somewhat adversely affect the local populations. If you are keeping a small group of frog-eating snakes and are successfully breeding them, maybe serious thought should be given to maintaining a frog colony (Frost 1982), which, within a few years, would make all sizes available without further depletion of your local populations. A point to note when feeding frogs to snakes, whether the frogs be wild caught, captive bred, or bought from a commercial source, is that Stoskopf and Hudson (1982) recommend encouraging the snakes to take dead frogs that have been kept in a freezer for at least 60 hours. After such a time in the freezer all trematodes seem to die, greatly reducing any chance of infection in the snakes. For insectivorous lizards, many foods—such as mealworms, locusts, and crickets—are available commercially, but when breeding and rearing young or small species, there is often a need for continuous access to small insects that necessitates breeding your own supply. Locust breeding cages are available and the accompanying instructions should be followed. Instructions for the breeding of mealworms (a giant form is now available, Batist 1984), wingless fruit flies, and crickets are presented on P. 24. Garthwaite (1984) gives details for breeding wax moths (*Galleria*) and flour moths (*Ephestia*). Richards (1978) gives details for breeding wax moths (*Galleria*), locusts, wood lice (Oniscoidea), flour beetles (*Tribolium*), house flies (*Musca*), blowflies (*Calliphora, Lucilia, Phormia*), white worms

(*Enchytraeus*), earthworms (Lumbricidae), and cockroaches (*Periplaneta*). Spoczy-nska (1974) discusses the maintenance of many insect species. One should note that two separate colonies must be kept so that if an accident should happen to one colony you still have a food supply in the second.

**Keeping reptiles outside.** The keeping of a local species out-of-doors should pose no real problem other than restricting the animals to a particular area. This can be done either by building a suitable brick wall finished with sand and cement or tiles on the inside so as to stop the animals escaping, or, alternatively, a circle of sheet metal could be put into the ground as suggested by Gray (1985). The area should have direct sunlight and cover, fresh water, and good drainage. Consider also the animals' food and hibernation needs. Langerwerf (1980) maintains large numbers of lacertids outside with continual breeding results. Pozio (1983) constructed a large vivarium off the floor for his studies on *Elaphe situla*. The maintenance of tropical reptiles outside in a temperate climate obviously presents many problems, but Visser (1972) recommends the use of hothouses or greenhouses.

A point of interest when keeping reptiles outside is the apparent qualitative and quantitative behavioural changes (in lizards) due to ultraviolet light and visible light intensity (Ditmars 1933, Moehn 1974, 1976). Ditmars (1933) also included fresh air in his comment on behavioural differences between reptiles kept inside or outside. See also the example *Bitis arietans* on p. 8 of this volume.

**Keeping reptiles inside.** Most reptiles, whether local or otherwise, are kept inside; to house them, a vivarium has to be constructed, with due consideration of the following points:

1. **Main structure.** This can be wood with a glass front; an all-glass aquarium; sheet metal cages with glass fronts; fibre glass with sliding glass doors on the front, or any combination of the materials. The choice is personal, while also considering the reptiles' needs. Obviously all-glass caging is needed for aquatic reptiles, and this writer prefers all glass or fibre glass for desert reptiles. Wood can be the most attractive when the vivarium is to be kept in the living room, though problems quickly appear if the wrong wood is used for reptiles requiring high humidity. One important point of structure in respect of venomous reptiles is to be able to clean the cage without endangering the keeper. One method used with heavy-bodied viperids is to place the snake in a bin or box while the cage is being cleaned. This method would obviously be impossible with, for example, mambas (*Dendroaspis*). Another method is to use a secure hide, which can be shut by the keeper from outside the vivarium after the reptile has entered; a more reliable method is to build a groove into the cage on three sides (back, top, and bottom or bottom, back, and front) with a slot in the fourth side (front or top respectively). Care should be taken to keep the slot

as narrow as possible so that any young or small inmates will not escape. When required, a sheet of metal or suitable board is inserted into the slot so as to run into the grooves, effectively dividing the cage in two. When this is done, the empty side of the cage is cleaned; then the process is repeated after the reptile has been encouraged into the clean half. Such a vivarium obviously needs two lids—one for each half and working independently. Actual structural arrangements within the vivarium for various habitats have been presented by Capezzone (1979) and Benson (1983) for semiaquatic reptiles; Pickering (1982), Willemsens (1971), Wales (1982), and Pearson (1984) for the African boid *Calabaria*; and Woerkom (this volume, pages 48–51) for *Eryx*. For those who intend to maintain large collections, Pawley (1971) suggests a very practical method for shelving all-glass vivariums in large numbers.

2. **Substrate.** This is often the point of most discussion amongst reptile keepers, trying to balance between what is pleasing to the eye and what is ideal for the reptile, while remembering that hygiene is the main consideration. There are various options open to the keeper, including:

a) gravel—The size of gravel used is of great importance as the animal is likely to consume gravel with its food. If the gravel is too large, this may cause serious internal problems.

b) sand—If swallowed in quantity, this may become impacted in the gut, particularly in pregnant females, also causing serious internal problems.

c) peat—Frequent changing is necessary, but it does retain moisture well.

d) leaf litter—The considerations are the same as with peat.

e) soil—This is not recommended.

f) newspaper—Newspaper has an immediately obvious advantage as it is easily replaced and has become standard with many keepers. This writer prefers to see the use of newspaper restricted to either quarantine, temporary, or nursery cages, or for animals temporarily separated from others. Tonge (1985) noted that skinks (*Leiolopisma telfairii*) kept on newspaper suffered with a variety of foot problems (long nails, twisted toes, accumulation of shed skin on the feet) that did not occur when the skinks were kept on a sand substrate.

With regard to substrate, this writer prefers to cover part of the floor with gravel and the remainder with a tray of a suitable substrate. The substrate can be discarded at regular periods, being immediately replaced with fresh material. Such an arrangement has been found essential in feeding *Cylindrophis rufus* (see Example, page 13). If such an arrangement is to be used, the tray can also be used as an egg-laying site, which would ease the removal of any eggs from the cage to an incubator. Care also must go to the choice of natural substrate, as each species has its own preference (Clark 1968).

3. **Light.** The lighting of a vivarium should be as unobtrusive as possible. One immediate question is the length of photoperiod, which varies with latitude (as shown by the lengthy tables of Jones 1978). Generally, most reptiles will respond to your local photoperiods. Secondary lighting (usually a light bulb, which can be one source, or the sole source, of heating) should be restricted to a short period of the day, thus allowing dawn and dusk to arrive

naturally. The second question regarding light is that of quality ultraviolet. As previously noted, Ditmars (1933) and Moehn (1974, 1976) reported behavioural changes in lizards that appeared to be linked to ultraviolet. Other problems that can occur due to lack of ultraviolet are reduced availability of D vitamins needed to absorb calcium (Tonge (1985) (Wallach 1970, 1971), increased deformities, and shorter lives (Tonge 1985). Tonge (1985) installed an ultraviolet source (in the 300–400 nm range) within 100 mm of the substrate surface, for full benefit, while Cooper and others (1983) suggested that the presence *or* absence of ultraviolet may trigger any underlying genetic problem. Recently, despite Tremper (1982) speaking in favour of black light fluorescent tubes, others have found that their use can be correlated with speeding up growth and causing severe eye damage to reptiles (A. S. Wright, personal communication) and should be avoided. Further references are Lang (1970); Laszlo (1969); Logan (1969); and Regal (1980).

4. **Heating.** As with lighting, the heating of a vivarium should be as unobtrusive as possible. A simple method—particularly when a number of cages are involved—is to heat the room to a suitable temperature and, when necessary, add a small amount of supplementary heating to each cage by way of a light bulb, which will encourage the reptiles to bask. Pickering (1982) suggests heating pads (as used by the plumbing trade) under the cages, supplemented by suitable light bulbs. In heating, thermoregulation requirements of the species are important, and one must not forget that nocturnal reptiles may also bask (Avery 1985). For further references, see Logan (1972) and Regal (1980).

5. **Air.** Ventilation is essential in a vivarium, and is usually obtained by vents of a suitable size in the lid or on one of the sides. Some species benefit from the introduction of cooler air at night.

> Example: *Bitis arietans*: a group of this heavy-bodied viper was maintained in captivity. All were feeding well but appeared somewhat limp in their general behaviour. Air was pumped into the cage at night, causing a rapid drop in temperature over a period of a couple of hours around dusk. Within a few days, the snakes became more active and their appetites increased. A slower air change had a similar effect on a group of *Bitis nasicornis*.

6. **Water.** Fresh water should always be available, even with desert reptiles—some of which may occasionally spend long periods bathing. Tap water should be avoided, in case of chlorine and other harmful substances. The cage and its occupants may require spraying, as many species are known to drink droplets of dew or rain. If the animal is semiaquatic, where a large quantity of water will be needed, the waste system used by the plumbing industry could be used. Furthermore, it is essential in a semiaquatic situation to ensure a dry area, as reptiles kept in overdamp conditions with no opportunity

to dry off will develop blisters. If blisters do develop in your reptile, remove it from the cage. Place it in a dry, warm temporary cage with only a small bowl of water for drinking. Rearrange the main cage to include a dry area before returning the reptile to it.

7. **Hides.** Two hides should be included in the vivarium. If only one is present, the animal has no choice of temperature at which to hide. Placing two hides at opposite ends of the temperature range within the vivarium at least gives your reptile a choice. Some reptile keepers neglect hides, which prevent them from seeing their animals for long periods of time. One solution is the use of transparent hides as suggested by Radcliffe and Chiszar (1983). This works well for snakes, in spite of the fact that the snakes can see out and be seen, suggesting that it is the confined space and not the darkness that the snakes need. Subterranean reptiles are often neglected, due to their greater need to hide, but they can be interesting to keep if given a hide in the form of a sheet of perspex, as suggested by Mehrtens (1962) for amphisbaenids. With arboreal species a branch is, at least in part, a hide. One must be sure that there is not just one high point (which is often immediately below a light bulb); there should be two, again at different ends of the temperature range, within the vivarium.

8. **Plants.** The decision about the use of real or artificial plants is a difficult and often personal point. Real plants are easily damaged or the soil around their base dug up by the inmates. This would require regular replacement. Plants may also carry unwanted germs into the cage. Goedings (1972) suggests careful choice and use of plastic plants, while Wright (this volume, p. 42) uses real plants in a tropical house.

9. **Labelling.** All cages should be clearly marked with the correct name and the number of inmates. If the inmates are venomous, this should be clearly stated where everyone can see.

You have decided on the species, you have researched its behaviour and needs, you have secured a supply of food, and you have prepared a vivarium. Now you are ready to obtain your specimen. Captive-bred specimens purchased from a breeder or friend are usually healthy specimens with few worries, though third/ fourth generation of some species (e.g., of the genus *Lampropeltis*) appear to be born with digestive problems that usually result in early death. However, both buying and collecting can have pitfalls, and the following points should be noted:

—the animal should appear alert; check whether it pulls back from sudden movement or lies in your hands when picked up.
—the animal should not be thin. Check the vertebrae on the back; if they are very obvious, the animal is undoubtedly underfed or unwell.
—with snakes, the animal should lie coiled up or partly so. A snake laid out straight is probably unwell.

—check the head and mouth. Does the mouth shut completely? Is the snout damaged? Are the eyes clear, with no eye scales left on from the last time the animal shed its skin?

—are there any ticks and mites? Scales sticking out can be a sign of mites even if none are visible.

—are there any scars on the animal, and if so, are they completely healed and clean?

—check if faeces are present in the cage. Are they clear? Check whether the vent of the animal is clean or gummed up.

—consider the age of the animal. How long do the species live? Many references on the ecology of a population of a specific species often tabulate known ages of the specimens in their study. Bowler (1977) lists known ages of many captive specimens. This point is of great importance when obtaining small lizards and snakes, as many species have a very short expected life span.

—notice the handling of the reptiles by the vendor. Many people, even with harmless snakes, freely use heavy leather gloves, resulting in careless handling. In snakes, this can so easily break off teeth, which may result in mouth infections.

—note any other signs of ill health (p. 26). Occasionally, due to personal reasons or the rarity of a species, you may decide to purchase a sick animal. If so, think long and hard. If possible, contact a knowledgeable vet before completing the purchase.

The animal has been purchased, brought home, and put into quarantine (p. 28). After a period of time, a healthy and thriving animal is transferred to its vivarium. Now there are other points to be considered.

**Handling reptiles.** Handle reptiles only when necessary, i.e., at the moment of capture, medical examination, moving house. To assist in handling or moving snakes, a variety of sticks are available (Coote 1984). Ionides (1965) details safe methods of handling venomous and nonvenomous snakes. A simple and often easy way to bag snakes prior to moving is to drop a bag onto the floor of the vivarium; with patience or encouragement, the reptile will enter the bag as if it was a hide. For long periods of handling large or dangerous reptiles, as in a veterinary examination, anaesthesia can be used (Harding 1977). Many methods have been detailed for the handling of snakes: King and Duvall (1984), Ward and Harrell (1978), Freed and Freed (1983), Murphy (1971), Gillingham and others (1983), Ball (1974), and Barker (1979); for the handling of large lizards: Barker (1979); and for the handling of large turtles: Galbraith and Brooks (1983). Small lizards are at great risk when being handled. For example, when collecting *Gonatodes vittatus* in Trinidad, this writer found some to have died from shock.

Gloves have been mentioned by many, but great thought should be given to their use. Thick strong leather gloves are useful when handling large lizards (e.g., *Varanus*) or medium crocodilians, to help prevent the handler from being injured by the reptile's tail or claws. Gloves should never be used when handling snakes or small lizards, as they interfere with your own degree of control. This can very quickly result in the injury of the animal. If it bites into the glove, it will more than likely break off some of its teeth, which could result in future mouth infection.

**Identifying individual specimens.** It is necessary for the records that are being kept on each specimen (p. 22) that each can, in turn, be positively identified. Ferner (1979) suggests many ways of marking individuals, most of which, though ideal for field work, are unwarranted in the vivarium—mainly due to the fact that rarely are many kept together at any time. Where more specimens than one are kept together, and there is no obvious difference in size, a note should be made in the records as to how each is identified. Two suggestions are the following:

—markings. Rarely will two specimens of one species have exactly the same pattern, and the head or the tail is the easiest place to note any differences. This writer found, while keeping a colony of *Crotalus adamanteus*, that the pale yellow markings on the front of the snout (upper and lower jaw) were ideal for individual identification. Observing the belly of many reptiles is another sure way, with your notes recording the markings of the first half-dozen ventrals.
—scars. If a specimen has a scar, this makes identification easy, though after a number of sheddings, small scars may disappear. It may be helpful to collect the shed skin of your reptile to keep with the records, thus confirming exactly where the scar is (Henley 1981). A broken tail is an obvious scar in lizards.

**Measuring.** It is always of great interest to keep a record of rate of growth of your reptile, but such a simple idea can have its problems. The first consideration must be to avoid stress in the animal. Chelonians can be readily turned on their back and their plastron measured from front to back. Large reptiles may need to be hand-held; with large pythons this may entail obtaining assistance, so that every metre of the animal is held firmly, with an extra person at the head. With the specimen held firmly but carefully, another person runs a length of string along the back of the snake and cuts it for length. The snake is returned to its vivarium and the string measured. Another successful and apparently easy method for measuring large pythons, where no help is needed, has been related to this writer. It is as follows:

Take two pieces of lightly adhesive tape—for example, masking tape—of a known length, say, 100 mm. Start from the back of the head and stick one piece of tape gently to the snake on the vertebral line. The second piece is than placed directly behind the first, again on the vertebral line. You have now measured 200 mm (excluding the head). Record this by marking two strokes on a piece of paper. Remove the foremost strip and place it directly behind the second and remaining strip. Add a further stroke on your paper. Repeat the process, being sure to make a note each time you do so, until you reach the tail tip. As with all methods for measuring large snakes, it is not 100% accurate, but this method can be done by only one or two operatives, with very little stress to the animal. The head can be measured with a hand-held ruler or estimated.

With small and medium-size reptiles, a fairly simple method is with a box—a piece of foam sponge covering its bottom—and a sheet of perspex just small enough to fit inside the box, plus a felt tip pen. The foam sponge is laid on the floor of the box and the reptile introduced. The perspex is then lowered into the box so as to trap the reptile between the sponge and perspex. Pressure is gently applied to stop the reptile from moving. Then, with the felt pen, a line is marked following the middle of the back of the specimen. The perspex is removed so the line can be measured, and the animal returned to its vivarium. Hudnall (1982) suggests chilling for slowing down the reptile, but many species would undoubtedly suffer from the process.

**Feeding problems.** Once in a vivarium, the animal must eat. Often this is a simple matter of putting food into the vivarium at the right time and temperature, where it is readily consumed. Occasionally, feeding can be a problem. There are various possible reasons for a reptile to refuse food:

—The animal may be unwell or hurt in some way.
—If the animal is wild-caught, it may have been caught just prior to its winter or summer rest, so it would have no interest in food. A. S. Wright (personal communication) found when keeping *Python regius* that although the animals' behaviour was as expected and the snakes were freely mating every year, the animals refused to eat for seven months of the year. During the remaining five months, the snakes ate avidly. The feeding and nonfeeding periods of the snakes appeared to coincide with the wet and dry seasons of their range in West Africa.
—Many species, especially snakes, do fast for long periods without suffering any ill effects.
—Many species, especially snakes, do not feed during mating season or while pregnant.

Presuming the problem is none of the above, check that the temperature is correct; check that you are feeding at the right time of day; and reconsider the arrangement within the vivarium.

Example: *Cylindrophis rufus*. A small colony of this fascinating Asian snake was kept in a vivarium with gravel floor. One-quarter of the floor was a tray of peat covered with damp moss and a piece of bark. The snakes were offered worms, frogs, snakes and pinkies (pink mice) but all the snakes eventually died without eating anything. A few years later, the opportunity arose to keep this species again. The snakes were put into a vivarium arranged as with the previous specimens and allowed a few weeks to settle down. An intensive program of encouraged feeding was then started. Finally, a method was found to feed this species. A snake was put into a jam jar barely big enough for the snake to coil up tightly on the floor of the jar. Food in the form of pinkies was dropped into the jar and then the jar was half filled with damp moss. Light was excluded from the jar. Half an hour later the snake had eaten three pinkies (compare this method with the feeding of *Eryx* in bags, as suggested by Woerkom, this volume, page 49). Next, the feeding had to be transferred to the vivarium. A small hollow was made on the peat floor in the vivarium and a nest of pinkies laid in it. These were covered with moss, and the moss was covered with a piece of bark. With such an arrangement, the mice were found and eaten. If the mice were left on the floor of the vivarium, whether on the gravel or the peat, they were still not eaten.

Change the food offered until the animal responds by feeding.

Example: *Ptyas carinatus*. A large (over two metres long) specimen, though appearing to be well, would not feed on mammals, birds, or amphibians, as suggested by the literature. Eventually a snake, *Natrix natrix helvetica,* nearly one metre in length was offered. The *Natrix* was immediately killed and eaten. From that day, the *Ptyas carinatus* would eat mammals, birds, and amphibians as long as snakes were also offered at least every fourth or fifth meal.

Example: *Boiga dendrophila*. Four large specimens of this beautiful Asian snake were kept in the same cage. Three were feeding regularly on a variety of mammals, birds, and frogs. The fourth was refusing all the food offered. The fourth was finally put into a cage with a specimen of *Ptyas korros* nearly as long as the *Boiga*. The *Ptyas* was immediately killed and eaten. This *Boiga dendrophila* continued to refuse all food offered other than snakes.

Example: *Crotalus horridus*. A collection of viperids, ten species of three genera were to be maintained on a diet of laboratory white mice, but one specimen of *Crotalus horridus* showed no interest in the food offered. Eventually it was fed on hamsters, which remained the only food that it would accept.

Example: *Ptyas mucosus*. A very large specimen of this snake (in excess of three metres) was kept in a proportionally large vivarium. It was essential that it had plenty of privacy and a varied diet. Rarely would it accept the same food at two consecutive feedings.

Another factor in feeding is that many species change their diet as they grow older, and their habits/habitat may also change.

Example: *Trimeresurus albolabris*. Welch (1978) showed that to encourage newborn *albolabris* to feed, their caging and food had to be very different from the adults. The adults fed readily on mice and lizards, and they spent all their time in the branches that had been put into the cage. Even when feeding, they rarely came to the floor, preferring to hang from a low branch and pluck their food off the floor. The young, however, had to be kept in a damp cage with a thick carpet of leaf litter. No branches were needed, and the only food accepted by the snakes was newly metamorphosed frogs. The snakes would only feed at night and the cage had to be freely sprayed around dusk.

If there is still no obvious reason why the animal is refusing to feed, the keeper may be forced to intervene in order to encourage the animal to begin to feed itself.

Odour manipulation can be of great use in cases where a snake generally eats mice as only part of its diet, but the particular snake you have comes from a population that tends away from mammals. These snakes often need great encouragement to eat mice alone. A mouse can be wrapped in shed snake or lizard skin, or the mouse can be rubbed with the body fluids of a dead snake or lizard. Often, after a few such meals, the snake will then take mice of its own accord.

Often a reptile will eat only rarely or eat so little that the animal is obviously wasting away. Its meals can be increased with the aid of a pair of tweezers. When the reptile is actually eating, have a second freshly killed prey ready. As the first is being swallowed, introduce the second into the reptile's mouth by using the tweezers. As long as you make no sudden movement, the animal will continue to eat, swallowing both as if they were one. Care must be taken with snakes that have good eyesight (e.g., *Elaphe*) as they may not take kindly to the intrusion.

Many reptile keepers do not want to feed their animals live food—either for fear of damage to the snake or a genuine revulsion to the act of a reptile killing a mouse—preferring to use freshly killed mice. Many reptiles, particularly nonsnakes, will readily take dead mice. Snakes occasionally can be encouraged by leaving the mouse in the cage overnight, though if there is more than one snake in the cage, this is not recommended. You may awake in the morning to find one plump snake, as a result of two snakes eating the same mouse from opposite ends. Other snakes may need encouragement at first and sometimes for a very long period of time. There are several ways of overcoming this problem:

—if the snake is obviously hungry, hunting for food, drop a dead mouse immediately in front of the snake's head; this may result in an immediate response.
—a mouse may be held by tweezers and shaken in front of the snake.
—a mouse held by tweezers may be gently slapped across the snout of the snake.
—a mouse held by tweezers may be dragged along the floor of the cage, across the path of the snake.

Live food must never be left overnight, or unsupervised for any length of time, in a vivarium. This writer left three mice in a cage with two large *Calloselesma rhodostoma*. The following morning, both snakes had eaten a mouse, but the third mouse had eaten half the head of the larger of the two snakes. The writer's entry into the reptile house disturbed the mouse, and the live snake struck out and immediately ate its second mouse. Warner (1979) also reports losing a young *Python molurus bivittatus* to a mouse.

Many reptiles are specialised feeders and do not respond to any number of tricks to change. You must ensure access to the necessary food before obtaining any such reptile. One example is the elapid genus *Bungarus* (the kraits), with which, on many occasions, this writer has made use of many tricks to no avail— all the specimens eating immediately when they were offered a live snake.

Occasionally one is unfortunate, particularly with snakes, in having a species or an old specimen which, despite your research and hard work, will still not eat. The ribs become more obvious, and the animal is steadily starving to death. It is now that force feeding has to be considered (Bogerd 1981), (Bruyndonckx 1981), (Kauffeld 1953), (Radcliffe 1975), (Stoel 1981). There are several different ways of force feeding. The following methods may be used, depending on the degree of cooperation on the part of the snake:

—a freshly killed prey is put into the mouth of the snake, which then accepts and swallows it. Often the snake may hang onto the prey without actually swallowing it. Carefully place the snake onto the floor of the cage, where it may lay for some time before swallowing or rejecting the prey. If the food is rejected, try again. Persistence often succeeds.
—a freshly killed prey is put into the mouth of the snake, which then tries to reject it. As the snake widens its mouth to reject, slowly and very carefully push the prey into the throat with the help of a blunt instrument. When the food is out of sight, the underside of the snake should be massaged to encourage the passage of the food down to the stomach. Often the passage into the throat can be made easier by dipping any prey into water, milk, or raw egg before starting.

—an artificial diet of minced beef, raw eggs, vitamins, glucose, and milk should be made up in a liquid form. Using a syringe with a fine rubber tube in place of a needle, insert the tube well down the throat of the reptile. Exert slow and steady pressure on the syringe. Great care must be taken, as it is easy to apply too much pressure too suddenly, causing the reptile's stomach to rupture. With the young or small reptile, the meat can be omitted for the first few feeds.

The feeding of young animals is often a simple matter of having smaller prey food. The feeding of baby snakes, however, even with the correct size and kind of food, can often be a problem (Applegate 1984), (Coote and Riches 1978). One of the following ideas should help:

—a different environment may be required. The adult animals may be thriving, feeding, and breeding in the vivarium, but many species require a different environment when young (this writer has found that this applies very often to arboreal species of snakes), for example, *Trimeresurus albolabris*, p. 14.
—try odour manipulation, p. 14.
—use methods for encouraged feeding, p. 14.
—some young snakes respond to movement of live prey, while others are apparently put off by movement, so dead prey may have to be used. Damage the nose of the prey to make it bleed and this will often evoke a feeding response.
—with young that have natural aggression, it is often easy to get the awkward feeders started by provoking them into striking at the prey by persistently prodding them with it—they strike, hold on, and, providing you keep still, will then proceed to devour their "aggressor".
—place the young in a bag with the prey (as for *Eryx*, p. 49).

**Sexing**. It should be the intention of all keepers to breed the animals in their care. The first step towards this is being sure of the sex of all the individual animals. Taxonomic revisions at species or genus level are an immediate reference, usually confirming if sex is determinable by colour, size, limb proportions, or subcaudal numbers. The sexing of many lizards of various families has been discussed by Howard (1984). In snakes, the males usually have a proportionally longer tail, which may also show a thickening at the base. Care should be taken with some species of snakes, e.g., *Lampropeltis*, in which the females have large scent glands at the base of their tail. Clark (1967) presented comparative morphological data correlating sexual differences in relative tail length in many species of fossorial North American snakes. Blanchard (1931) discussed several secondary sex characteristics. Sex probing in snakes (Fitch 1960; Laszlo 1975; Schaefer 1934) is NOT recommended. This can be difficult and dangerous, and it is always stressful to the snake. The widely practised probing of newborn snakes is totally unnecessary as light pressure at the base of the tail will often help to determine sex (Gregory 1983) and is probably just as reliable.

**What happens when they mate or the female is pregnant?** Many articles list "stimuli used," but as already stated, there is no need for stimuli other than good husbandry. The latter may include fluctuation in food supply, separation of the sexes until the mating season, temperature and light (Laszlo 1977) (Jones 1978), rainfall and moisture (Brown and Sexton 1973) (Stamps 1976), and even the idea of recorded thunderstorms could be useful. Before keeping reptiles, all these points must be considered, although their individual importance can vary with the species. The breeding of various specific groups has been generally discussed by others: boas (Huff 1980), pythons (Ross 1980), colubrids (Coote 1985), (Osborne 1985), lacertids (Langerwerf 1980c). General notes on mating times and size of clutch or brood have been presented for many species by Fitch (1970).

When a female is known to be pregnant, it is recommended that she be moved to a cage of her own, where the temperature can be increased by a few degrees. With oviparous species, a suitable substrate (p. 7) can be made available for her to lay her eggs on or in. While pregnant, many snakes do not eat. If the keeper is unsure, food should be offered but, presuming that the female is otherwise healthy, do not worry unduly if the food is refused.

In an indoor vivarium and with viviparous species all the keeper can do is ensure cleanliness, correct temperature, clean water, food if required, and be patient. When the young are born, it is advisable to remove them all to a nursery vivarium, with separate vivariums for each if possible, as this will make controlled feeding that much easier for the keeper. A habit observed with snakes of the subfamily Boinae is the eating of stillborn young (Groves 1980) (Huff 1980) (Neill and Allen 1962) (Townson 1978, 1985) and occasionally the eating of living young (Huff 1980). Though I have found no record of other species eating their stillborn young, it is known that many species are cannibalistic, and it would be wise to be cautious.

Occasionally an oviparous reptile may fail to ovoposit. The reasons for this can include general malnutrition, wrong environment or temperature, and unsuitable egg-laying substrate (McGurty 1982). If these criteria are satisfied, the reason for nonoviposition is probably medical and a vet should be consulted (Feldmann 1984). In the case of oviparous species, especially in snakes, egg laying is usually preceded by a period of noticeable hyperactivity in the female in her search for an egg site. There is usually also a postcoital slough, seven to twenty-seven days prior to actual laying (Coote 1985). When the eggs are laid, it is wise to remove them to an incubator. Reptiles kept out-of-doors will undoubtedly lay eggs unnoticed by the keeper. If you do notice egg laying in an outdoor vivarium, you could fence off the site and leave them to the elements.

The fence would give some protection to the eggs while incubating and would also restrict the movement of the hatchlings until you can collect and remove them to a nursery.

Whether laid outside or inside, the moving of reptile eggs provokes great debate. Many writers say it is imperative that the eggs remain in the same position as they are laid; if not, careless handling can result in suffocation of the embryo due to alteration of the air space within each egg (Ross 1978) (Schouten 1985) (Tryon 1978b). Pritchard (1979) states that the removal of the eggs from the laying site should be done immediately, for when removed more than one day later, the young will be killed. After a few months, with the young well developed within the egg, they may again be moved. Others such as Feldman (1983) and Marcellini and Davis (1982), have found little difference in hatch rate between disturbed and undisturbed eggs. Riches (1976) reports successful hatching of eggs of *Natrix natrix natrix* sent to him through the post. Many reptiles lay eggs that adhere to each other, which promotes further debate. Coote and Riches (1978) recommended separation of *Lampropeltis* eggs, while Riches (1976) advocated nonseparation. Wright (1986) successfully separated and hatched eggs of *Lampropeltis getulus floridana*.

If the keeper decides to remove the eggs, this should be done quickly and with great care. The eggs should be put immediately into a secure and safe incubator (Gray 1984), on a suitable substrate (McGurty 1982), or in a container (Tryson 1975) in an incubator. All containers should be clearly marked with the name of the species, the number of eggs laid, and the date they were laid. Appendix II lists recorded lengths of incubation for a variety of species. The keeper should note that some chelonians may hatch in as little as eight weeks, but some species are known to actually overwinter in the egg. Therefore, unless an egg is obviously spoiled, do not break it open (Pritchard 1979) until the majority have been hatched for a period of time.

Claessen (1979), in his discussion on the mechanics of egg incubation, states that eggs absorb water predominantly from the substrate, so it is essential that the eggs are placed on or in moist substrate and not just left in moist air. A popular substrate is vermiculite. Tryon (1975) recommends (for semiaquatic chelonian eggs) one ounce of vermiculite to one fluid ounce of water, in sealed jars or aquaria. A well-sealed lid removes the need to add any extra water, though the lid should be removed for one or two minutes every two weeks to replenish the oxygen, the lid then being resealed. Pritchard (1979) states that tortoise eggs should be kept dry, with the eggs of semiaquatic chelonians being kept in humid conditions. Suitable humidity is obtained by blowing up a plastic bag with the eggs inside, and tying the mouth of the bag straightaway. The humidity contained in one's breath is then maintained throughout incubation. Coote (1985), in his discussion on hatching colubrid eggs, recommends a heater pad below a false mesh floor controlled by a solid-state aquarium thermostat keeping the temperature at 25 to 30 °C. Higher temperatures are not recommended, as excessive incubation temperatures are being linked with a vareity of hatchling deformities. Equal weights of vermiculite and water are used as the incubation medium, with each clutch being in its own styrofoam box. The boxes are opened daily to allow adequate air exchange, as there is some evidence that inadequate oxygen availability during incubation leads to spinal deformities in hatchlings. Many species of geckos lay their eggs and adhere them to the walls of the vivarium; these are best incubated where they are (see pages 38–41).

Fungus occasionally appears on eggs. This should be gently wiped off and the egg returned to a drier medium. Eventually, with little trouble, the eggs will hatch or live young will be born. Although the young will undoubtedly give immense pleasure to the keeper, the first few months of life are the most difficult and important. The main problem is the food supply, and the actual act of feeding by the young (p. 16). Tremper (1978) discusses the care of hatchling tortoises.


**Ill health in reptiles.** There is no intention here to include treatments for sick reptiles, as it is essential that the keeper develop a good relationship with his local veterinary surgeon. Many veterinary surgeons have either limited or no experience of treating reptiles, so it may be beneficial to introduce to the veterinarian in the early days the works of Frye (1973) (1981); Marcus (1981); Hoff, Frye, and Jacobson (1984); Cowie (1976); Cooper and Jackson (1981); Townson and Lawrence (1985); Townson and others (1980); Cooper and others (1985); Murphy (1975); Claessen (1982) (1983); Reichenbach-Klinke and Elkan (1965); Hingley (1983); and Ippen, Schroder, and Elze (1985).

If the animal becomes unwell (p. 26), the veterinary surgeon should be visited immediately. Problems that most keepers may deal with themselves include mites (p. 30) and ticks. Most cases of these come with new stock, so quarantine (p. 28) is essential. If ticks are found, each should be covered with a drop of alcohol and then gently picked off with tweezers. The cage should be thoroughly cleaned and all its furniture disposed of.

Prevention is better than cure; a healthy specimen kept in hygienic conditions should give few problems. One area where the keeper can help prevent any problems is that of nutritional diseases (Berger 1983; Claessen 1982; Millichamp 1981). After an initial period of quarantine, when ticks and mites will be cleared and the faeces sent for examination, the animal should be fed a varied diet, and where possible, ultraviolet light should be used. Calcium and vitamin $D_3$ are of some importance to reptiles, the latter apparently more so for lizards than snakes. When snakes are healthy and fed a varied diet, a multivitamin supplement should not be needed, and is believed by many to be harmful. If the snake is fed poultry, $D_3$ will have to be added, while snakes fed on plain meat will need calcium and $D_3$. With regard to lizards, Langerwerf (1980)—who has considerable experience with breeding lacertids in extremely large numbers—recommends adding one teaspoon of calcium lactate and

10,000 i.u. of $D_3$ to one litre of drinking water, with pregnant females being fed insects sprinkled with the mixture. One should take care, as too much $D_3$ results in hard, wiry-appearing animals. Lang (1970) urges the use of ultraviolet light in preference to any $D_3$ supplement.

# 2

# Supplementary Notes

# 2.1

# Record Keeping

## Oliphant F. Jackson

I have found, over the years, that I learned a great deal from the study of the records that I kept. They may seem of little consequence at the time, but when things go wrong, that is when records are worth their weight in gold. In fact, it is only by the study of good records that some of the diseases of reptiles have come to be recognised. When compiling a record, it is useful to follow a pattern for different species and I suggest the following.

*For snakes ·*
Start by giving the species of snake, both by its common and by its scientific name, then its sex and how it was sexed. Note from whom or where it was obtained and as much information about its diet and habitat in the wild as you are able to glean from books. From this stage on, record things in a tabular form:

| Date | Quantity and type of food eaten | Weight at a particular stage, such as after sloughing | Length measured at the same time as weight | General comments and observations (sloughs, odd signs, medications given, etc.) |
|------|------|------|------|------|

*For any kind of lizard*

As with snakes, name the reptile, give the origin, and write about its diet and habitat in the wild.

| Date | Food preferences noted | Activity pattern in the vivarium | Weight | General comments and observations |
|------|------|------|------|------|

*For chelonians*

The type of record that is kept will vary, depending on whether the animal is an aquatic, semiaquatic, or terrestrial species; also, far fewer records can be maintained if the chelonian is free in a garden or pond. Nevertheless, it is important to weigh and measure chelonians on a regular basis. It is important because that is about the only way in which you will be able to tell what goes on inside the "bony box."

Use the preliminary headings as for snakes and lizards:

| Date | Carapace length between verticals in millimetres | Weight in grams | Comments such as on weather conditions, temperature, moving of animal inside or outside and data about hibernation, etc. |
| --- | --- | --- | --- |

## 2.2

# Maintenance of a Food Supply:
# Mealworms, Fruit Flies, and Crickets

A note on the maintenance of a breeding stock of mealworms, fruit flies, and crickets is here included. The three are probably the easiest and most convenient to maintain for insectivorous reptiles. Again the reader is reminded that at least two separate colonies should be maintained, so that if any mishap befalls one, another is immediately available.

*Mealworms:* A glass or metal container should be filled up to within 100 mm of the top with alternating layers of bran (50 mm deep) and sacking/heavy cotton. A starting culture of a minimum 100 g of mealworms is then introduced and the lid securely fitted. This lid should also keep out all light. Fresh food in the form of bread and vegetable and fruit peelings should be given every two days, after removing the remains of all previous meals. Vegetable peelings will keep the general humidity up and help prevent cannibalism. The life cycle is slow if the stock is kept at room temperature, an ideal temperature being between 25 and 30 °C.

Risdon (1982) recommends one layer of bran covered with a flat electrically heated pad (as used by greenhouse workers), under which the mealworms will group and where their life cycle is greatly speeded up. A combination of the above methods would undoubtedly give the keeper great control over quantity and size as needed.

*Fruit flies:* First, a medium has to be prepared with the following ingredients: wholemeal flour, sugar, agar, methyl-p-hydroxybenzoate and water. Mix 300 g of wholemeal flour, 150 g of sugar, 15 g of agar and 500 cm$^3$ of cold water. Add this steadily, continually stirring into one litre of freshly boiled water. Return the whole mixture to the heat and simmer for 20 minutes, with occasional stirring. Remove from the heat and stir in 12 cm$^3$ of 10% methyl-p-hydroxybenzoate (an antifungus preservative) in 96% ethanol. Pour the medium, while it is still warm, into suitable containers and then store in the deep freeze. As required, a container of medium can be thawed and placed with a suitable number of adults in a large glass jar with a lid of fine gauze. If the fruit flies are needed only for a short period—perhaps the first few months of a newborn lizard's life, until the lizard is large enough for other more readily available insects—the flies could be maintained on a medium of agar and rotting fruit juices such as banana, apple, and melon. Care should be taken with rotting fruit as it is prone to fungal attacks.

*Crickets:* Use an all-glass or plastic container measuring 300 x 300 x 300 mm, with a close-fitting mesh lid for good ventilation. Half the floor area should be covered with cardboard tubes, crumpled newspaper, and such to provide the crickets both with plenty of hiding places and an increased surface area. The other half of the floor should have a food container (bran, flour, vegetable and fruit peelings), a water container (it is advisable to use cotton wool soaked in water), and a couple of small trays of moist peat for egg laying. Breeding is best at a temperature of 27 to 33 °C. After eggs have been laid the trays can be left in the colony, removed to another cage to start a fresh colony, or put into a vivarium, where the lizards can feed themselves on the crickets as they hatch and emerge.

# 2.3

## Signs of Ill Health

### Oliphant F. Jackson

Herpetologists should watch for the following signs, which often indicate that a reptile is ill. Under these conditions, you should make an appointment to see your veterinary surgeon; do not forget to take your records along with you to the consultation.

*Symptoms of illness:*

Periods greater than six weeks when the reptile (snake) refuses food.

Periods longer than one week when the reptile (lizard) refuses food.

Any regurgitation of food.

A loss of 10% of the body weight.

Open mouth breathing.

Noisy respirations.

The presence of a constantly wet runny discharge from the nostrils of tortoises.

A reptile that is unable to open its mouth.

A snake or lizard that never flicks its tongue in or out.

Any redness or swellings inside the mouth.

Any redness, ulceration, or necrotic (grey) plaques inside the mouths of tortoises.

The presence of any lump, bump, or blister on or under the skin.

Any tear or cut on the skin.

Frequent skin sloughing.

Incomplete skin sloughs.

Retained spectacles over the eyes after a slough.

Any "reptile with eyelids" that is unable to open its eyes.

Any terrapin with very swollen eyes.

The loss of good skin colour, especially in lizards.

Any swelling of the toes in lizards.

Any swelling at the end of the limbs in chelonians.

Any persistent protrusion or swelling by, or out of, the cloaca.

Any loss of shields (scutes) in chelonians.

Any discoloration on top of or underneath the shields of chelonians.

If you are able to see fluid moving about underneath a shield when you press on that shield.

The passage of very wet faeces. (Take a fresh sample to your veterinary surgeon in a small pot or bottle).

When the reptile is seen to be drinking water much more frequently than normal. Again, be prepared and take along any freshly excreted material from the cloaca.

On any occasion when you see any form of worm that has been passed out. It sometimes helps the veterinary surgeon if you take the worm along in a small plastic bag.

Any lack of muscle tone: Snakes tend to hang like a bit of limp rope, while lizards refuse to climb, and chelonians are so weak that they are unable to lift their plastron off the ground.

Swellings of the jaws or limbs of the larger lizards, like iguanas.

If the bones of the spine and/or the pelvis become very prominent.

Any tortoise of the *Testudo* species in which the weight for carapace length ratio is below the mean.

Maggot infestation.

# 2.4

# The Isolation of Newly Purchased Reptiles

## Oliphant F. Jackson

One of the things that happens with the greatest of regularity to the novice herpetologist is that a disease is introduced when a new reptile is purchased. The following are the diseases most commonly transmitted in this way.

*Ectoparasites,* including mites. Many reptiles purchased from pet shops and dealers have mites on them. These are so small and so well concealed that neither the purchaser nor the pet shop owner may be aware that mites are present. Mites multiply rapidly and are easily spread from vivarium to vivarium so that within a few weeks the whole collection is infested. The other problem with both mite and tick infestations is that when these insects bite, they carry, and are able to transmit, blood parasites from reptile to reptile.

*Helminths,* such as the *Kaliciphalus* nematode. This nematode is a very important and common parasite that has a direct life cycle. In the faeces there are often live larvae, and these can affect snakes either by penetrating the skin or by contaminating the food before it is swallowed. The worms themselves damage the intestinal mucosa, causing erosions and ulcers; in severe infestations, they carry a poor prognosis. For this reason, it is always wise to have a faecal sample examined before a snake is introduced into a vivarium with another snake.

There are virus diseases, protozoan organisms as well as bacterial diseases that are infectious and contagious. There are still some conditions in reptiles where the casual agent has yet to be identified, like that of the runny nose syndrome (RNS) in chelonians. Yet this RNS disease entity is able to spread very easily. If you are the owner of several tortoises, you may be lucky enough not to have this condition present, but with the introduction of a new tortoise, the whole herd may become infected. This commonly occurs when one kind owner offers to look after a friend's tortoise while the family goes off for their summer holiday, though the RNS disease may be spread either way! So, if you have been kind and offered to look after someone else's tortoises, do keep them separated from your own while you are looking after them.

The length of time that you have to keep a new reptile in isolation is variable, but certainly it should not be too short. Observe the reptile carefully, offer it food, and see that it does eat. Take a faecal sample to a veterinary surgeon and have it checked by microscopic examination for the presence of pathogenic organisms. With snakes, always examine the freshly sloughed skin very carefully, and never leave them in the vivarium. If in doubt, at the end of about four weeks, take both your records and your reptile along to your veterinary surgeon. Ask him to give the reptile a clinical examination and tell you if it is safe to allow it out of isolation.

# 2.5

# Mite Infestations in Snakes and Lizards

## Oliphant F. Jackson

Recently, some herpetologists have been talking about "Vapona resistant mites." This is nonsense, but the reason it has arisen is that the organophosphorus insecticidal strip has been used incorrectly.

Before telling you the correct way to treat a mite infestation, let me give you some warnings about the poisonous properties of these organophosphorus insecticides. They are absorbed into mammalian fat and stay "bound" to that fat for a very long time inside the animal or reptile body. This is one reason why there is a warning on the packets that they must not be used in kitchens or where food is being prepared. The organophosphorus can kill reptiles if they are exposed to it for a long time and, of course, it builds up in the reptilian "fat body."

The signs of organophosphorus poisoning are inappetence, regurgitation, incoordination, convulsions, coma, and eventually death.

Then, there is the length of time that the strip itself continues to give off the poisonous insecticidal vapour; this is about 3 months. After this 3 months, there will be insufficient organophosphorus being given off to kill a single mite.

This is one reason why people have jumped to the conclusion that the mites have become resistant, for I have heard of herpetologists who leave a Vapona strip hanging in the reptile room all the year round. This must never be done.

Now, before I go further, there is another important set of facts to know, and they concern the life cycle of the reptile mite, *Ophionyssus natricis,* although other species of mites may sometimes be involved. Under optimal conditions, at 30 °C the life cycle takes 21 days. Each female lays about 60 to 80 eggs, some on the reptile but the majority in tiny crevices and holes on woodwork round the vivarium. The eggs are impervious to Vapona vapour and therefore, if there is insufficient Vapona vapour when the nymphs hatch out of the egg, a repeat infestation will rapidly occur.

*The efficient treatment of a mite infestation will take three weeks* and requires that a clean small hospital vivarium be used. Set up a small hospital vivarium (B) with paper on the bottom and a clean water bowl. Place the Vapona strip, encased in a protective cardboard or plastic container, and the reptile into vivarium B for three days (a maximum of four days). This will kill all mites on the reptile but will not endanger the reptile. You will not feed the reptile during these three days but you may feed it as usual thereafter.

Take out all wood and bark from the original vivarium (A) and burn it, but leave the rest untouched for the first three days; otherwise, you will merely spread the mites around. Burning the wood and bark is the only way to ensure that the mites and mite eggs in them get destroyed. When you take the Vapona strip out of hospital vivarium B, place it in vivarium A and cover the hole with a plastic bag. Leave it for 21 days, at the end of which time all the nymphs that have hatched out will have been killed. Now you may dismember the entire vivarium, wash it, clean it, disinfect it, and reconstitute it with clean "furniture." It will then be ready to rehouse the reptile. You must remember that if you have several vivaria housing different reptiles, they too may harbour mites; each vivarium must be treated in the same manner if you are to eliminate mites from your collection.

Remember that the Vapona strip will continue to give off organophosphorus vapour for a little over two months after you finish treating vivarium A; at the end of that time, it will have expired and must be thrown away in the dustbin.

One authority advises that only a "1 cm portion" of a Vapona strip be used for every cubic foot of vivarium space, but I have never cut up a strip, although I certainly used a "small space" version rather than the large room strips.

# 2.6

# A Note on Aquatic Reptiles

The maintenance of aquatic chelonia has been discussed in detail by Tryon (1978a, 1978b); most of his comments stand good for aquatic snakes (e.g., *Enhydris bocourti*), so only a few comments are made here.

Ultraviolet apparently destroys many harmful bacteria and fungi and therefore should be available at all times. One should avoid using domestic water and change the water only once a week to avoid undue stress. A separate tank specifically for feeding should be maintained, which will reduce the need to clean the main tank. (Also, if food is left in the main tank, it will increase the likelihood of disease.) At least in the case of chelonians, feeding usually stimulates defecation, which would occur in the feeding tank. The animals should be left for several hours in the feeding tank to ensure that they are well fed.

# 2.7

# Desert Reptiles

## J. L. Cloudsley-Thompson

The desert environment is characterised by drought and extremes of temperature. The Sahara, one of the world's hottest deserts, experiences mean annual temperatures exceeding 30 °C (85 °F). A shade temperature of 58 °C (136.4 °F) was registered at El Aziza, Libya, in September 1922. An annual shade temperature from − 2.0 °C (28 °F) to 52.5 °C (126.5 °F) has been recorded at Wadi Halfa, Sudan; and a fluctuation from − 0.5 °C (31 °F) to 37.5 °C (99 °F) within 24 hours at Bir Mighla, southern Tripolitania, in December. These may be exceptional, but meteorological stations are by no means common in the desert, and many other even more exceptional thermal fluctuations have probably passed unrecorded. In any case, desert reptiles certainly do inhabit a harsh environment in which thermal fluctuations are marked and frequent.

Among modern reptiles, metabolic heat production probably reaches significant proportions only in larger forms, such as pythons and boas. Smaller species are ectothermal and obtain their heat from their environment rather than from metabolic sources. Although environmental temperatures fluctuate violently in the desert, the body temperatures of desert reptiles are, in nature, maintained at a remarkably constant level by behavioural rather than by physiological means. Reptiles sun themselves, until their bodies reach the optimum temperature, and then seek shelter in the shade. All day-active reptiles do this—shuttling between sun and shade—but it is most marked in species that inhabit the desert, where differences between sun and shade temperatures are most extreme (Cloudsley-Thompson 1971, 1972; Gans & Dawson 1976; Gans & Pough 1982).

These points should be taken into account when attending to the requirements of captive reptiles. Day-active species require a heating lamp, so that they can raise their body temperatures to about 35–38 °C by basking. It would not be satisfactory to maintain the vivarium at such high temperatures because the animals would not then be able to behave naturally and select the temperatures they require. Nor would they be able to change their preferred temperatures seasonally. In addition to a heat source, day-active desert reptiles also need rock shelters in which they can secrete themselves at will. A U. V. lamp is also necessary for their health, and as much sunlight as possible.

Many desert lizards are day-active, including representatives of the families Iguanidae, Agamidae, Scincidae, Lacertidae, and Varanidae (Gadow 1901; Lambert 1984; Mayhew 1968). Of these, probably the Agamidae take least readily to life in captivity. It is difficult to keep the *Agama* species alive for more than a year or two, and they tend to suffer from infections of the jaw. The *Uromastix* species are also notoriously difficult to keep satisfactorily in captivity. Individual lizards vary greatly in their behaviour, some becoming surprisingly tame within a few days, whilst others remain nervous and shy throughout their lives. The same applies to a wide variety of reptile species. Lacertidae are among the easiest of the lizards to maintain in a vivarium.

Most desert snakes, amphisbaenids, and geckos are nocturnal in habit. African geckos, such as *Tarentola annularis, Ptyodactylus hasselquisti,* and *Hemidactylus brookii,* are comparatively easy to keep. The former, at least, is extremely resistant to desiccation and can withstand long periods without food or water. This is not true of day-active Scincidae and Agamidae, which are surprisingly susceptible to desiccation. It is therefore wise to provide water, in the form of a dish containing moist cotton wool, for all desert reptiles, even though in nature they may have to make do with the body fluids of their prey. Excess moisture may be harmful.

Geckos should be provided with suitable retreats, such as broken flower pots, beneath which they can establish their territories and hide away during the daytime. Some individuals may become quite tame and even emerge into the daylight to take food.

One evening, some years ago, I drove with a friend from Tucson, Arizona, through the Lower Sonoran desert to the research station at Puerto Penasco in Baja California, Mexico. When darkness fell, we saw, as expected, several Western diamondback and Sidewinder rattlesnakes on the road, in addition to a number of scorpions and tarantulas. They were all, presumably, attracted to the warmth of the tarmac. We collected some of the snakes in sacks for research purposes. The following morning I tipped one of the Western diamondbacks onto the scorching sand in order to photograph it. The animal immediately turned towards me. Fearing a possibly hostile intent, I stepped backwards, for it must have been about 2 m long. It soon became apparent, however, that the poor creature was merely trying to escape into my shadow from the glare of the sun. Within a minute or two, it began to show signs of heat stress; so I returned it to its sack in the shade. Under similar conditions, desert lizards will also run towards shade or, if none is available, dig themselves into the sand. Sidewinders, likewise, bury themselves when overheated.

Heat death in desert reptiles is not preceded by particularly striking symptoms. After an initial burst of vigorous struggling, the animals lose the capacity for coordinated movement. At the critical thermal maximum, they become lethargic and finally paralysed if not removed from the exposure. For ecological purposes, the critical thermal maximum at which the power of locomotion is lost, even though recovery is initially possible, is more important than the absolute lethal temperature. In most day-active desert lizards that have been studied, this lies in the range 40–45 °C, while in desert snakes, it is probably about 5 °C lower—depending upon the duration of exposure (Cloudsley-Thompson 1971; Mayhew 1968). Heat death appears to be associated with a decreased affinity of haemoglobin for oxygen above 45 °C, enzyme failure, cytoplasmic coagulation in the muscles, and direct effects upon tissue proteins. Maximal lethal temperatures of 43–44 °C have been recorded for a variety of desert snakes and of 48–49 °C for lizards. Day-active species are, understandably, more sensitive to cold than are nocturnal species, but the lethal low temperatures of reptiles are less precise than critical thermal maxima.

Desert snakes require a layer of sand deep enough to burrow into, as well as rocks and broken flower pots into which they can retreat when disturbed. They do not require the high temperatures preferred by desert lizards, and they do not appear to be any more difficult to maintain in captivity than snakes from other biomes. American desert bullsnakes (*Pituophis* species) readily settle down and may live for years in a small cage.

Land tortoises mostly inhabit semiarid regions and the requirements of desert species do not differ noticeably from any other kind of tortoise, apart from the need for an abundance of sand in which to burrow. A lamp for basking under, a U. V. light, a varied diet rich in vitamins, and water to drink will provide for most of their requirements. Winter hibernation does not appear to be important; desert tortoises remain active throughout the year when provided with continuous warmth and food.

The special characteristic features of the reptiles that inhabit deserts, which should not be overlooked when they are in captivity, include the following.

(i) *Speed*. The lizards and snakes are slender and speedy. Many desert lizards have the digits broadened out or extended by fringes of long scales so that they do not sink into the sand. In captivity, desert reptiles should be given as much space as possible.

(ii) *Adaptations for burrowing*. These include the hardened epidermis and scales, and strong claws. Desert tortoises dig deep burrows, in nature. Snakes, such as the *Typhlops* and *Eryx* species, have specially modified snouts, and their tails are very short and blunt. Sand vipers (*Echis* species) have scales on their backs arranged in oblique rows so that they can heap sand upon their bodies by wriggling and shaking. Horned toads (*Phrynocephalus* species) do the same by means of lateral folds of the skin. In many burrowing species, the nostrils are directed upwards instead of forwards as a protection against the entry of sand. In most snakes, the nostrils are protected by complicated valves, or are reduced to small pinholes. The eyes may be overhung by head shields, as in the *Typhlops* species, or protected by scales. In some skinks (*Mabuya* species) the lower lid is much enlarged, with a transparent window in it, so that the eye can be closed without impeding sight. The ear apertures are either small, absent, or protected by fringes of scales. In captivity, burrowing desert reptiles should be housed in vivaria containing large quantities of sand for burrowing.

(iii) *Colour change.* Many desert lizards are able to change colour so that they match their background. The vivarium housing these animals can be made more interesting by providing a variety of coloured rocks and sands to which the inhabitants can adapt themselves.

# 3

# Specific Notes on a Variety of Reptile Species

# 3.1

# Geckos: *Eublepharis macularius, Gehyra mutilata, Hemidactylus brooki,* and *Phelsuma dubia*

## D. G. Garthwaite

*Eublepharis macularius:* Leopard Gecko.

**Distribution:** This species ranges from southern Transcaspia and Iraq eastwards to the northwest Frontier Provinces and south to Rajputana and the Khandish District of India. In Pakistan this large, nocturnal, ground-dwelling gecko lives in colonies (Minton 1966). *Adults:* The snout- vent length is approximately 11–13 cm and up to 16 cm in males. Males are easily distinguished from females by having a broader head, a heavier build, and a V-shaped row of femoral pores.

**Vivarium conditions:** A glass-fronted wooden vivraium, 45 x 30 x 30 cm is ideal for housing a pair of adult *E. macularius.* Pieces of bark provide cover on a newspaper substrate. Light and heat is provided by a 15 W pearl electric light bulb. Lights come on at 08.00 hrs. and go off at 22.30 hrs. During the day, the bulb raises the temperature to between 27 °C and 30 °C, and at night a radiator in the room prevents the temperature falling below 20 °C.
**Diet:** In the wild, this species takes a variety of large invertebrates and small vertebrates. In captivity, adults thrive on a diet of locusts, moths, crickets, and pink mice. Food can be dusted with the multivitamin powder SA 37. Multivitamins are also provided once a week, using the water-soluble Ocevital, and fresh water is provided for the rest of the time. The addition of multivitamins appears to be essential for the successful husbandry of a number of species, and in particular for rearing young, which are inclined to have fits and die if fed solely on insects. Although not strictly food, the addition of calcium in the form of cuttlefish bone is appreciated by all geckos, especially by females in breeding condition. Both males and females of this species will eat quite large pieces of cuttlefish (3 mm$^2$) and smaller species will eat correspondingly smaller pieces of cuttlefish bone.

**Breeding:** In captivity, mating normally occurs in the spring (March to April) with a pair of eggs being laid a month later. At the start of a laying season, females may produce only a single egg, as will young females or those in poor condition. During the laying season, three to four clutches of two eggs are produced. Occasionally three eggs are laid.

Once mating has been observed, the female should be provided with an adequate egg-laying site. Leopard geckos and other members of the Eublepharinae, such as *Coleonyx* and *Hemitheconyx,* lay parchment-shelled eggs, which desiccate easily unless provided with suitable conditions. A suitable site is a plastic box, 18 x 18 x 10 cm, two-thirds filled with damp sand or potting compost. A hole 25 mm in diameter is made in one side, allowing access for gravid females. The female will scrape a hole in the laying medium, deposit the eggs, and then cover them over. Once laid, eggs are best removed and incubated outside the vivarium. Damp vermiculite is an ideal incubation medium and eggs should be half buried in damp vermiculite. Under ideal conditions, the eggs will absorb water and swell. During incubation, care must be taken to ensure that the vermiculite does not dry out. As with crocodilians and chelonians, the sex of a hatchling is determined by temperature. With leopard geckos, temperatures over 32 °C produce mainly males, those under 29 °C produce mainly females (Wagner 1980). At a constant temperature of 27 °C, eggs hatch after 56 to 63 days (Thorogood and Whimster 1979).

Hatchlings can be reared either singly or in colonies, and maturity is normally reached within a year. Vivarium conditions should be the same as for the adults, although the actual size of the vivarium can be smaller. Feeding presents no problems and young will thrive on a diet of wax moth larvae, crickets, moths, and locusts. Multivitamins and calcium provided for the adults should also be used for the young.


*Gehyra mutilata.*
**Distribution:** Madagascar, Sri Lanka, S. E. Asia, Japan, Philippine Islands, New Guinea, much of Oceania and Mexico (McCoy 1980). *Adults:* The average snout-vent length is 55 mm, with the tail being slightly longer. Males possess both pre-anal and femoral pores and females with access to calcium have extremely well-developed calcified endolymphatic sacs.
**Vivarium conditions:** as for *Hemidactylus brooki.*
**Diet:** as for *H. brooki.*
**Breeding:** As with *H. brooki,* there appears to be no definite breeding season, with eggs being laid in every month of the year. Eggs are normally laid between sheets of newspaper, one month after mating, and further pairs of eggs are laid at two- to three-week intervals. Incubation is as for *H. brooki.* At a constant temperature of 25 °C, eggs take approximately 65 days to hatch. The care of the young is as for *H. brooki.* The eggs measure about 11 x 8 mm. Hatchlings measure around 21 mm snout to vent, tail 20 mm. Average weight 0.3 gram.


*Hemidactylus brooki*
**Distribution:** Borneo, south China, tropical Asia and northern half of Africa.

It has been introduced into the West Indies and South America (Minton 1966). *Adults:* the snout-vent length is approximately 50 mm with females being slightly larger than males. Males have pre-anal and femoral pores, and females when provided with calcium have obvious calcified endolymphatic sacs. **Vivarium conditions:** As for *Eublepharus macularius,* although the vivarium should be taller, e.g., 30 x 35 x 40 cm.

**Diet:** A diet of wax moth larvae, small crickets, and moths is suitable for *H. brooki.* Water and multivitamins should be provided as for *E. macularius.* Calcium should be given in the form of flakes of cuttlefish bone.

**Breeding:** In captivity there appears to be no definite breeding season, with eggs being laid at all times throughout the year. In Pakistan, egg laying seems to be almost continuous from March to October (Minton 1966). Once mated, eggs may be laid at fortnightly intervals, with up to 22 pairs of eggs being laid in 13 months. As with the majority of gekkonine geckos, a single pair of calcareous eggs is laid at one time. Females will lay eggs in dry potting compost, burying the eggs and then covering again with compost, under pieces of bark, or between sheets of newspaper. Eggs laid under bark are often covered with moss if this is provided (Garthwaite 1984). Eggs are best removed from the main vivarium for incubation and placed carefully on dry vermiculite in a sealed plastic box. Cotton wool soaked in water and placed in a separate container within the plastic box provides humidity. Care must be taken to keep the humidity to a minimum, as an excess can be detrimental to successful hatching (Pashley 1981). At a constant temperature of 30 °C, the mean incubation period is 50 days (Garthwaite 1984) and produces mainly females. Newly hatched geckos are best removed and reared separately in individual containers; in this way the progress of individuals can be monitored. Groups of *H. brooki* will fight and compete for food, with the smaller and weaker individuals usually dying. Transparent plastic boxes (175 x 115 x 60 mm) complete with a 25 mm ventilation hole, covered with gauze, are ideal for rearing young *H. brooki.* The floor of the box is covered with newspaper, a piece of cardboard egg tray provides a hide, and two shallow dishes—one containing water and the other, crushed cuttlefish bone—complete the setup. Food consists of small crickets, wax moth larvae, and fruit flies. Care must be taken not to overfeed the young as this can lead to stress. The young are best fed daily for the first month of their life; after this they can be fed every other day. Water is provided as for the adults. Under ideal conditions, maturity is normally reached within a year. Juveniles can be sexed after 6–8 months. Cleanliness and a reliable food source are essential in rearing hatchlings to adulthood. Eggs average 11 x 9 mm. Hatchlings average snout-vent length of 22 mm, tail 25 mm.

*Phelsuma dubia*
**Distribution:** Comoro Islands, Zanzibar, introduced into Tanzania and Madagascar.
*Adults:* average snout-vent length 65 mm. Females have well-developed calcified endolymphatic sacs.


**Vivarium conditions:** as for *Hemidactylus brooki*.
**Diet:** as for *H. brooki.*


**Breeding:** This is an extremely prolific species, with pairs of eggs being laid as close as 9 days apart. Eggs are laid a month after mating and throughout the year. In captivity, the eggs are normally laid on the walls or front glass of the vivarium. Eggs laid in such a position should be covered with a clear plastic container (no ventilation holes needed) and taped in position (does not need to be removed until the eggs hatch), so as to prevent the adults from either eating the eggs or mauling the newly hatched young. Eggs hatch after approximately 60 days at the temperature regime experienced by the adults. The care of the young is as for *H. brooki*. The eggs average 11 x 9 mm. Hatchlings have an average snout-vent length of 21 mm, tail length 22 mm.

## 3.2

## *Basiliscus vittatus,* the Two-Banded Basilisk

## A. S. Wright

**Size:** This is a medium-sized iguanid. Four females in the care of the author average approximately 55 cm total length, the snout-vent length being around 15 cm. Thus, most of the lizard is tail, and the overall appearance is a slender, streamlined long-legged species.

**Colour:** A variably marked lizard, its ground colour ranges from rich brown in some specimens to an orange/brown or even olive green in others. Two broken lines of cream or beige run longitudinally down each side of the body. These stripes do not extend onto the tail, which is uniformly coloured.

**Sexual dimorphism:** Sexing of adult basilisks presents no problems—the males are endowed with a large crest on the nape, and in most species, a pronounced sail along the dorsum and tail. In contrast, females have just a small crest on the nape and a very small series of sawlike scales running down the dorsum.

**Conditions in Captivity:** Four females are on public display in a large vivarium comprised of two octagonal sections. Each measures 2 m x 2 m (floor area) and they are joined by an interconnecting section 1 m x 1 m. The vivarium is 2 m high throughout. The whole area is planted with living plants—mainly bromeliads, epiphytic orchids and *Maranta* species, but *Ficus pumila, Monstera deliciosa,* and *Philodendron* species are also present. The substrate is a deep layer of peat moss and forest bark, into which two ponds have been sunk (one in each octagon). One pond is approximately 1 m x 70 cm x maximum depth 10 cm; the other is 1.2 m x 80 cm x maximum depth 35 cm.

Lighting is provided by six 60 cm True-Light tubes and six 60 cm Grolux tubes, with six 100 W spotlights providing concentrated areas of heat for basking. The Grolux tubes are purely for the benefit of the plants. The spotlights are not normally all used simultaneously, and three of the six are only employed periodically. Day length is varied through the year by means of timeclocks. The daytime temperature in the majority of the vivarium is 25–27 ° C, but the spotlights provide basking areas of up to 31 ° C. At night, the temperature does not normally fall below 22 ° C.

The humidity of the vivarium is high—normally 70% or more, due to the presence of the water in the ponds, the "bowls" of the bromeliads and the periodic sprayings which the plants receive.

It is worth noting that the vivarium containing the basilisks is set up as a community vivarium; other inhabitants include *Anolis carolinensis*, *Bombina orientalis*, and *Rhacophorus multimaculatus*.

**Habits and observations:** The basilisks were chosen for this tropical display because of their high tolerance of humid conditions in captivity, and the specimens certainly appear to thrive in these conditions. Prior to their introduction, the quarantine vivarium housing the specimens was sprayed regularly with water from a "plant mister." Standing water was also always available, but the specimens never looked as healthy as they do in their current surroundings. All four individuals have been seen periodically entering the ponds in the vivarium and partially submerging themselves.

These lizards are as agile as their appearance would suggest, and the much publicised ability to run across water without breaking the surface tension and "sinking" has been observed on a score of occasions.

Whilst the specimens were extremely skittish in the small (1.3 m x 60 cm x 60 cm) quarantine tank, they have become surprisingly docile on their release into the tropical vivarium. Entrance to the vivarium by staff for cleaning and routine maintenance rarely provokes any response, and provided the approach does not take the individual by surprise, specimens can be caught with little difficulty. However, if startled, these lizards can take flight at astonishing speed. On a handful of occasions, warning head-bobbing movements and even gaping mouths have greeted intruders—these defensive postures are a complete sham, since no attempt to bite is ever made.

The basilisks show no territorial behaviour in this vivarium (although since all four are females, this should perhaps be anticipated) and show absolute tolerance of the other species sharing their environment (my initial worries that they might harass the *Anolis* have been completely unfounded). Furthermore, none of the other species present appear to worry about the presence of *Basiliscus*.

**Feeding:** A varied invertebrate diet is avidly taken. Locusts (up to final instar for *Schistocerca migratoria*), crickets, mealworm larvae, earthworms, and house flies are all taken. The metabolic rate appears to be quite high—specimens which appear rotund one day can be quite slim three days later, although the stored fat in the hind limbs and tail base remains. As stated earlier, the other vertebrates in the vivarium (reptiles, amphibians, and fish) are ignored. Apart from Vionate added to the mealworms supplied to them, no other extra source of vitamins is offered.

**Breeding:** Having only managed to acquire young female specimens for the display, I had no expectations of breeding this species until males could be obtained. The females were released into the tropical vivarium in June 1984. In September 1984 three eggs were found—one infertile, one fertile but laid in the water bowl of a bromeliad and thus ruined, and one apparently perfect egg. This was incubated in moist vermiculite in a sealed container and inspected regularly to check progress and allow circulation of fresh air. The egg went to full term with no signs of complications, but the young failed to hatch. On opening the egg, a fully developed but dead basilisk was revealed. The reason for the failure to hatch has not been ascertained.

The following points are of interest: the eggs were laid over 6 months after acquisition of the specimen; therefore, at least this period must have elapsed since the individual mated. Normally, basilisk eggs are laid about 3 months after fertilisation, indicating that this female retained sperm for around 3 months (possibly longer) before fertilisation occurred. This gives an actual date for fertilisation of within a fortnight of the female's introduction to the tropical display vivarium. This presumably indicates that the specimen found these conditions favourable.

The author is pleased to report that a suitable male specimen for introduction to the vivarium has been found and hopes to be able to report breeding success in the foreseeable future.


**Further Comments:** It is a common complaint of keepers of these lizards that they remain very nervous in captivity; they often physically damage themselves by running into vivarium walls when disturbed. Although this was encountered in the quarantine cage, it has never happened in the display vivarium, where the specimens seem very placid. I would therefore advocate the use of a large, well-planted and humid vivarium for keeping basilisks.

# 3.3

## *Ctenosaura acanthura,* the Mexican Spiny-Tailed Iguana

## A. S. Wright

**Characteristics of Species:** This is an extremely confused genus. Although Smith (1972) has undertaken a considerable amount of taxonomic work on the subspecies of *C. hemilopha,* and Smith and Taylor (1950) produced a key for Mexican reptiles in 1950, there has been little recent work on the taxonomy of the genus as a whole as far as I can ascertain. The only monograph I have managed to find for the genus is that of Bailey (1928). The number of species in the genus varies from four to eight, according to the authority consulted. Burghardt and Rand (1982) give eight species.

The specimens under discussion in this article lack the typical off-white bars which extend onto the flanks of *C. pectinata.* All species have a well-developed dorsal crest of spines in both sexes, and a heavily spined tail. There are large bumps behind the eyes, reminiscent of those found on Rhinoceros Iguanas (*Cyclura cornuta*); these appear to function as fat-storage organs.

**Size:** A large, robust iguanid, adult specimens of *C. acanthura* are somewhat over 1 m in length (snout-vent approximately 35 cm).

**Sexual Differences:** Male has much larger (and sharper) spines on the tail. There are no obvious colour differences between the sexes. Both have a black head, body, and legs. The tail is coloured in alternate bands of black and a deep beige brown. When basking, both sexes develop a metallic blue sheen in patches on the flanks and occasionally all over the abdomen.

**Range:** Central and northern South America; the stronghold for the genus is Mexico, which is also the country of origin of the specimens under discussion.

**Conditions in Captivity:** The specimens are on public display in a cage measuring 1.8 x 1.8 x 2 m (1 x b x h). The lizards (one male, two females) are kept on a gravel substrate in an arid vivarium. Climbing opportunities are provided by branches and false rockwork, which allow the lizards to bask 1.3 m above floor level. The rockwork also provides shelter and hiding places. Lighting is provided by three 1.3 m True-Light fluorescent tubes, one 1.3 m Grolux tube (these provide the background heat), and two Par 38 150 W spotlights which produce considerable heat in a discreet beam. The floor temperature is 25 ° C, but the hottest basking areas reach 43 ° C. Day length can be easily varied since all lighting is on a timeswitch, but in reality we only vary daylength slightly over the year, between 12 and 16 hours per day.

**Habits:** These iguanids are relatively inactive lizards, and spend most of the day basking on rocks and branches approximately 1 m above floor level. However, they do retire to the ground periodically to seek shade and to feed. The male specimen is extremely inquisitive, and the presence of the keeper in the vivarium (for cleaning and routine maintenance) results in his immediate attention.

**Handling:** Despite the inquisitiveness, and the fact that the male will come and eagerly take locusts (a special delicacy) from a pair of feeding forceps, there is a very strong resentment to actual handling, which for this reason is kept to a minimum. Attempts at capturing the specimens result in the following response: The tail, which is quite formidably armed with spines, is lashed at the keeper in powerful blows. Upon grasping the specimen, the mouth is opened fully, and on occasions the whole head is arched back over the body with the jaws stretched wide open—forming a considerable gape. In the author's experience, once the lizard is held firmly in the typical "monitor" hold (head held firmly but not too tightly behind the jaws with left hand, right hand supporting belly and restraining hind legs, and with the tail held against the keeper's body with the right elbow), most specimens quickly become calm— although one female in my care is extremely aggressive and continues to attempt to escape and to bite even when firmly held.

Although the author has never seen them deliberately employed as a weapon, the claws on all limbs of this species are long and powerful, and rip human flesh easily during the course of routine handling of specimens. Certainly, if the lizards chose to employ them as a deterrent, they could cause considerable lacerations.

Leather handling gauntlets prevent damage by the claws, and the author tends to wear these for protection (having been cut on numerous occasions when not wearing them!).

Although the author has handled juvenile specimens of *Ctenosaura* on several occasions, and invariably found them completely docile, he has yet to meet a "tame" adult specimen. It would be interesting to ascertain whether juveniles can be raised to maturity without turning aggressive.

**Feeding:** One aged specimen (a female) in my care will only take a mixed diet of fruit (tomato, banana, orange, pear, dandelion flowers, plums). She rejects grapes, melon, peach, and tinned pulses. This specimen is force-fed animal matter in the form of raw egg and bone broth to supplement her diet. A newly acquired female and the male both eat animal matter avidly. The male shows a definite preference for locusts, although dead pink mice, day-old chicks, dog food, half-grown rats, and eggs are also eaten. The remaining female accepts dead mice readily.

I have yet to see these lizards drinking water, although they will drink pure fruit juices (either orange or mixed fruits). The vitamin supplement Abidec is added to this fruit juice on a weekly basis. Additionally, Vionate multivitamin compound and Stress, a high calcium and protein powder designed originally for lactating bitches, are added to the fresh fruit once every 10 days.

*Additional comments:* The taxonomy of the genus certainly merits further study, or at least greater publicity. Despite their intractability in terms of handling, I have found these creatures extremely rewarding to keep.

# 3.4

# The Snakes of the Genus *Eryx*

# A. B. van Woerkom

**Identifications:** The head is compressed, with small eyes, which may be on the sides of the head as in *Eryx tataricus,* or on the top of the head as in *Eryx miliarius.* The rostral shield is large and well developed, producing an upper jaw that is longer than the lower jaw. The head is not distinct from the neck, due to the heavy muscle of the latter. The body is thick compared to its length and the muscles of the body are strong. The snakes of this genus feel different in the hand; for example, *Gongylophis conicus* feels very hard and stiff, whilst *Eryx johnii johnii* feels like soft rubber. The tail is very short and ends in a blunt tip (*Eryx colubrinus*) or a sharp spine (*Eryx somalicus*), or else it appears like a second head (*Eryx johnii*). Snakes of the genus *Eryx* differ from all other snakes by the shape of the vertebral bones. They also have small head scales, small body scales (36–67 rows at midbody), and a narrow row of ventral scales. The subcaudal scales are not divided. Most species, when adult, measure 60–70 cm in length, with species maximum lengths varying between 40 cm in *Eryx elegans* and 1 m in *Eryx tataricus.* The males are generally smaller than the females, particularly in *E. colubrinus* and *Gongylophis conicus.* Sex can be determined by the length of the spurs. A male has clearly visible spurs (except when very young); they are very small or not visible in females. Also, comparison of tail lengths is helpful, with the male having a much longer tail in proportion to body length than the female (this is the only way of sexing very young sand boas).

**Distribution:** In contrast to the pythons, which live in the Old World, most boas inhabit the New World. *Eryx* is one of the exceptions, being found in West Africa, East Africa, and North Africa northeast through Asia Minor to southeastern Europe in the north and India and central Asia in the east.

**Systematics:** There are about ten species of sand boas belonging to the genera *Eryx* and *Gongylophis.* In central Asia, there is great confusion over the validity of several species (e.g., are *jaculus* and *tataricus* the same species?); however, there are people working on the problem, and it is hoped that in the not too distant future it will be solved.

**Habitat:** The shape of the head, neck, and body immediately suggests subterrestrial living. Sand boas are to be found in deserts, semideserts and other dry, arid terrains. They are able to disappear very quickly into the sand and

48

creep through the sand just beneath the surface. A furrow along the middle of the back and, sometimes, strongly keeled scales prevent the sand from sliding off their backs and showing their presence.

**Behaviour:** Sand boas are active above the ground at twilight and during the night, hiding under stones, in rodent holes, or just under the surface of the sand during the day. Central Asian species such as *E. jaculus, E. tataricus,* and *E. miliarius* hibernate in the winter. Food consists of small rodents, lizards, and small birds, whilst the smaller species also prey on insects. The snakes lie in ambush under the sand, with only the eyes and nostrils above the surface. When a prey is within striking distance, they strike out of the sand and either constrict the prey or squeeze it to death against an object such as a rock. Nest rodents are swallowed alive. Sand boas are usually not aggressive and it is rare for them to bite if handled with care, extra care being needed with *E. miliarius* and *Gongylophis conicus.*

**Terrarium:** Sand boas do not need a large terrarium. The smaller species need a surface area of about 1,500 cm$^2$, the larger species 5,000 cm$^2$, both these sizes being adequate for two or three snakes. The ground surface can be enlarged by constructing a horizontal shelf about 100 mm wide across the entire back of the terrarium and fixed 100 mm above the ground floor. The ideal substrate is 100–200 mm of clean sand. Flat stones should be present in and on the sand, but care should be taken, as the sand boas are strong enough to push the stones against glass fronts and cause damage. The water dish (all sand boas like to drink and some will even lie in the water bowl for a period of time) and any flower pots should also be secured. Many species will climb, so a branch should be in the cage. Light and temperature are regulated by means of one or two bulbs close to the substrate and a heating cable on one side of the terrarium, which will provide a temperature gradient across the terrarium. It is preferable to situate the water bowl on the cool side of the terrarium. During the day, the temperature should be 25–30 °C, with a hot spot under a bulb of a maximum 35 °C. Night temperatures can be around 20 °C, which can be lower for west and central Asian species.

   If the snakes have problems with sloughing, it is recommended to create a humid spot (using a layer of sphagnum) at the cool end of the terrarium.

   Almost without exception, sand boas will accept mice and young rats, in captivity. If any snake refuses food, use nestling mammals. It may be that the temperatures are too low; increase the temperature and the hot spot. If a snake continues to refuse food for no apparent reason, put the snake in a linen or cotton snake bag with two or three nestling mammals. Close the bag and leave for an hour or so. You will find that the snake usually will have eaten the food. This bagging can also be used for young sand boas, some of which are difficult in the early days.

**Reproduction:** Not much is known with regard to stimulus for reproduction in sand boas, though it is known that for west and central Asian species it is essential that they are hibernated for three or four months in dry sand at 6–10 °C. For *Eryx johnii johnii,* high pressure and alterations of air pressure in general have a positive influence on sexual activity. Copulation takes place in spring. The male shows an interesting behaviour in that he tries to dig the posterior half of the female up out of the sand prior to copulation. During pregnancy the female refuses all food. After successful mating, young are born within four to four and one-half months:

| | |
|---|---|
| *Eryx miliarius* | up to 10 young in June/July |
| *Eryx johnii* | 5–6 young in July/August |
| *Eryx jaculus* | 5–12 young in July/August |
| *Eryx tataricus* | 10–15 young in August/September |
| *Eryx colubrinus* | 10–15 young in October |

The average length of the newborn young is 200 mm, varying from 120 to 130 mm in *Eryx jaculus* and *E. miliarius* to 270–290 mm in *E. johnii.*
 The first slough takes place when the young are 8–10 days old in *E. colubrinus* and 14–16 days old in *E. johnii.* Soon after this, the young will accept pinkies, which may be fed by bagging (see above).

**Growth rate:** The growth rate of sand boas is illustrated by the following examples from specimens kept in captivity:
*Eryx colubrinus loveridgei*

| | | |
|---|---|---|
| 1. a female newborn | : 200 mm | |
|     5 years old | : 510 mm | |
|     8½ years old | : 630 mm | |
| 2. a male | : 390 mm | |
|     after 2½ years | : 485 mm | |
| 3. six newborn young | : 200 mm; | 8½ g |
|     after 2½ months | : 270–310 mm; | 25–35 g |

*Eryx jaculus*

| | |
|---|---|
| 1. newborn young | : 120 mm |
|     after 1 year | : 250–280 mm |

*Eryx johnii johnii*

| | | |
|---|---|---|
| 1. five newborn young | : 270–280 mm | ; 20–22 g |
|     after 6 months | : 340–350 mm | ; 36–37 g |
| 2. young female newborn | : 280 mm | ; 22 g |
|     after 1½ years | | ; 125 g |

|   |   |   |
|---|---|---|
| after 2½ years | : 800 mm | ; 365 g |
| 3. young male | : 370 mm | ; 46 g |
| after nearly 3 years |   | ; 115 g |
| after 3½ years | : 680 mm | ; 220 g |
| 4. young female | : 350 mm |   |
| after 8 years | : 850 mm |   |

# 3.5

# *Boiga dendrophila,* the Mangrove Snake

## C. J. Howard

**Introduction:** The beautiful mangrove or black and yellow tree snake is found in a wide area from Thailand to the Philippines and south to Malaya and Sumatra. It is a rear-fanged snake that generally does well in captivity and is often seen in public collections of reptiles. Despite this, records of its successful breeding and rearing of the young are scarce. The notes here presented refer to data collected at Twycross Zoo, where several successful breedings have taken place.

**Housing:** The mangrove snake can exceed two metres in length, so the vivarium should be of suitable dimensions to allow adequate exercise. The snake is partially arboreal and prefers to spend the daylight hours coiled up on a branch well above the ground. The vivarium should therefore be relatively high and should include a few stout branches.

The substrate can be gravel, peat, bark, or newspaper—the latter being the most convenient and the easiest to replace, when soiled, on a regular basis.

If possible, a large pool should be included to allow the snakes to bathe, as they often encounter difficulty when sloughing if conditions are too dry. Alternatively, the snakes can be regularly sprayed with tepid water when about to slough.

Vivarium temperatures should reflect a diurnal and a seasonal variation in order to promote breeding. Suggested limits are 18–20 ° C minimum winter nighttime temperatures and 32–34 ° C maximum during hot summer days. It is easier for the snakes to choose their own preferred temperatures if the heating source is confined to one end of the vivarium.

Photoperiod can be adjusted seasonally to produce a variation throughout the year. Under natural conditions, the day length probably does not alter greatly throughout the year, as the species is found close to the equator in some parts of its range. However, in captivity, a regime of 8 hours light and 16 hours dark during the winter period and a 12 hours light and 12 hours dark period during the summer has led to breeding. These periods are probably not critical.

**Diet:** Under natural conditions, the mangrove snake seems to eat a wide variety of food items including bats, birds, lizards, snakes, frogs, and fish. In captivity, adults are best fed on dead mice or rats. Chicks can also be used on occasion.

Difficult feeders can sometimes be tempted to accept hen eggs initially. Feeding usually occurs during the hours of darkness or at twilight. It is best to feed the snakes separately to avoid accidental cannibalism, as they become very active and aggressive when food is offered.

**Breeding:** Copulation presumably occurs at night; at least, I have never observed it during the daylight hours. Eggs can be laid throughout the year and have been produced in every month.

Females of approximately equal size may lay large numbers of small eggs (e.g., 12 eggs ranging in size from 36 x 27 mm to 39 x 29 mm) or they may lay small numbers of larger eggs (e.g., 6 eggs ranging in size from 46 x 25 mm to 55 x 29 mm). A single egg with the dimensions of 49 x 28 mm weighed 25 grams.

Oviposition is usually preceded by a pre-egg-laying slough about 8–11 days before its occurrence. A suitable egg-laying site should be provided for the gravid female. A plastic bucket half filled with damp newspapers will suffice and should be placed in the vivarium once the pre-laying slough has taken place. Increased diurnal activity is often a sign of the imminence of oviposition.

Eggs can be incubated in sterilized vermiculite or in peat. The eggs should be half to three-quarters buried in the damp medium. The container used should be well aerated to allow a plentiful supply of fresh oxygen to reach the incubating eggs. Eggs incubated at about 28 °C hatch in 90–108 days.

**Rearing the young:** Hatchlings from the smaller-sized eggs measure from 340 to 398 mm in total length. Those from the larger eggs range from 432 to 460 mm in total length. One of these larger hatchlings would weigh about 25 grams. Twins have been noted in two different eggs on two occasions but none survived to hatch out.

The hatchlings have a ground colour of dark greyish brown (rather than the black or blue/black of adults). The crossbands are orange or pinkish orange on the latter half of the body and change later to the yellow crossbands seen in the adult snake. The yellow crossbands are attained gradually over the first 10 months of the young snake's life, starting with the anterior bands and finishing with the caudal bands.

The hatchlings first slough about 10–12 days after their emergence from the egg. Some babies will readily accept pink mice and are not difficult to feed. Others, however, are more difficult to get to feed. These may have to be force-fed on mouse tails initially. Some respond to assisted feeding of pink mice, swallowing food placed gently between their jaws.

The young snakes are ideally housed individually in plastic aquaria with newspaper substrate, a hide box, and a small water container. A small twig for exercise and to help with sloughing can also be incorporated in the aquarium or vivarium.

Temperature and photoperiod regimes can be similar to that employed for adults, but to promote rapid growth, the minimum temperatures can be raised slightly. The hatchlings can be fed twice per week on one pink mouse each to start with. After several weeks, two pink mice or more can be fed once per week. Growth can be rapid once the snake has settled down to feed voluntarily.

Some hatchlings are nervous and aggressive while others are of a more peaceful nature. Most seem to feed better when they are presented with food at night and when the presence of a hide box offers security for them.


**Discussion:** The mangrove snake is generally hardy and easy to care for in captivity. With appropriate environmental control, it will breed regularly. The main problem is in getting the hatchlings to feed on a regular basis. In my experience, it is the diurnal, and possibly the seasonal, variation in temperatures which promotes successful breeding. Snakes housed under more-or-less constant temperatures have produced only infertile eggs.

As the mangrove snake grows to a large size—and since it can be an irritable and aggressive species—care should be exercised when handling it. The fact that in the United Kingdom it is included on the list of "Dangerous Wild Animals" indicates that great respect should be shown to this commonly kept snake. When this is done, much pleasure can be gained from keeping this beautiful and interesting species of snake.

# 3.6

## *Coluber constrictor,* the Black Racer

## A. S. Wright

Despite the scientific name, this snake does not actually constrict its prey. The northern limits of its range are in Canada, but it is found through most of the U.S. and one subspecies (*Coluber constrictor stejnegerianus*) reaches as far south as Mexico. Wright and Wright (1957) recognised nine subspecies. The specimens referred to in this account are of the typical subspecies *Coluber c. constrictor.*

**Size:** Although records of lengths up to 2 m are recorded, those in the author's care comprised an adult male of approximately 1.5 m and a subadult female of 0.8 m.

**Colour:** Much variation occurs within the species as a whole, but specimens of *Coluber c. constrictor* are a uniform black on the dorsal surface. The ventral surface is an attractive deep gray except in the chin and throat region, where it is white.

**Conditions in captivity:** These snakes are active and diurnal, and agile climbers. Because of their habits, they require a large vivarium. The author housed the two specimens in a vivarium measuring 1 m x 0.7 m x 1 m (l x b x h). Heating was provided by incandescent light positioned at one end of the vivarium to give a temperature gradient within the cage. Daytime temperature in the warmest part reached 28–30 ° C. At night this was reduced to around 20 ° C.

It is often reported that these snakes are nervous and generally difficult to acclimatise to captive conditions; the author's own experiences bear this out. These snakes have good eyesight, and the presence of the author in the snake room was quickly noticed. Rapid movements near to their vivarium resulted in tail vibrations, particularly in the female. This specimen was particularly nervous and struck defensively whenever handled. The male was more placid but, nonetheless, resented handling. I found that the best way to hold these snakes was to allow the male to have the first 40 cm of his length completely unrestricted. This appeared to give the animal a feeling of security, since after gliding through the hands for a short period, he would usually settle. Any attempts to touch the specimen in the head or neck region would result in concerted efforts to escape.

**Feeding:** Both specimens accepted dead food—adult mice, in the case of the male, newly weaned mice and "pinkie" rats and mice by the female. However, it was not easy to induce the snakes to feed initially, and the female fasted for several weeks before finally accepting food. During this period, a wide variety of possible foods were offered, including dead day-old chicks, pullets' eggs, and locusts, but only the rodents elicited any interest at all. It is worth noting that other snakes figure quite largely in the diets recorded for this species, so it would be inadvisable to house it with other snake species.

**Additional comments:** This extremely attractive species of North American colubrid is only likely to settle if given a spacious vivarium in a relatively quiet corner of the reptile house.

# 3.7

# European Species of the Colubrid Genera
## *Coluber, Coronella, Elaphe, Malpolon,* and *Natrix*

## D. Wright

*Coluber viridiflavus:* This species shows an enormous variation in temperament, though usually a most active and irritable snake which is best kept in isolation until it is feeding regularly. This may take several months. It needs a large vivarium and must not be handled more than strictly necessary, as it is likely, due to its excitable nature, to succumb to rupture of the gall bladder. It thrives much better under the influence of True-Light.

*Coronella austriaca:* This snake adapts readily to captivity, needs no True-Light, and with hibernation will readily breed. Most freshly caught specimens will only eat lizards but can be encouraged to take baby mice if these are previously rubbed against live lizards. This species, like *V. ammodytes* (p. 66), can be kept in a small vivarium, though overcrowding should be avoided or cannibalism may occur.

*Elaphe longissima:* All of the European *Elaphe* species can do without True-Light but need a well-lit cage. This species, which may be vicious at first, prefers voles or gerbils and usually settles down to do very well in captivity. Older specimens seem more adaptable than young.

*Elaphe quatuorlineata:* This species is the most active of all European *Elaphe* and thrives under almost any conditions provided it is kept warm and dry. Most specimens are docile from the start.

*Elaphe scalaris:* It usually takes well to captivity, although most specimens are irritable, usually trying to bite when handled. This is a very shy snake and it is essential that the vivarium contain plenty of hiding places for this species to thrive. As with *Elaphe longissima,* this species may only eat voles or gerbils at first.

*Malpolon monspessulanus:* This species requires a high temperature, especially at first, to persuade it to eat. It will feed on voles and brown mice but may be

57

difficult to establish due to its simple refusal to feed. Once feeding, problems rarely reoccur. This irritable species readily bites if handled. Though not essential, True-Light does have obvious benefits for the snake.

*Natrix:* All three species tend to be temperamental, so one should avoid any disturbances or unnecessary handling. If allowed to hibernate, all three will readily breed when their eggs are incubated in damp sterilised peat at 26–29 °C.

*Natrix maura:* This is the most aquatic of the three species and can be kept in a small vivarium provided it contains a large bowl of water. Fish forms the bulk of its diet. True-Light is not essential.

*Natrix natrix* (subspecies: *helvetica* and *natrix*): The food preferences of this species vary considerably and appear to depend on the type of terrain where the animal is found. Snakes caught on dry commons where amphibians are rare will readily take whole litters of newborn mammals (avoiding adults due to inability to protect themselves from mammals biting back), whilst those from marshy areas will only consume amphibians. This species is very active and requires a large vivarium with plenty of branches. It is chiefly a terrestrial species, only entering water in search of food. Real sunlight or True-Light is essential for this species; otherwise, its colour will fade, its condition will deteriorate, and eventually it will die (this process taking about 18 months).

*Natrix tessellata:* Basically the data as given for *Natrix natrix* applies, though this species is slightly more ready to enter water and thus should have a larger water bowl, compared with *N. natrix.* This species readily takes fish as well as amphibians.

# 3.8

## *Drymarchon corais erebennus,* the Mexican Indigo Snake

## A. S. Wright

*Subspecific distinctions:* Sixth upper labial in contact with lower anterior temporal, or with small scale cut off from it. (In *D. corais couperi* the sixth upper labial is truncated due to the fact that the seventh curves forward to touch the fifth). *D. c. erebennus* normally has 14 scale rows at the vent (there are 15 in *D.c. couperi*) and the subcaudal count is usually in the range 55–65 (fewer than in *D. c. couperi*). In specimens where the head is not black, *D. c. erebennus* has distinctive black streaks running from the eye to the upper lip.

**Size:** *Drymarchon corais* is a large, robust colubrid. Of the two specimens currently in the author's care, the male is a little over 2 m; the female 1.8 m. They both have considerably larger girths than rat snakes (*Elaphe*) of the same lengths.

**Colour:** There is considerable colour variation among specimens of this subspecies, although these differences do not appear to be linked with the sex of specimens. The female under discussion is virtually the same colour as a Florida Indigo (*D. c. couperi*), i.e., totally black except for the throat, which is carmine red, and the undersurface of the head, which in this individual is white. The extremely bright sheen for which Florida Indigos are famed is not so highly developed in this individual. (I cannot state whether or not this applies to all black specimens of the subspecies *erebennus*).

The male looks totally different. Two-thirds of the animal's length, from the tip of the head backwards, is a brick red/brown with irregular black lateral blotches. These blotches become more abundant (and larger) posteriorly, and the last portion of the trunk and the entire tail are jet black above and beneath. For the first two-thirds of its length, the ventral surface is salmon pink. Although the description makes the snake sound somewhat gaudy, in life it is a singularly attractive snake.

**Range:** From Texas through to Mexico, it is found from sea level to 600 m.

**Conditions in Captivity:**
There are a true pair of specimens on public display in a vivarium measuring

59

1.8 m x 1.8 m x 2 m (l x b x h). The snakes are kept on a substrate of pea gravel. Hiding spaces are provided by massive blocks of sandstone, and air-dried branches provide climbing opportunities.

The vivarium is lit by 3 x 1.3 m True-Light tubes and one 1.3 m Grolux tube. The latter is of no benefit to the reptiles; it is included because the adjacent vivarium is a tropical house containing many live plants that rely on Grolux lighting for their health. The walls of all the display vivaria are painted the same colour, and since the Grolux affects the shade of the paint, a tube is included so that the background colour differences are minimised.

These four fluorescent tubes provide background heat, but two areas of higher temperature are created by 150 W spotlights. The daytime floor temperature is 24 ° C, but in the spotlit areas this rises to 29 ° C. Although *Drymarchon corais* is thought of as a dweller of arid regions, its tolerance of hot, dry conditions is surprisingly low *in vitro* (Wright and Wright 1957).

**Activity of Specimens:** Although long periods are spent hiding amongst the rocks, when the snakes are active they fully utilise the space provided, climbing regularly and spending considerable periods basking both at floor level and among the branches.

**Feeding:** The specimens, which were wild-caught imports, were originally offered dead mice. While these were taken, they were not avidly received. Dead day-old chicks, however, are favoured. The male, a robust example, normally consumes five chicks per feed; the female (which is of slighter build) tends to take three. Food is offered at intervals of between 7 and 12 days. Fresh drinking water is always available—the vitamin supplement Abidec is added to this once a week.

**Temperament:** On initial receipt, when housed in a smaller quarantine vivarium, neither specimen showed any signs of objection to handling. Indeed, unshed eye scales were removed and antibiotic cream was applied to nasal scale damage received in transit without any signs of objection. While the female remains a singularly placid specimen, the male's temperament has changed considerably since his release into the display vivarium. This may simply be a reaction to less frequent handling than initially, but the author speculates that it may include other factors, such as territorial defense, or even be partially attributable to the presence of virtually natural sunlight as supplied by the True-Light. There appears to be a correlation between aggression and sunlight in several species of reptile (Welch, p. 6). Attempts to touch this specimen produce the following response: audible hissing, with flattening of the neck region vertically for approximately 12 cm and rapid vibration of the tail. Further "interference" causes the individual to coil tightly into a strike position, with the head and neck slightly raised (not unlike a rattlesnake threat posture). The strike itself is rapid and violent—the reach approaches 80 cm.

**Transportation of Specimens:** This species is constantly seeking to find a way out of a standard cloth carrying bag, and confinement in such a bag for relatively short periods can lead to a badly rubbed nose. For some reason, confinement in a box (be it polystyrene or cardboard) does not seem to elicit the same response. The author would strongly recommend, therefore, that these snakes be transported in a box rather than a bag.

**Breeding:** Although mating between the specimens was not observed, the female deposited eight large, elongate eggs on May 21, 1984. Like those of the Florida subspecies, the eggs of *Drymarchon corais erebennus* possess calcareous granules on the surface. These eggs were incubated in moist vermiculite (equal weights of vermiculite and water) in sealed containers. All eggs were separated from each other by a gap of at least 2 cm to prevent fungal spread and were half submerged in the vermiculite. Incubation temperature was 28 ° C, and the lids were removed from the containers every other day to inspect the eggs and allow fresh air to circulate.

Unfortunately, a mechanical failure in the incubator resulted in an overheating of the eggs (55 ° C for three hours until the fault was discovered) on 21.6.1984. Despite their removal to an alternative incubator at the correct temperature, all the eggs collapsed rapidly. Upon opening them a few days later (26.6.1984), seven well-developed embryos were revealed; the eighth egg was infertile.

# 3.9

## *Spilotes pullatus,* the Black and Yellow or Tiger Rat Snake

## P. S. Cooke

Of Central and South America's colubrid snakes, *Spilotes pullatus* is one of the largest. Although relatively slender, this serpent often reaches lengths of 3 to 4 metres. It has a beautiful glossy black and yellow colouration and is an inhabitant of the hot humid bush environments ranging from Mexico south through Honduras and Costa Rica to Bolivia and Paraguay. It leads a mainly arboreal existence, feeding on birds, rodents, frogs, and other reptiles.

This snake is considered to be one of the most difficult to manage in captivity, as it presents two main problems. First, due to being nervous and alert—and therefore commonly aggressive—it will often show little interest in food. It is best offered small mice or day-old chicks, and if the food animals are wetted first, this will often encourage a little more interest. Food should be offered at intervals of no less than 14 days to prevent upsetting the snake too much. Even well-acclimatized specimens will feed infrequently, as shown by the following:

| month | number of mice accepted | month | number of mice accepted |
|---|---|---|---|
| September | 2 | May | 5 |
| October | 2 | June | 4 |
| November | 2 | July | 6 |
| December | 3 | August | 0 |
| January | 7 | September | 11 |
| February | 4 | October | 0 |
| March | 5 | November | 0 |
| April | 6 | December | 1 |

*Spilotes pullatus* will seize prey in their mouth and overcome it by pressing down on it with a coil of the body.

The second problem in keeping this species is the large vivarium it requires, with plenty of climbing opportunities and hiding places. The temperature must be kept at 25 to 30 ° C, with a slight drop at night, and with a daytime photoperiod of approximately 12 hours. A high humidity is necessary in the vivarium, which can be achieved by means of a large water container and occasional spraying with warm water, or by providing a substrate of damp leaf litter; however, if using the latter method, plenty of thought must be given to cleanliness because of increased risk of bacterial infection.

Once settled, *Spilotes pullatus* can be expected to live for many years in captivity, but will remain aggressive, frequently rattling its tail, vertically inflating its neck, and striking with little provocation. It is, therefore, advisable that this species be kept in a part of the reptile room that will receive the least disturbance. *Spilotes pullatus,* although known to be an egg-laying species, has not yet been bred in captivity; this is understandable considering its large size, unfavourable disposition, and the fact that it is rarely available.

# 3.10

# *Trimeresurus albolabris,* the Green Pit Viper

# J. W. Verkerk

**Description:** *Trimeresurus albolabris* is an arboreal snake found in India, Nepal, south China and the Indonesian Archipelago. It lives high in the trees as well as in rice fields (where it can be a danger to man). In the wild, this species feeds on small mammals and birds, with the young snakes also eating frogs.

Sex can be determined by the length of the snake and by the number of ventrals and subcaudals. Males have 151–169 (= 159 ± 4.4) ventrals, 61–78 (= 69.8 ± 4) subcaudals and reach a maximum length of 760 mm. Females have 149–173 (= 161 ± 4.6) ventrals, 48–67 (= 55.5 ± 4) subcaudals and reach a maximum length of 1130 mm. The colour of the snake is light green or yellow green dorsally with a yellowish venter. The upper side of the tail is brown red. Specific to *T. albolabris* is that the interstitual skin (that which is under the scales) is ringed black and white, which is obvious when the snake is feeding. If these rings are absent, the snake is not *albolabris.* Young snakes all have a white stripe, and sometimes a black one running the length of the body on the first row of dorsal scales. As the snake grows, this stripe disappears in females while being retained by males.

**The vivarium:** My snakes (a female, 1080 mm, and a male, 610 mm) are kept in a vivarium measuring 80 x 40 x 80 cm (1 x d x h). The vivarium is made of wood and all the sides are lined with cork tiles. The front is two sliding panes of glass which can be locked. The furniture is kept simple. On the floor there is a large (35 x 40 x 5) water basin, always full of fresh water, the rest of the floor being covered with fine river sand. There are also several branches and plastic plants where the snakes can hide. The cage is lit with a 30 W tungsten lamp and a 40 W glowlamp. The latter is primarily for heat and is turned off during the winter. The temperature in the vivarium is about 27 ° C in the summer (21 ° C at night) and 22 ° C in the winter (17 ° C at night). The lamps are on 13.5 hours in the summer and 10 hours in the winter. Relative humidity is maintained at about 80%.

**Behaviour and reproduction:** *T. albolabris* is a quiet snake, spending much of the time laying motionless in the branches. Noticeable is the fact that they never lie together, leading, as they do in nature, a solitary life. The snakes are sprinkled with water, which seems to make them more active, both in drinking the droplets (they do not drink from the basin in the cage) and their search for food. It is of interest that if the snakes are sprayed during the day there is no apparent reaction, but if they are sprayed at night they react very aggressively, particularly the male. When searching for prey, they hang from the branches with their necks held in an S shape ready for striking. The female will eat once a week, the male only once a month. Both are offered mice, and the female will also take small birds (when offered birds, the male has refused them).

Mating takes place in autumn. Both animals become restless and start to spend some time close to each other or even together. Copulation (which can last for one-half to four hours) takes place in the evening, and immediately after separating the male will move up into the branches and away from the female. During pregnancy, the female refuses to eat; so will the male, if left in the same cage. It is recommended that the male be removed to a separate cage where he will continue feeding. Pregnancy lasts about 5–7 months, depending on the temperatures in the cage. When the young are finally born, they measure 130–160 mm in length and weigh only a few grams each. Young females produce 10–15 young, with older females producing much larger broods (up to 40). In the wild, the young feed almost exclusively on very young frogs and my young are fed *Lymnodynastes perroni*. If young frogs are not available, they can be force-fed with newborn mice for a short period before they freely take mammals.

**Conclusion:** *T. albolabris* is not particularly venomous and is easy to maintain in captivity. Under the right conditions, this snake will readily breed.

# 3.11

# European Species of the Genus
## Vipera (V. ammodytes, V. aspis, V. berus)

## D. Wright

*Vipera ammodytes:* This species is well suited for laboratory work as it will thrive in a very small vivarium. It requires a high temperature, at which it usually feeds well. As a species, it is not as sensitive as *V. berus.*

*Vipera aspis:* Very similar in its requirements to *V. berus* (see below), it is less sensitive. With little disturbance and a high temperature, this snake feeds well, initially on voles.

*Vipera berus:* Newly caught specimens must be kept in isolation apart from all disturbances in a very hot vivarium (26–30 ° C during the day) until they have started feeding. Once feeding, they can be put together in numbers in a large vivarium at a lower temperature. Initially they should be fed dead voles. Hibernation is essential for physiological reasons and to encourage breeding. True-Light or something similar is essential or the snakes will die after about two years. Problems are rarely encountered with newborn or very young adders.

# 4

## Species—Reference List

# 4.

# Species—reference list

*Acanthodactylus erythrurus*: Busack (1976); Busack and Jaksic (1982)
*Acanthodactylus erythrurus erythrurus*: Sautereau (1980)
*Acanthophis antarcticus*: Shine (1980)
*Acanthosaura*: Wallace (1978)
*Acrantophis dumerili*: Huff (1983)
*Acrantophis madagascariensis*: Branch and Erasmus (1976) (1977)
*Acrochordus granulatus*: Voris and Glodek (1980)
*Agama*: Langerwerf (1980)
*Agama agama*: Chetwynd (1983); Cloudsley-Thompson (1981); Harris (1964);
    James and Porter (1979); Marshall and Hook (1960)
*Agama agama africana*: Daniel (1960) (1961)
*Agama atra*: Bruton (1977)
*Agama atricollis*: Curry-Lindahl (1979)
*Agama bibroni*: Capel-Williams and Patten (1978)
*Agama stellio*: Langerwerf (1977) (1981)
*Agama stellio picea*: Childress (1970)
*Agkistrodon bilineatus*: Peters (1979); West (1981)
*Agkistrodon bilineatus taylori*: Burchfield (1982)
*Agkistrodon blomhoffi blomhoffi*: Merzec (1980)
*Agkistrodon contortrix laticinctus*: Schuett (1978)
*Agkistrodon halys caraganus*: Hübers and Fricke-Hübers (1983)
*Agkistrodon piscivorus*: Burkett (1966); Wharton (1966)
*Agkistrodon piscivorus piscivorus*: Blem (1981)
*Ahaetulla*: Henderson and Binder (1980)
*Algyroides*: Langerwerf (1980)
*Alligator*: Bustard (1980)
*Alligator mississipiensis*: Joanen and McNease (1980)
*Amblyrhynchus cristatus*: Pawley (1966) (1969)
*Ameiva ameiva*: Vitt (1982)
*Ameiva fuscata*: Somma and Brooks (1976)
*Ameiva undulata amphigramma*: Perez-Higareda (1981b)
*Amphibolurus barbatus*: Almandarz (1969); Van Aperen (1969)
*Amphibolurus barbatus barbatus*: Bustard (1966)
*Amphibolurus inermis*: Pianka (1971)
*Amphibolurus isolepis*: Pianka (1971)
*Amphibolurus nullarbor*: Smith and Schwaner (1981)
*Amphibolurus vitticeps*: Johnston (1979)
*Amphiesma vibakari*: Moriguchi and Naito (1982)

*Anadia brevifrontalis*: Swain and others (1980)
*Angolosaurus skoogi*: Hamilton and Coetzee (1969)
*Anguis fragilis*: Patterson (1983)
*Anniella pulchra*: Bury and Balgooyen (1976)
*Anolis acutus*: Ruibal and others (1972); Ruibal and Philibosian (1974)
*Anolis aeneus*: Gorman and Licht (1975); Stamps (1973); (1976) (1977); Stamps and Crews (1976)
*Anolis bimaculatus sabanus*: Blok (1971)
*Anolis biporcatus*: Henderson (1972)
*Anolis carolinensis*: Burghardt (1964); Cooper (1971) (1979); Greenberg and Noble (1944); Sigmund (1984); Tokarz and Jones (1979)
*Anolis frenatus*: Scott and others (1976)
*Anolis gadovii*: Fitch and Henderson (1976)
*Anolis limifrons*: Sexton and others (1972); Scott and others (1976)
*Anolis lucius*: Allen and Neill (1957)
*Anolis nebulosus*: Jenssen (1970)
*Anolis oculatus*: Somma and Brooks (1976)
*Anolis oculatus montanus*: Welzel (1981)
*Anolis polylepis*: Hertz (1974)
*Anolis pulchellus*: Gorman and Harwood (1977)
*Anolis sagrei*: Brown and Sexton (1973)
*Anolis taylori*: Fitch and Henderson (1976)
*Anolis trinitatis*: Gorman and Licht (1975)
*Anolis tropidolepis*: Fitch (1972)
*Antillophis parvifrons alleni*: Franz and Gicca (1982)
*Aporosaura anchietae*: Goldberg and Robinson (1979); Louw and Holm (1972); Robinson and Cunningham (1978)
*Aspidites melanocephalus*: Charles and others (1985); Neumann (1978)
*Aspidites ramsayi*: Fyfe and Harvey (1981)
*Atheris squamiger*: Wallach (1980)
*Basiliscus basiliscus*: Barden (1943); Echelle and others (1972); Fleet and Fitch (1974); Lieberman (1980)
*Basiliscus plumifrons*: Banks (1983); Bloxam (1980); Pawley (1972)
*Basiliscus vittatus*: Echelle and others (1972); Mudde (1980)
*Bipes*: Papenfuss (1982)
*Bitis arietans*: Hartmann and Steiner (1984); Rosselot (1980)
*Bitis caudalis*: Akester (1983); Douglas (1981)
*Bitis gabonica gabonica*: Akester (1979) (1980); Huffman (1974)
*Bitis gabonica rhinoceros*: Vandeventer and Schmidt (1977)
*Bitis peringueyi*: Robinson and Hughes (1978)
*Blanus cinereus*: Langerwerf (1974)
*Boa constrictor*: Chapon and others (1976); Visch (1985)
*Boa constrictor constrictor*: Kivit (1983); Kivit and Kivit (1981); Schilt (1981a) (1981b); Tielemans (1981) (1982a) (1982b)

*Boa constrictor imperator*: Jarvis and Jarvis (1980)
*Boa constrictor ortonii*: Vries (1983)
*Boaedon fuliginosus*: Hartmann and Steiner (1984)
*Boaedon fuliginosus fuliginosus*: Nägele (1984)
*Boaedon lineatus*: Blackwell (1954b); Fertard (1982)
*Boiga blandingi*: Groves (1973)
*Boiga cyanea*: Coote (1979)
*Boiga cynodon*: Quinn and Neitman (1978)
*Boiga dendrophila*: Groves (1974); Nägele (1984)
*Boiga dendrophila melanota*: Peels (1981)
*Boiga trigonata*: Bulian and Bulian (1983)
*Bothrops atrox*: Burchfield (1975)
*Bothrops atrox asper*: Pawley (1969)
*Bothrops caribbaea*: Groves and Altimari (1979)
*Bothrops nasutus*: Ripa (1983)
*Bothrops nummifer*: Ankenman (1982)
*Bothrops schlegeli*: Antonio (1980); Blody (1983)
*Brachylophus fasciatus*: Arnett (1979)
*Cacophis*: Shine (1980)
*Caiman*: Bustard (1980)
*Caiman crocodilus*: Alvarez del Toro (1969)
*Caiman crocodilus crocodilus*: Hunt (1969); Staton and Dixon (1977)
*Calabaria reinhardtii*: Bartlett (1982); Gartlan and Struhsaker (1971); Pols (1981)
*Callisaurus*: Clarke (1965)
*Callisaurus draconoides*: Kay and others (1970); Pianka and Parker (1972); Vitt and Ohmart (1977a)
*Calotes*: Wallace (1978)
*Calotes versicolor*: Asana (1931); Pandha and Thapliyal (1967); Raut and Ghose (1984)
*Candoia bibroni*: Murphy and others (1978)
*Candoia carinata*: Murphy and others (1978)
*Candoia carinata paulseni*: Fauci (1981)
*Carphophis amoenus amoenus*: Barbour and others (1969)
*Carphophis vermis*: Clark (1968) (1970)
*Cemophora coccinea*: Nelson and Gibbons (1972)
*Cemophora coccinea copei*: Palmer and Tregembo (1970)
*Chalarodon madagascariensis*: Blanc and Carpenter (1969)
*Chalcides ocellatus*: Badir (1968); Badir and Hussein (1965)
*Chalcides ocellatus tiligugu*: Gilpin (1969); Riches (1981)
*Chamaeleo*: Wagemaker (1972)
*Chamaeleo chamaeleon*: Fertard (1978)
*Chamaeleo dilepis*: Brain (1961)
*Chamaeleo hohnelii*: Bustard (1965)
*Chamaeleo jacksonii*: Bech (1982); Poel-Hellinga (1974) (1977); Schley (1976)

*Chamaeleo namaquensis*: Burrage (1973)
*Chamaeleo pumilis pumilis*: Burrage (1973)
*Chamaesaura anguina*: Berger (1978); Niekisch (1981)
*Chelodina expansa*: Legler (1978)
*Chelodina longicollis*: Armstrong (1982); Kennerson (1980); Pickering (1982)
*Chelonia mydas*: Booth and Peters (1972)
*Chelydra serpentina*: Yntema (1976) (1978)
*Chelydra serpentina osceola*: Punzo (1975)
*Chelydra serpentina serpentina*: Froese (1978)
*Chersina angulata*: Krzystyniak (1984)
*Chionactis occipitalis*: Warren (1953)
*Chondropython viridis*: Bumgardner (1985); Hollander (1979); Schouten (1984)
    (1985); Walsh (1977)
*Chrysemys floridana*: Gibbons (1977)
*Chrysemys picta belli*: Legler (1954)
*Chrysemys picta marginata*: Raney and Lachner (1942)
*Chrysemys picta picta*: Mitchell (1985)
*Chrysemys scripta elegans*: Thornhill (1982)
*Chrysemys scripta taylori*: Davis and Jackson (1973)
*Clemmys guttata*: Ernst (1970) (1976) (1982)
*Clemmys insculpta*: Meritt (1980)
*Clemmys muhlenbergii*: Arndt (1972) (1977); Bloomer and Holub (1977);
    Nemuras (1967); Tryon and Hulsey (1977); Zovichian (1971a) (1971b)
*Clonophis kirtlandi*: Tucker (1976) (1977)
*Cnemidophorus*: Asplund (1974)
*Cnemidophorus arubensis*: Schall (1974)
*Cnemidophorus calidipes*: Duellman (1960)
*Cnemidophorus communis communis*: Walker (1982)
*Cnemidophorus deppei*: Kennedy (1968)
*Cnemidophorus flagellicaudus*: Stevens (1980)
*Cnemidophorus guttatus*: Kennedy (1968)
*Cnemidophorus hyperythrus beldingi*: Bostic (1965) (1966)
*Cnemidophorus inornatus*: Christiansen (1971)
*Cnemidophorus labialis*: Walker (1966)
*Cnemidophorus lemniscatus*: Mueller (1971)
*Cnemidophorus martyris*: Walker (1980)
*Cnemidophorus neomexicanus*: Christiansen (1971); Leuck (1985)
*Cnemidophorus ocellifer*: Vitt (1983)
*Cnemidophorus parvisocius*: Maslin and Walker (1973)
*Cnemidophorus scalaris*: Barbault (1977)
*Cnemidophorus sexlineatus*: Brown (1956); Carpenter (1960); Clark (1976); Fitch
    (1958); Hardy (1962); Hoddenbach (1966); Leuck (1985)
*Cnemidophorus sonorae*: Routman and Hulse (1984)
*Cnemidophorus tesselatus*: Leuck (1985)

*Cnemidophorus tigris*: Barbault (1977); Burkholder and Walker (1973); Pianka (1970); Vitt and Ohmart (1977b)
*Cnemidophorus tigris multiscutatus*: Goldberg (1976)
*Cnemidophorus tigris tigris*: Mahrdt (1976)
*Coleonyx brevis*: Dial (1978)
*Coleonyx reticulatus*: Dial (1978); Gallo and Reese (1978)
*Coleonyx variegatus*: Berger (1984b); Cooper and others (1985); Denardo (1985); Greenberg (1943); Parker and Pianka (1974)
*Coluber constrictor*: Fitch (1963); Lillywhite (1985)
*Coluber rhodorhachis*: Murthy and Sharma (1975)
*Coluber viridiflavus carbonarius*: Steehouder (1984)
*Constrictor constrictor*: Howard (1983)
*Constrictor constrictor constrictor*: Martin and Martin (1984)
*Cophosaurus*: Clarke (1965)
*Cophosaurus texanus*: Barbault (1977)
*Corallus annulatus annulatus*: Murphy and others (1978)
*Corallus caninus*: Groves (1978); Murphy and others (1978); Riel (1984); Savage (1973)
*Corallus enhydris*: Pendlebury (1974)
*Corallus enhydris cookii*: Brederode (1982); Foekema (1974); Renkema (1981); Verstappen (1981)
*Corallus enhydris enhydris*: Abuys (1985); Gaal (1983); Pols (1980) (1982) (1983)
*Cordylus cordylus cordylus*: Burrage (1974)
*Cordylus giganteus*: Marais (1984)
*Cordylus vittifer*: Jacobsen (1972)
*Coronella austriaca*: Kozak and Simecek (1977); Spellerberg and Phelps (1977)
*Coronella girondica*: Street (1973)
*Corucia zebrata*: Honeggar (1975) (1985)
*Corythophanes cristatus*: Davis (1953)
*Corythophanes hernandezi*: Perez-Higareda (1981a)
*Cosymbotus platyurus*: Church (1962)
*Crocodylus*: Bustard (1980)
*Crocodylus johnstoni*: Compton (1981); Dunn (1977) (1981)
*Crocodylus moreletii*: Hunt (1973) (1980)
*Crocodylus niloticus*: Pooley (1962) (1969)
*Crocodylus palustris*: David (1970); Yadav (1969)
*Crocodylus porosus*: Webb and others (1977)
*Crotalus*: Murphy and Armstrong (1978)
*Crotalus adamanteus*: Burchfield (1975); Sayers (1982)
*Crotalus atrox*: Beaver (1976); Landreth (1973); Tinkle (1962)
*Crotalus cerastes laterorepens*: Moore (1978)
*Crotalus confluentus oreganus*: Storer and Wilson (1932)
*Crotalus enyo enyo*: Tryon and Radcliffe (1977)
*Crotalus horridus*: Allen (1982)

*Crotalus horridus atricaudatus*: Gibbons (1972)
*Crotalus horridus horridus*: Keenlyne (1972)
*Crotalus mitchelli pyrrhus*: Moore (1978)
*Crotalus polystictus*: Hubbard (1980)
*Crotalus unicolor*: Carl and others (1982)
*Crotalus vegrandis*: Carl and others (1982)
*Crotalus viridis oreganus*: Baron (1976); Fitch and Twining (1946)
*Crotalus viridis viridis*: Gannon and Secoy (1984)
*Crotalus willardi*: Quinn (1977)
*Crotalus willardi obscurus*: Marcus (1976b)
*Crotalus willardi willardi*: Tryon (1978)
*Crotaphytus collaris*: Fitch (1956)
*Crotaphytus wislizeni*: McCoy (1967); Parker and Pianka (1976)
*Crotaphytus wislizeni silus*: Montanucci (1965)
*Cryptophis nigrescens*: Shine (1984)
*Cryptophis pallidiceps*: Shine (1984)
*Ctenosaura pectinata*: Evans (1951)
*Ctenotus robustus*: Saylor Done and Heatwole (1977)
*Cuora amboinensis*: Inskeep (1984a) (1984b); Olliff (1980)
*Cyclemys dentata*: Norris (1983)
*Cyclura carinata*: Iverson (1980)
*Cyclura cornuta*: Haast (1969)
*Cyclura cornuta cornuta*: Shaw (1969)
*Cyclura macleayi caymanensis*: Carey (1966)
*Cyclura macleayi macleayi*: Shaw (1954)
*Cylindrophis rufus*: Foekema (1970)
*Cyrtodactylus kotschyi*: Gooding (1982)
*Dasypeltis scabra*: Bardulla (1984)
*Deirochelys reticularia*: Gibbons (1969)
*Demansia*: Shine (1980)
*Dendroaspis jamesoni kaimosae*: Leloup (1964)
*Denisonia*: Shine (1983)
*Dermatemys mawi*: Campbell (1972)
*Diadophis punctatus*: Myers (1965); Wijk (1985)
*Diadophis punctatus arnyi*: Carl (1978); Clarke (1968)
*Diadophis punctatus edwardsi*: Prieto (1975)
*Diadophis punctatus regalis*: Parker and Brown (1974)
*Dinodon rufozonatum*: Simmons (1977)
*Diplodactylus vittatus*: Bustard (1968)
*Diploglossus curtissi aporus*: Ober (1970)
*Dipsosaurus dorsalis*: Carpenter (1961); Davis (1976); Minnich and Shoemaker (1970); Muth (1977); Norris (1953); Pianka (1971)
*Draco volans*: Hairston (1957)
*Drymarchon corais couperi*: Beardsley and Barten (1983); Brunner (1981); Coote (1978); Edmondson (1979); Gillingham and Chambers (1980); Hine (1984); LeBuff (1953); Welch (1978a)

*Dryophis nasuta*: Zwinenberg (1976)
*Echiopsis curta*: Shine (1982)
*Echis colorata*: Goode (1979)
*Egernia depressa*: Day (1980)
*Egernia dorsalis*: Adler (1958)
*Egernia whitii whitii*: Adler (1958)
*Eirenis collaris*: Weber-Semenoff (1977)
*Elaphe*: Coote and Riches (1978); Riches (1978)
*Elaphe carinata*: Chapman (1983)
*Elaphe climacophora*: Fukada (1976) (1978); Mishima and others (1976) (1977a)
   (1977b)
*Elaphe dione*: Tiser (1980)
*Elaphe guttata*: Gillingham (1979); Leach (1978); Riel (1977)
*Elaphe guttata emoryi*: Reid (1983)
*Elaphe guttata guttata*: Bechtel and Bechtel (1958); Boerema (1985); Brand
   (1981); Hartmann and Steiner (1984); Nägele (1984); Oosten (1981); Riel
   (1982)
*Elaphe helena*: de Silva (1977)
*Elaphe longissima*: Werb (1979)
*Elaphe obsoleta*: Gillingham (1979)
*Elaphe obsoleta bairdi*: Brecke and others (1976)
*Elaphe obsoleta lindheimeri*: Eerden (1985)
*Elaphe obsoleta obsoleta*: Fitch (1963); Kieve (1979); Littleford and Keller (1946);
   Nijhof (1984; Pelt (1983)
*Elaphe obsoleta quadrivittata*: Brand (1982); Ford (1974); Friend and Friend
   (1984);Koore (1985); Moss (1985)
*Elaphe obsoleta rossalleni*: Allen and Neill (1950); Bryant (1982); Chapman
   (1979); Vokins (1981); Woerkom (1984)
*Elaphe obsoleta spiloides*: Nägele (1984)
*Elaphe porphyracea nigrofasciata*: Romer (1979)
*Elaphe quadrivirgata*: Fukuoka (1975)
*Elaphe quatuorlineata quatuorlineata*: Haan (1982)
*Elaphe radiata*: Schmidt (1983)
*Elaphe rosaliae*: Ottley and Jacobsen (1983)
*Elaphe rufodorsata*: Sura (1981)
*Elaphe schrenkii schrenkii*: Peels (1982)
*Elaphe situla*: Pozio (1983); Sigg (1984); Werb (1980)
*Elaphe subocularis*: Campbell (1972); McIntyre (1977); Morgan (1984)
*Elaphe vulpina*: Gillingham (1979)
*Elaphe vulpina vulpina*: Gillingham (1974) (1977); Zehr (1969)
*Emoia atrocostata*: Alcala and Brown (1967)
*Emys orbicularis*: Grundy (1982); Haan (1981); Lancon and Lancon (1981)
*Enhydrina schistosa*: Voris and others (1978); Voris and Jayne (1979)
*Enyaliosaurus clarki*: Duellman and Duellman (1959)
*Epicrates*: Groves (1980); Huff (1980)

*Epicrates angulifer*: Huff (1976); Murphy and others (1978); Nowlinski (1977)
*Epicrates cenchris*: Andreotti (1977); Chapon and others (1976); Murphy and others (1978); Wolf (1985)
*Epicrates cenchris cenchris*: Lemke (1978)
*Epicrates cenchris crassus*: Brunner (1978) (1979)
*Epicrates cenchris maurus*: Koore (1985b)
*Epicrates fordii fordii*: Murphy and Guese (1977); Murphy and others (1978)
*Epicrates gracilis gracilis*: Murphy and others (1978)
*Epicrates inornatus*: Huff (1978)
*Epicrates monensis monensis*: Campbell and Thompson (1978)
*Epicrates striatus*: Hanlon (1964)
*Epicrates striatus striatus*: Markx (1985); Riel (1982); Stoel (1982); Townson (1978); Verstappen (1982)
*Epicrates subflavus*: Bloxam (1977); Huff (1979)
*Eridiphas slevini*: Hunt and Ottley (1982)
*Eryx*: Bartlett (1982)
*Eryx colubrinus loveridgei*: Lamers (1984); McLain (1982)
*Eryx conicus*: Giffiths (1984)
*Eublepharis macularius*: Hingley (1985); Spruyt (1984); Thorogood and Whimster (1979); Wagner (1974)
*Eumeces callicephalus*: Campbell and Simmons (1961)
*Eumeces copei*: Guillette (1983)
*Eumeces egregius*: Mount (1963)
*Eumeces fasciatus*: Burghardt (1964); Cagle (1940); Fitch (1954); Fitch and Achen (1977)
*Eumeces laticeps*: Douglas (1965)
*Eumeces latiscutatus*: Hikita (1976)
*Eumeces obsoletus*: Fitch (1955); Hall (1971)
*Eumeces septentrionalis septentrionalis*: Breckenridge (1943)
*Eumeces skilotonianus*: Berger (1984a)
*Eunectes murinus*: Belluomini and Veinert (1967); Chapon (1976); Deschanel (1978); Holstrom (1980)
*Eunectes notaeus*: Townson (1985)
*Euspondylus brevifrontalis*: Fouquette (1968)
*Farancia abacura*: Meade (1937)
*Farancia abacura abacura*: Reynolds and Solberg (1942); Wells (1980)
*Farancia erythrogramma*: Gibbons and others (1977)
*Furina*: Shine (1981)
*Gavialis*: Bustard (1980)
*Gehyra australis*: Rösler (1983)
*Gehyra mutilata*: Rose (1982)
*Gehyra variegata*: Bustard (1967) (1970)
*Gekko gecko*: Brodsky (1969)
*Gekko stentor*: Tho and Ho (1979)

*Gekko tawaensis*: Hara (1975)
Gekkonidae: Garthwaite (1984)
*Geochelone carbonaria*: Davis (1979)
*Geochelone denticulata*: Auffenberg (1970)
*Geochelone elephantopus*: Bacon (1980)
*Geochelone pardalis*: Coles (1984) (1985); Cairncross and Greig (1977); Hine (1978)
*Geochelone pardalis babcocki*: Bennefield (1982); Coakley and Klemens (1983)
*Geochelone radiata*: Auffenberg (1978)
*Geochelone sulcata*: Grubb (1971)
*Gerrhonotus multicarinatus*: Langerwerf (1980) (1981); Parker (1981)
*Gerrhonotus multicarinatus nanus*: Burrage (1964); Milstead (1965)
*Gerrhonotus multicarinatus webbi*: Milstead (1965)
*Gerrhosaurus major*: Howard (1980)
*Glyphodon*: Shine (1981)
*Gopherus agasizii*: Luckenbach (1982)
*Gopherus berlandieri*: Weaver (1970)
*Gopherus polyphemus*: Auffenberg (1966); Douglass (1978); Douglass and Layne (1978); Iverson (1980)
*Graptemys pseudogeographica ouachitensis*: Moll (1976)
*Gymnophthalmus multiscutatus*: Vitt (1982)
*Haemorrhois hippocrepis hippocrepis*: Welch (1982)
*Heloderma suspectum*: Wagner and others (1976)
*Heloderma suspectum cinctum*: Peterson (1982)
*Hemidactylus brooki*: Avery (1981); Pashley (1981)
*Hemidactylus frenatus*: Bustard (1970); Cheng and Lin (1977); Chruch (1962); Marcellini (1971)
*Hemidactylus turcicus*: Gilpin (1972)
*Hemitheconyx caudicinctus*: Rösler (1981)
*Heterodon nasicus*: Platt (1969)
*Heterodon platyrhinos*: Nichols (1982); Platt (1969)
*Holbrookia*: Clarke (1965)
*Holbrookia maculata*: Axtell (1960)
*Holbrookia propinqua*: Judd and Ross (1978); Selcer and Judd (1982)
*Holbrookia texana*: Johnson (1960)
*Homalopsis buccata*: Berry and Lim (1967)
*Homonota uruguayensis*: Gudynas and Gambarotta (1980)
*Hoplocephalus bungaroides*: Wells (1981)
*Hoplodactylus pacificus*: Rowlands (1978)
*Hydromedusa tectifera*: Benefield (1979)
*Hydrosaurus pustulosus*: Gonzales (1974)
*Hypnale hypnale*: de Silva and Toriba (1984)
*Hypsiglena torquata*: Clark and Lieb (1973)
*Iguana iguana*: Bakhuis (1982); Billiau (1972); Drummond and Burghardt (1983); Fitch and Henderson (1977); Hirth (1963); Licht and Moberly

(1965); Mendelssohn (1980); McGinnis and Brown (1968); Mueller (1972); Oliver (1984); Rand (1972); Reid (1984); Van Aperen (1969); Werner and Miller (1984)
*Iguana iguana iguana*: Howard (1980)
Iguanidae: Burghardt and Rand (1982)
*Imantodes cenchoa*: Henderson and Nickerson (1976)
*Imantodes gemmistratus*: Henderson and Nickerson (1976)
*Imantodes lentiferus*: Henderson and Nickerson (1976)
*Japalura swinhonisii*: Blok (1973)
*Japalura swinhonisii formosensis*: Cheng and Lin (1977)
*Kinixys belliana*: Kragh (1982)
*Kinosternon baurii*: Coote (1983)
*Kinosternon baurii baurii*: Coote (1978)
*Kinosternon flavescens flavescens*: Lardie (1975) (1978) (1979); Mahmoud (1967)
*Kinosternon leucostomum*: Rudloff (1982)
*Kinosternon leucostomum leucostomum*: Perez-Higareda (1981c)
*Kinosternon scorpoides scorpoides*: Fretey (1976)
*Kinosternon subrubrum*: Iverson (1979)
*Kinosternon subrubrum hippocrepis*: Mahmoud (1967)
*Lacerta*: Langerwerf (1980)
*Lacerta armeniaca*: Langerwerf (1980)
*Lacerta danfordi anatolica*: Sautereau and Langerwerf (1981)
*Lacerta graeca*: Langerwerf (1984)
*Lacerta lepida*: Howard (1985)
*Lacerta lepida lepida*: Hofmann (1963)
*Lacerta lepida pater*: Langerwerf (1977); Mantel (1984); Meeuwen (1974)
*Lacerta mosorensis*: Langerwerf (1983)
*Lacerta sicula sicula*: Botte and others (1976)
*Lacerta strigata*: Langerwerf (1980); Sautereau (1982)
*Lacerta viridis*: Appleyard (1978) (1979); Blanc (1979); Phillips (1983)
*Lacerta vivipara*: Avery (1962) (1966) (1971) (1975a) (1975b); Avery and McArdle (1973); Bauwens and Verheyen (1985); Gilpin (1969)
Lacertidae: Davies (1983) (1984a) (1984b) (1984c)
*Lachesis muta*: Burchfield (1975); Switak (1969)
*Lampropeltis*: Coote (1985); Riches (1978)
*Lampropeltis calligaster calligaster*: Clarke (1954); Coote (1981)
*Lampropeltis calligaster rhombomaculata*: Tryon and Carl (1980)
*Lampropeltis doliata doliata*: Palmer (1961)
*Lampropeltis getulus*: Alberico (1978); Jauch (1984); Zweifel (1980)
*Lampropeltis getulus californiae*: Clark and others (1984)
*Lampropeltis getulus floridana*: Bryant (1981)
*Lampropeltis getulus getulus*: Norrie (1982)
*Lampropeltis getulus nigritus*: Neitman (1980)
*Lampropeltis mexicana alterna*: Assetto (1978); Cranston (1985); Murphy and others (1978)

*Lampropeltis pyromelana*: Marcus (1976a); Tanner and Cox (1981)
*Lampropeltis triangulum*: Fitch and Fleet (1970); Williams (1978)
*Lampropeltis triangulum arcifera*: Herman (1979)
*Lampropeltis triangulum elapsoides*: Barten (1981); Dloogatch and Zaremba (1981); Herman (1979); Hingley (1982); Riel (1982)
*Lampropeltis triangulum hondurensis*: Howard (1985)
*Lampropeltis triangulum nelsoni*: Kardon (1979)
*Lampropeltis triangulum polyzona*: Kardon (1979)
*Lampropeltis triangulum sinaloae*: Gillingham and others (1977); Kardon (1979); Nolan (1981)
*Lampropeltis triangulum syspila*: Kamb (1978)
*Lampropeltis triangulum temporalis*: Miller and Grall (1978)
*Lampropeltis triangulum triangulum*: Henderson and others (1980)
*Lampropeltis zonata multicincta*: Coote (1984)
*Lamprophis fuliginosus*: Nägele (1985)
*Laticauda laticaudata*: Klemmer (1967)
*Leioheterodon madagascariensis*: Campbell and Murphy (1977)
*Leiolopisma otagense*: Watchman (1979)
*Leiolopisma rhomboidalis*: Wilhoft (1963)
*Leiolopisma telfairii*: Tonge (1985)
*Leiolopisma zelandica*: Barwick (1959)
*Lepidophyma tuxtlae*: Greene (1970)
*Leptodeira annulata*: Petzold (1969)
*Leptophis ahaetulla*: Zwinenberg (1976)
*Leptotyphlops dulcis dulcis*: Clark (1968); Punzo (1974)
*Leptotyphlops humilis*: Brattstrom and Schwenkmeyer (1951)
*Leptotyphlops humilis humilis*: Punzo (1974)
*Lerista bougainvillii*: Smyth and Smith (1974)
*Liasis albertisii*: Ross and Larman (1977); Trutnau (1984)
*Liasis childreni*: Barnett (1980) (1982); Chiras (1982); Dunn (1979); Ross (1973) (1983); Sheargold (1979)
*Liasis fuscus*: Charles and others (1985)
*Liasis mackloti*: Ross and Larman (1977)
*Liasis olivaceus*: Christian (1978)
*Lichanura trivirgata gracia*: Granger (1982)
*Liocephalus carinatus*: Petzold (1962)
*Liolaemus magellanicus*: Jaksic and Schwenk (1983)
*Liolaemus multiformis multiformis*: Pearson (1954)
*Lycodonomorphus bicolor*: Madsen and Osterkamp (1982)
*Lygodactylus*: Mobbs (1981)
*Lygosoma laterale*: Brooks (1967)
*Mabuya brevicollis*: Daele (1980)
*Mabuya buettneri*: Barbault (1974) (1976)
*Mabuya mabouya*: Somma and Brooks (1976)
*Mabuya maculilabris*: Barbault (1976)

*Mabuya multifasciata*: Hingley (1983)
*Mabuya quinquetaeniata*: Simbotwe (1980)
*Mabuya striata*: Simbotwe (1980)
*Macrelaps microlepidotis*: Marias (1980)
*Madagascariophis colubrina*: Campbell and Murphy (1977); Erasmus and Branch (1982)
*Malaclemys terrapin*: Burger (1976); Burger and Montevecchi (1975)
*Malaclemys terrapin pileata*: Burns and Williams (1972)
*Masticophis lateralis euryxanthus*: Hammerson (1978)
*Masticophis taeniatus taeniatus*: Parker and Brown (1980)
*Mehelya capensis*: Pewtress (1983)
*Menetia greyii*: Smyth and Smith (1974)
*Meroles cuneirostris*: Goldberg and Robinson (1979); Robinson and Cunningham (1978)
*Microsaura damarana*: Spence (1966)
*Micrurus fulvius*: Jackson and Franz (1981)
*Micrurus fulvius fulvius*: Allen (1940)
*Micrurus fulvius tenere*: Campbell (1973); Quinn (1979)
*Moloch horridus*: Pianka and Pianka (1970)
*Morelia amethistina*: Charles and others (1985)
*Morelia oenpelliensis*: Charles and others (1985)
*Morelia spilota*: Charles and others (1985)
*Morelia spilotes variegata*: Riel (1982) (1984)
*Morethia boulengeri*: Smyth and Smith (1974)
*Naja haje*: Behler and Brazaitis (1974)
*Naja haje annulifera*: Krzystyniak (1984)
*Naja melanoleuca*: Leloup (1962); Tryon (1979); Wilson (1959)
*Naja naja*: Quinn and Hulsey (1978); Campbell and Quinn (1975)
*Naja naja naja*: Agrawal (1979)
*Natrix maura*: Dennis (1982); Dumont (1979); Koppel (1979)
*Natrix natrix*: Koppel (1979)
*Natrix natrix helvetica*: Dennis (1980)
*Natrix natrix natrix*: Meek (1983)
*Natrix rhombifera rhombifera*: Bowers (1966)
*Natrix rigida*: Brown (1978)
*Natrix sipedon sipedon*: Littleford and Keller (1946)
*Natrix tessellata*: Steward (1958); Wolk (1984)
*Naultinus elegans*: Rowlands (1979)
*Nerodia cyclopion*: Mushinsky and others (1980)
*Nerodia erythrogaster*: Mushinsky and others (1980)
*Nerodia fasciata*: Mushinsky and others (1980)
*Nerodia fasciata fasciata*: Friend and Friend (1983)
*Nerodia harteri*: Carl (1981)
*Nerodia rhombifera*: Mushinsky and others (1980)
*Neusticurus ecpleopus*: Sherbrooke (1975)

*Opheodrys aestivus*: Palmer and Braswell (1976); Plummer (1981); Steehouder (1983)
*Opheodrys vernalis*: Groves (1976); Sexton and Claypool (1978)
*Ophiophagus hannah*: Acharjyo and Murthy (1983); Biswas (1976); Burchfield (1977); Dobbs (1967); Oliver (1956); Polder (1969)
*Ophisaurus apodus*: Claffey and Johnson (1982)
*Ophisaurus compressus*: Bartlett (1985)
*Osteolaemus*: Bustard (1980)
*Osteolaemus tetraspis*: Tryon (1980)
*Osteolaemus tetraspis tetraspis*: Beck (1978); Hara and Kikuchi (1978); Sims and Singh (1978); Teichner (1978)
*Oxybelis*: Henderson and Binder (1980)
*Oxybelis aeneus*: Henderson (1974); Henderson and Nickerson (1977)
*Oxybelis fulgidus*: Henderson and Nickerson (1977)
*Oxyuranus*: Shine and Covacevich (1983)
*Paleosuchus*: Bustard (1980)
*Paleosuchus trigonatus*: Jardine (1981)
*Panaspis nimbaensis*: Barbault (1976)
*Pelamis platurus*: Zeiller (1969)
*Pelomedusa galeata*: Cloudsley-Thompson (1971)
*Pelomedusa subrufa*: Ernst (1981); Harding (1981)
*Pelomedusa subrufa subrufa*: Bels (1983)
*Peropus mutilatus*: Church (1962)
*Phelsuma*: Mobbs (1981)
*Phelsuma guentheri*: Bloxam and Tonge (1980); Bloxam and Vokins (1978); Langebaek (1979)
*Phelsuma laticauda*: Howard (1980)
*Phelsuma lineata*: Vosjoli (1978)
*Phelsuma madagascariensis*: Demeter (1976); Switak (1966)
*Phelsuma quadriocellata*: Vosjoli (1978)
*Phrynops gibbus*: Mittermeier and others (1978)
*Phrynosoma*: Gray (1984a); Pianka and Parker (1975)
*Phrynosoma cornutum*: Cahn (1926)
*Phrynosoma m'calli*: Norris (1949)
*Phrynosoma platyrhinos*: Banta (1961)
*Phrynosoma solare*: Lowe (1954)
*Phyllodactylus marmoratus*: Hudson (1981); King (1977)
*Physignathus cocincinus*: Blake (1985); Howard (1982)
*Pituophis melanoleucus*: Bryant (1981)
*Pituophis melanoleucus catenifer*: Vejerslev (1985)
*Pituophis melanoleucus lodingi*: Reichling (1982)
*Pituophis melanoleucus melanoleucus*: Hine (1980)
*Pituophis melanoleucus mugitus*: Bruno (1983)
*Pituophis melanoleucus stejnegeri*: Parker and Brown (1980)
*Platynotus semitaeniatus*: Vitt and Goldberg (1983)

*Platysternon megacephalum*: Buskirk (1982)
*Podarcis*: Mattison (1981)
*Podarcis erhardii*: Quayle (1983)
*Podarcis lilfordi*: Norrie (1981)
*Podarcis muralis*: Appleyard (1979); Avery (1978)
*Podarcis sicula*: Avery (1978)
*Podarcis taurica ionica*: Chondropoulos and Lykakis (1983)
*Podocnemis expansa*: Alho and Padua (1982)
*Polychrus acutirostris*: Vitt and Lacher (1981)
*Psammophis elegans*: Spawls (1980)
*Psammophis sibilans*: Blackwell (1954a)
*Psammophis subtaeniatus sudanensis*: Steehouder (1984)
*Pseudechis colletti*: Charles and others (1983)
*Pseudechis guttatus*: Charles and others (1980)
*Pseudemys scripta*: Moll and Legler (1971)
*Pseudemys scripta elegans*: Davis and Jackson (1970)
*Pseudemys scripta troosti*: Cagle (1950)
*Pseudocerastes persicus fieldi*: Lehmann (1982)
*Pseudonaja nuchalis*: Banks (1983)
*Pseudonaja textilis*: Banks (1983)
*Pseudonaja textilis textilis*: Wells (1980)
*Ptyas mucosus*: Riel (1976)
*Ptychozoon*: Mudde (1980)
*Ptychozoon kuhli*: Mobbs (1979); Tiwari (1961)
*Ptyodactylus hasselquistii*: Werner and Goldblatt (1978)
*Python*: Katuska (1982)
*Python anchietae*: Patterson (1978)
*Python boeleni*: Murphy and others (1978)
*Python curtus*: Bowser (1979); Lang (1984); Stafford (1980) (1982)
*Python molurus*: Barker and others (1979); Vinegar (1973); Yadav (1967)
*Python molurus bivittatus*: Gaten (1982); Martin and Martin (1984); Van Mierop
    and Barnard (1976) (1978); Wagner (1976)
*Python regius*: Armstrong (1979); Edmondson (1976); Hawes (1974); Hingley
    (1983); Lehmann and Lehmann (1985); Logan (1973); Van Mierop and
    Bessette (1981)
*Python sebae*: Branch and Patterson (1975); Dunn (1979); Munnig Schmidt
    (1971) (1973); Patterson (1974); Sclater (1862)
*Python spilotus*: Murphy and others (1978)
*Python timoriensis*: Murphy and others (1978)
*Regina alleni*: Franz (1977)
*Regina grahamii*: Mushinsky and others (1980)
*Regina septemvittata*: Branson and Baker (1974)
*Rhabdophis tigrinus*: Moriguchi and Naito (1982); Sura (1981) (1983)
*Rhamphiophis oxyrhynchus rostratus*: Walsh and Davis (1978)
*Rhampholeon brachyurus*: Berrie (1981)

*Rhinocheilus lecontei*: Kronen (1980)
*Rhinocheilus lecontei tessellatus*: Lardie (1965)
*Rhinoclemmys pulcherrima incisa*: Hidalgo (1982)
*Sacalia bealei*: Praedicow (1984)
*Sanzinia madagascariensis*: Branch and Erasmus (1976) (1977); Foekema (1975); Groves and Mellendick (1973)
*Sauromalus hispidus*: Carl and Jones (1979); Sylber (1985)
*Sauromalus obesus*: Berry (1974); Case (1972) (1976); Mayhew (1963); Nagy (1973)
*Sauromalus obesus obesus*: Crooks (1983); Sanborn (1972)
*Sauromalus obesus tumidus*: Prieto and Ryan (1978); Prieto and Sorenson (1975) (1977)
*Sauromalus varius*: Sylber (1985)
*Scaphiophis albopunctatus*: Cahill (1971)
*Sceloporus cyanogenys*: Greenberg (1976)
*Sceloporus graciosus*: Marcellini and Mackey (1970); Rose (1976); Tinkle (1973)
*Sceloporus graciosus graciosus*: Burkholder and Tanner (1974)
*Sceloporus grammicus*: Ortega and Barbault (1984)
*Sceloporus grammicus disparilis*: Axtell and Axtell (1970)
*Sceloporus horridus*: Medica and Arndt (1976)
*Sceloporus jarrovi*: Carpenter (1960); Ruby (1977) (1978); Simon (1975) (1976); Tinkle and Hadley (1973)
*Sceloporus malachiticus*: Laurens (1976); Marion and Sexton (1971)
*Sceloporus merriami merriami*: Carpenter (1961)
*Sceloporus occidentalis*: Davis and Verbeek (1972); Goldberg (1974); Marcellini and Mackey (1970); Rose (1976)
*Sceloporus occidentalis occidentalis*: Davis and Ford (1983); Johnson (1965)
*Sceloporus olivaceus*: Kennedy (1956)
*Sceloporus orcutti*: Mayhew (1963)
*Sceloporus poinsetti*: Ballinger and others (1977)
*Sceloporus scalaris*: Anderson (1958); Ballinger and Congdon (1981)
*Sceloporus undulatus*: Sexton and Marion (1974)
*Sceloporus undulatus erythrocheilus*: Ferner (1976)
*Sceloporus undulatus garmani*: Ballinger and others (1981); Mayer (1977)
*Sceloporus undulatus hyacinthinus*: Trautwein (1983)
*Sceloporus undulatus undulatus*: Crenshaw (1955)
*Sceloporus woodi*: Jackson and Telford (1974)
*Scincella laterale*: Fitch and Achen (1977)
*Scincus scincus*: Badir and Hussein (1965)
*Siaphos equalis*: Bustard (1964)
*Sistrurus*: Murphy and Armstrong (1978)
*Sistrurus catenatus catenatus*: Reinert (1981); Reinert and Kodrich (1982)
*Sistrurus catenatus tergeminus*: Chiszar and others (1975)
*Sistrurus miliarius*: Carpenter (1960)
*Sistrurus miliarius miliarius*: Palmer and Williamson (1971)

*Sistrurus miliarius streckeri*: Fleet and Kroll (1978)
*Sitana ponticeriana*: Subba Rao (1983)
*Sonora episcopa episcopa*: Kassing (1961)
*Sonora semiannulata linearis*: Staedeli (1964)
*Spalerosophis cliffordi*: Dmi'el (1967)
*Sphaerodactylus cinereus*: Rösler (1983)
*Sphenodon punctatus*: Gans and others (1984)
*Sphenomorphus kosciuskoi*: Saylor Done and Heatwole (1977)
*Sphenomorphus pardalis*: Rankin (1978)
*Sphenomorphus quoyi*: Saylor Done and Heatwole (1977); Veron (1969a) (1969b); Veron and Heatwole (1970)
*Sphenomorphus tryoni*: Bustard (1964)
*Sternotherus carinatus*: Mahmoud (1967)
*Sternotherus minor*: Cox and others (1980)
*Sternotherus odoratus*: Mahmoud (1967); Olexa (1969)
*Stilosoma extenuatum*: Mushinsky (1984)
*Storeria dekayi*: Clausen (1936); Mitchell (1976)
*Takydromus septentrionalis*: Cheng and Lin (1977)
*Takydromus tachydromoides*: Jackson and Telford (1975); Minobe (1927); Takenaka (1980); Telford (1969); Yamamoto (1975)
*Tantilla gracilis gracilis*: Clark (1968)
*Tarentola annularis*: Cloudsley-Thompson (1972)
*Tarentola mauritanica*: Lopez-Jurado and others (1982)
*Telescopus semiannulatus*: Balvers (1982)
*Terrapene carolina*: Nichols (1939)
*Terrapene carolina carolina*: Cohen (1977); Evans (1953)
*Terrapene carolina triunguis*: Reagan (1974)
*Terrapene coahuila*: Brown (1974)
*Terrapene ornata ornata*: Legler (1960)
*Testudo denticulata*: Mowbray (1966)
*Testudo elephantopus*: Shaw (1961); Throp (1969)
*Testudo elongata*: Dunn (1976)
*Testudo graeca*: Collins (1980)
*Testudo hermanni*: Blake and Blake (1978); Cheylan (1981); Collins (1980)
*Testudo hermanni robertmertensi*: Cheylan (1982); Lancon and Lancon (1981)
*Testudo horsfieldi*: Broucko (1981)
*Testudo marginata*: Collins (1980); Hine (1982); Jenvey (1982); Walsh (1980)
*Testudo radiata*: Burchfield (1975); Peters (1969)
*Testudo sulcata*: Cloudsley-Thompson (1970)
*Thamnophis butleri*: Carpenter (1952); Ford and Killebrew (1983)
*Thamnophis elegans*: Arnold (1977)
*Thamnophis elegans terrestris*: Butler (1985)
*Thamnophis melanogaster*: Ford and Ball (1977)
*Thamnophis ordinoides*: Stewart (1965) (1968)
*Thamnophis radix*: Quartero (1982); Zwart and Van Ham (1980)

*Thamnophis radix haydeni*: Wolverkamp (1985)
*Thamnophis sauritus proximus*: Meerman (1981); Reijst (1980) (1981); Tinkle (1957)
*Thamnophis sauritus sauritus*: Carpenter (1952)
*Thamnophis sirtalis*: Alpaugh (1980); Fitch (1965); Heijnen (1983)
*Thamnophis sirtalis concinnus*: Stewart (1965) (1968)
*Thamnophis sirtalis infernalis*: Riches (1979)
*Thamnophis sirtalis parietalis*: Manders (1985); Marle (1982); Reijst (1980) (1981); Stoffels (1981)
*Thamnophis sirtalis similis*: Vanhoof (1985)
*Thamnophis sirtalis sirtalis*: Carpenter (1952); Healy (1953); Heijnen (1982)
*Thelotornis*: Henderson and Binder (1980)
*Thrasops jacksonii*: Pillich (1984)
*Thrasops jacksonii jacksonii*: Reil (1976)
*Tiliqua gerrardi*: Adler (1958); Field (1980); Stephenson (1977)
*Tiliqua nigrolutea*: Adler (1958); Bartlett (1984)
*Tiliqua occipitalis multifasciata*: Adler (1958)
*Tretanorhinus variabilis*: Petzold (1967)
*Trimeresurus albolabris*: Hartmann and Steiner (1984); Oosten (1982a) (1982b); Welch (1978b)
*Trimeresurus flavoviridis*: Ankenman (1981); Koba (1971); Koba and Morimoto (1978); Minakami and Nakamoto (1980)
*Trimeresurus gramineus*: Boerema (1981)
*Trimeresurus popeorum*: Janssen (1982)
*Trimeresurus trigonocephalus*: de Silva (1983)
*Trionyx muticus*: Plummer (1976) (1977a) (1977b) (1977c)
*Trionyx spiniferus spiniferus*: Robinson and Murphy (1978)
*Tropidechis carinatus*: Shine and Charles (1982)
*Tropidoclonion lineatum*: Force (1931)
*Tropidoclonion lineatum lineatum*: Clark (1968)
*Tropidurus peruvianus*: Huey (1974)
*Tropidurus torquatus*: Vitt and Goldberg (1983)
*Tupinambis nigropunctatus*: Jarvis (1981)
*Tupinambis teguixin*: Gudynas (1981); Hall (1978)
*Uma exsul*: Pough and others (1978)
*Uma notata*: Mayhew (1966); Pough (1970)
*Uma notata notata*: Sugerman and Applegarth (1980)
*Uma scoparia*: Mayhew (1966)
*Uromacer*: Henderson and Binder (1980)
*Uromacer frenatus dorsalis*: Henderson and Horn (1983)
*Uromacer oxyrhynchus*: Groves and Altimari (1977)
*Uromastix acanthinurus*: Grenot (1978); Watson (1969)
*Uromastix hardwicki*: Murthy and Arockiasamy (1977)
Uropeltinae: Murthy (1980)
*Urosaurus ornatus*: Asplund (1964); Parker (1973)

*Uta*: Ferguson (1970)

*Uta mearnsi*: Hain (1965)

*Uta stansburiana* Asplund (1964); Best and Gennaro (1984); Goldberg (1977); Medica and Turner (1976); Nussbaum and Diller (1976); Parker (1974); Parker and Pianka (1975); Tinkle (1967)

*Varanus acanthurus*: Husband (1979)

*Varanus acanthurus brachyurus*: Murphy (1971)

*Varanus dumerili*: Sprackland (1976)

*Varanus gouldii*: Barnett (1979); Green and King (1978)

*Varanus gouldii rosenbergi*: King and Green (1979)

*Varanus griseus*: Billiau (1972); Vernet (1978) (1982)

*Varanus komodoensis*: Osman (1967)

*Varanus niloticus*: Cowles (1930)

*Varanus salvator*: Acharjyo and Molapatra (1980); David (1970)

*Varanus storri*: Bartlett (1981) (1982)

*Varanus timoriensis*: Sautereau and Bitter (1980)

*Vermicella annulata*: Shine (1980)

*Vipera ammodytes*: Janssen (1981)

*Vipera ammodytes montandoni*: Ripa (1983)

*Vipera aspis*: Naulleau (1970) (1973) (1983)

*Vipera berus*: Andren (1982); Prestt (1971); Wright (1982)

*Vipera berus berus*: Howard (1976)

*Vipera lebetina*: Bogdanov and Zinjakova (1980)

*Vipera russelli*: Naulleau (1977); Naulleau and Brule (1980)

*Vipera ursinii ursinii*: Baron (1980)

*Virginia striatula*: Clark (1964); Mitchell (1976)

*Xantusia*: Brattstrom (1952)

*Xantusia henshawi*: Lee (1974); Mautz and Case (1974)

*Xantusia vigilis*: Cowles (1944); Miller (1951) (1954); Morafka and Banta (1973); Zweifel and Lowe (1966)

*Xenocalamus bicolor lineatus*: Branch and Patterson (1976)

# Appendix I

## Venomous Colubrids

The following list is of snakes known or believed to be capable of causing varying degrees of envenomation in man. For further information on venomous colubrids, see McKinstry (1983) and Taub (1967).

| Species | Reference |
|---|---|
| *Ahaetulla nasuta* | Alcock and Rogers (1902) |
| *Alsophis angulifer* | Neill (1954) |
| *Alsophis portoricensis* | Heatwole and Banuchi (1966); Hegeman (1961) |
| *Atractaspis dahomeyensis* | Warrell and others (1976) |
| *Atractaspis engaddensis* | Chajek and others (1974) |
| *Atractaspis irregularis* | Corkill and others (1959) |
| *Atractaspis microlepidota* | Corkill and Kirk (1954) |
| *Boiga blandingi* | Levinson and others (1976) |
| *Boiga dendrophila* | Burger (1974); Welch, personal observation |
| *Cerberus rhynchops* | Alcock and Rogers (1902) |
| *Coluber ravergieri* | Mamonov (1976) |
| *Conophis lineatus* | Ditmars (1931) |
| *Crotaphopeltis hotamboeia* | Broadley (1959); Chapman (1968) |
| *Dendrelaphis papuaensis* | Neill (1949) |
| *Dispholidus typus* | Fitzsimons (1962); Pope (1958) |
| *Dromicus chamissonis* | Schenone and Reyes (1965) |
| *Enhydris bocourti* | Welch, personal observation |
| *Enhydris enhydris* | D'Abreu (1913) |
| *Heterodon nasicus* | Bragg (1960) |
| *Heterodon platyrhinos* | Grogan (1974) |
| *Leptophis ahaetulla* | Zwinenberg (1977) |
| *Leptophis diplotropis* | Hardy and McDiarmid (1969) |
| *Macrelaps microlepidotus* | Fitzsimons and Smith (1958) |
| *Oxybelis fulgidus* | Crimmins (1937) |
| *Philodryas olfersii* | Nickerson and Henderson (1976) |
| *Pliocercus elapoides* | Seib (1980) |
| *Psammophylax rhombeatus* | Fitzsimons (1962); Fitzsimons and Smith (1958) |
| *Psammophylax tritaeniatus* | Chapman (1968) |
| *Rhabdophis tigrinus* | Kono and Sawai (1975); Mittleman and Goris (1974) (1978) |

86

| | |
|---|---|
| *Stenorrhina freminvillei* | Cook (1984) |
| *Tachymensis peruviana* | Schenone and Reyes (1965) |
| *Thamnophis elegans elegans* | Vest (1981) |
| *Thamnophis sirtalis sirtalis* | Hayes and Hayes (1985) |
| *Thelotornis kirtlandi* | Broadley (1959); Fitzsimons and Smith (1958); Loveridge (1956) |

# Appendix II

## Incubation of Reptile Eggs: Temperature and Length of Incubation in Days

| Scientific name | Temperature °C | Number of days | Eggs laid/ hatched | Reference |
|---|---|---|---|---|
| **PELOMEDUSIDAE** | | | | |
| *Pelusios castaneus* | 30–31 | 54 | 15/3 | Slavens (1984) |
| *Podocnemis unifilis* | | 42 | 3/2 | Slavens (1984) |
| **CHELIDAE** | | | | |
| *Chelodina novaeguineae* | 29.5 | 102–107 | 16/2 | Slavens (1984) |
| **KINOSTERNIDAE** | | | | |
| *Kinosternon baurii* | 28 | 71–100 | | Coote (1983) |
| **TESTUDINIDAE** | | | | |
| *Geochelone carbonaria* | | 192 | – /2 | Slavens (1984) |
| *Geochelone emys* | | 63 | 37/24 | Slavens (1984) |
| *Geochelone radiata* | 29.5 | 101–121 | – /9 | Slavens (1984) |
| **EMYDIDAE** | | | | |
| *Chinemys reevesi* | | 64 | 2/2 | Slavens (1984) |
| *Clemmys insculpta* | | 46 | 7/2 | Slavens (1984) |
| *Cuora trifasciata* | | 74 | 5/2 | Slavens (1984) |
| *Emys orbicularis* | 25.5 | 72–73 | 5/3 | Grundy (1982) |
| *Emys orbicularis* | | 90 | 3/2 | Slavens (1984) |
| *Pseudemys scripta elegans* | | 63 | 10/10 | Slavens (1984) |
| *Rhinoclemmys pulcherrima incisa* | 29.5 | 119 | –/4 | Slavens (1984) |
| **GEKKONIDAE** | | | | |
| *Ailuronyx seychellensis* | 23 | 96 | –/ 2 | Slavens (1984) |
| *Coleonyx variegatus* | | 45 | | Fitch (1970) |
| *Diplodactylus ciliaris* | 27 | 49 | –/1 | Slavens (1984) |
| *Diplodactylus elderi* | 30 | 43 | | Bustard (1965) |

88

| Scientific name | Temperature °C | Number of days | Eggs laid/ hatched | Reference |
|---|---|---|---|---|
| *Eublepharis macularius* | 30 | | 13/4 | Slavens (1984) |
| *Eublepharis macularius* | 28–32 | 40–42 | –/12 | Slavens (1984) |
| *Eublepharis macularius* | 23.5–29 | | –/6 | Slavens (1984) |
| *Eublepharis macularius* | 27 | 56–63 | | Thorogood and Whimster (1979) |
| *Eublepharis macularius* | 27 | 50 | | Werb (1980) |
| *Gehyra australis* | 27 | 58 | –/4 | Slavens (1984) |
| *Gehyra australis* | 25 | 87–143 | | Bustard (1969) |
| *Gehyra mutilata* | 25 | 65 | | Garthwaite, this vol., p. 39 |
| *Gekko gecko* | | 100 | 4/2 | Slavens (1984) |
| *Gekko gecko* | 27 | 161 | | Brodsky (1969) |
| *Gekko japonicus* | | 55 | | Fukada (1965) |
| *Gekko monarchus* | 26–30 | 60 | –/18 | Slavens (1984) |
| *Gonatodes vittatus* | 27 | 91 | | Mobbs (1980) |
| *Gymnodactylus geckoides* | | 206 | | Vanzolini (1953) |
| *Hemidactylus brooki* | 30 | 50 | | Garthwaite (1984) |
| *Hemidactylus flaviviridis* | | 57 | | Minton (1966) |
| *Hemitheconyx caudicinctus* | 29.5 | 56 | 9/8 | Slavens (1984) |
| *Heteronotia binoei* | 25 | 47–48 | | Bustard (1968c) |
| *Lygodactylus picturata* | 27 | 59 | | Mobbs (1981b) |
| *Oedura castelnaui* | 30 | 60 | | Bustard (1967) |
| *Oedura l.lesueurii* | 30 | 58 | | Bustard (1967) |
| *Oedura marmorata* | 30 | 88 | | Bustard (1967) |
| *Oedura ocellata* | 30 | 55 | | Bustard (1967) |
| *Oedura tyroni* | 30 | 49 | | Bustard (1967) |
| *Pachydactylus geitje* | 25 | 122 | | Bustard (1963a) |
| *Phelsuma dubia* | | 60 | | Garthwaite, this vol., p. 41 |
| *Phelsuma guentheri* | 21–29 | 75–90 | –/13 | Slavens (1984) |
| *Phelsuma guentheri* | 30 | 70 | | Bloxham and Tonge (1980) |
| *Phyllodactylus marmoratus* | 25 | 88 | | Bustard (1963b) |
| *Phyllodactylus porphyreus* | 25 | 115 | | Bustard (1963b) |
| *Ptychozoon kuhli* | 21 | 100 | | Mobbs (1980) |
| *Ptychozoon lionatum* | 21–29 | 77 | –/20 | Slavens (1984) |
| *Sphaerodactylus notatus* | | 74–79 | | Duellman and Schwartz (1958) |

AGAMIDAE

| | | | | |
|---|---|---|---|---|
| *Agama stellio* | 29 | 50–52 | | Langerwerf (1980) |
| *Agama stellio* | 30 | 47 | | Langerwerf (1980) |

| Scientific name | Temperature °C | Number of days | Eggs laid/ hatched | Reference |
|---|---|---|---|---|
| *Physignathus cocincinus* | 26.5–38 | 59–63 | | Howard (1982) |
| *Physignathus cocincinus* | 31 | 60 | 171–111 | Slavens (1984) |
| **CHAMAELEONIDAE** | | | | |
| *Chamaeleo basiliscus* | | 169–183 | | Shaw (1960) |
| **IGUANIDAE** | | | | |
| *Basiliscus plumifrons* | 28 | 67 | 14/7 | Banks (1983) |
| *Basiliscus plumifrons* | 31 | 61 | 81/55 | Slavens (1984) |
| *Basiliscus vittatus* | 31 | 47 | 70/36 | Slavens (1984) |
| *Cyclura macleayi* | | 119 | | Shaw (1954) |
| *Dipsosaurus dorsalis* | 36.5 ± .4 | 43–45 | 16/15 | Muth (1977) |
| *Iguana iguana* | 30 | 73 | 5/4 | Licht and Moberly (1965) |
| *Sauromalus obesus obesus* | 32 | 67 | 10/1 | Crooks (1983) |
| **LACERTIDAE** | | | | |
| *Lacerta agilis* | 31 | 35–36 | | Langerwerf (1980) |
| *Lacerta danfordi anatolica* | 30 | 43 | | Langerwerf (1980) |
| *Lacerta lepida* | 25.5–29 | 69–75 | 18/11 | Howard (1985) |
| *Lacerta pater* | 29 | 88–89 | | Langerwerf (1980) |
| *Lacerta schreiberi* | 28–29 | 42–47 | | Langerwerf (1980) |
| *Lacerta strigata* | 29–30 | 44 | | Langerwerf (1980) |
| *Lacerta strigata* | 28–32 | 50–60 | | Sautereau (1982) |
| *Lacerta viridis* | 30 | 42 | 38/37 | Slavens (1984) |
| *Lacerta viridis* | 28 | 77 | 15/1 | Phillips (1983) |
| *Lacerta viridis* | 30 | 63 | 15/1 | Phillips (1983) |
| **SCINCIDAE** | | | | |
| *Eumeces callicephalus* | | 8 | | Zweifel (1962) |
| *Lygosoma quadrupes* | | 32 | | Smith (1935) |
| **ANGUIDAE** | | | | |
| *Gerrhonotus multicarinatus* | 28 | 50–52 | 23/6 | Langerwerf (1981) |
| *Gerrhonotus multicarinatus* | 30 | 40–42 | 24/13 | Langerwerf (1981) |
| *Gerrhonotus multicarinatus* | 27 | 42–44 | 20/20 | Langerwerf (1981) |
| *Gerrhonotus multicarinatus* | 27 | 40–43 | 55/50 | Langerwerf (1981) |
| *Gerrhonotus multicarinatus* | 29 | 40–43 | | Langerwerf (1980) |
| *Ophisaurus attenuatus* | 27–31 | 36 | 12/11 | Slavens (1984) |

| Scientific name | Temperature °C | Number of days | Eggs laid/ hatched | Reference |
|---|---|---|---|---|
| **BOIDAE** | | | | |
| *Chondropython viridis* | 29.5 | 56 | –/16 | Slavens (1984) |
| *Chondropython viridis* | 20–30.5 | 54 | 23/23 | Slavens (1984) |
| *Python molurus bivittatus* | 29.5–32 | | 46/35 | Slavens (1984) |
| *Python regius* | 29–33 | 58–69 | 10/8 | Lehmann and Lehmann (1985) |
| *Python sebae* | 29–30 | 79 | 30/16 | Slavens (1984) |
| **COLUBRIDAE** | | | | |
| *Boaedon fuliginosus* | 23.5–29 | 70 | –/25 | Slavens (1984) |
| *Boaedon fuliginosus fuliginosus* | 24–28 | 72 | 7/7 | Nägele (1984) |
| *Boaedon fuliginosus fuliginosus* | 23–30 | 71–75 | 10/7 | Nägele (1984) |
| *Boaedon fuliginosus fuliginosus* | 23–30 | 71–75 | 8/8 | Nägele (1984) |
| *Dasypeltis scabra* | 24–28 | 61 | 13/2 | Bardulla (1984) |
| *Elaphe guttata guttata* | 28 | 61–62 | 23/23 | Boerema (1985) |
| *Elaphe obsoleta quadrivittata* | 30 | 49 | 22/21 | Koore (1985) |
| *Elaphe obsoleta quadrivittata* | 30 | 46 | 22/16 | Koore (1985) |
| *Elaphe obsoleta quadrivittata* | 26.5–29.5 | 72–75 | 10/10 | Friend and Friend (1984) |
| *Elaphe situla* | 26 | 66–69 | 4/3 | Werb (1980) |
| *Elaphe subocularis* | 26–29 | 83 | 4/4 | Morgan (1984) |
| *Gonyosoma oxycephala* | 30.5 | 105–119 | 5/5 | Bryant (1982) |
| *Heterodon nasicus* | 24.5–27.5 | 42 | 13/9 | Slavens (1984) |
| *Lampropeltis getulus floridana* | 29–30 | 46–48 | 12/12 | Steehouder (1985) |
| *Lampropeltis zonata multicincta* | 24.5–28.5 | 67 | 4/3 | Coote (1984) |
| *Mehelya capensis* | 20–23 | 99 | 10/7 | Pewtress (1983) |
| *Pituophis melanoleucus catenifer* | 25–28 | 59/60 | 5/4 | Vejerslev (1985) |
| *Pituophis melanoleucus melanoleucus* | 26–31 | 55 | 5/2 | Hine (1980) |
| *Psammophis elegans* | 26–33 | 67 | 6/6 | Spawls (1980) |
| *Rhabdophis tigrinus* | 20–30 | 34–35 | 13/3 | Sura (1981) |
| *Rhabdophis tigrinus* | | 35–38 | 12/7 | Sura (1983) |

| Scientific name | Temperature °C | Number of days | Eggs laid/ hatched | Reference |
|---|---|---|---|---|
| *Rhabdophis tigrinus* | | 43 | 9/2 | Sura (1983) |
| *Rhinocheilus antoni* | | 64 | 14/13 | Slavens (1984) |
| **ELAPIDAE** | | | | |
| *Aspidelaps scutatus* | | 58 | 9/9 | Slavens (1984) |
| *Naja haje annulifera* | 21–27 | 72 | 21/18 | Krzystyniak (1984) |

# Appendix III

# Herpetological Societies

There can be nothing but benefits from joining a local herpetological society where opinions can be exchanged and questions asked and answered. This list of societies and their last known addresses includes those known to publish either regularly or irregularly. The first part lists journals, with the names of the societies that publish them. Note: Such parts of titles as: Newsletter of , Journal of the , Bulletin of the , Bulletin, Newsletter, and Journal are obviously omitted here.


## 1. Journals.

*Amphibia-Reptilia*: Societas Europaea Herpetologica
*Aquarien Terrarien*: Kulturbund der DDR
*Australian Journal of Herpetology*: Australian Herpetologist's League
*British Journal of Herpetology*: British Herpetological Society
*Catesbeiana*: Virginia Herpetological Society
*Chelonia*: Chelonia—Sociedad para el estudio de los Quelonios
*Copeia*: American Society of Ichthyologists and Herpetologists
*Das Aquarium*: Isis
*De Schildpad*: Nederlandse Schildpadden Vereniging
*Die Schildkröte*: Interessen-Gemeinschaft Schildkrotenschutz
*Hamadryad*: Madras Snake Park Trust
*Herp*: New York Herpetological Society
*Herp Happenings*: Toledo Herpetological Society
*Herp News*: Palm Beach County Herpetological Society
*Herpetofauna*: Herpetofauna, Federal Republic of Germany
*Herpetofauna*: Australian Affiliation of Herpetological Societies
*Herpetologica*: Herpetologist's League
*Herpetological Review*: Society for the study of Amphibians and Reptiles
*Herpetology*: Southwestern Herpetological Society (U.S.A.)
*Herpeton*: Southwestern Herpetological Society (U.S.A.)
*Herptile*: International Herpetological Society (U.K.)
*Herpwise*: Greater Dayton Herpetological Society
*Japanese Journal of Herpetology*: Herpetological Society of Japan
*Journal of Herpetology*: Society for the study of Amphibians and Reptiles
*Lacerta*: Nederlandse Vereniging voor Herpetologie en Terrariumkunde
*Litteratura Serpentium*: Nederlandse Doelgroep Slangen
*Mountain Boomer*: Oklahoma Herpetological Society

*Notes from NOAH*: Northern Ohio Association Herpetologists
*Rephiberary*: Association for the study of reptilia and Amphibia
*Salamandra*: Deutschen Gesellschaft für Herpetologie und Terrarienkunde
*Snoken*: Swedish Herpetological Society
*Terra*: Terra, Herpetologic Society
*Testudo*: British Chelonia Group
*The Forked Tongue*: Greater Cincinnati Herpetological Society
*The Plastron Papers*: New York Turtle and Tortoise Society
*The Snake*: The Japan Snake Institute
*Tortuga Gazette*: California Turtle and Tortoise Club
*Turtle Power*: Bay Area Turtle and Tortoise Society
*Voice of the Turtles*: San Diego Turtle and Tortoise Society.

## 2. Herpetological Societies.

### Argentina

Asociacion Latino-Americana Ictiologo y Herpetologo
Dr. M. A. Freiberg
Museo Argentina Ciencias Naturales
Avenida Angel Gallardo 470
Buenos Aires, Argentina.

### Australia

Australian Affiliation of Herpetological Societies
Dr. H. Ehmann
School of Biological Sciences
Sydney Technical College
Broadway N.S.W. 2007 Australia
(There are five member societies, all of which receive the journal *Herpetofauna*: Australin Herpetological Society, South Australian Herpetology Group, Victorian Herpetological Society, Western Herpetological Group, and New Zealand Herpetological Society.)

Australian Herpetologist's League
G.P.O. Box 864
Sydney, N.S.W. 2001 Australia

### Belgium

Centre d'Observation Belge des Reptiles et Amphibiens
A. Goethals
Avenue General Medecin Derache, 153
1050 Brussels, Belgium

Terra, Herpetologic Society
F. Vanderstraeten
Wolterslaan 93
9110 Gent– Sint-Amandsberg, Belgium

## Canada

Canandian Amphibian and Reptile Conservation Society
9 Mississauga Road North
Mississauga, Ontario L5H 2H5, Canada

Venomous Animal Society of Canada
S. Allen
11 Knightsbridge Road, no. 1010
Bramalea, Ontario L6T 3X4, Canada

## Denmark

Nordisk Herpetologisk Forening
U. Olsen
Ørnevej 6
4040 Jyllinge, Denmark

## France

Société Herpetologique de France
Université de Paris VII
Laboratoire d'Anatomie comparée
2 Place Jussieu
75230 Paris cedex 05, France

## Germany, Democratic Republic of

Kulturbund der DDR (Zentraler Fachausschuss Terrarisktik)
1030 Berlin
PSF 34
Democratic Republic of Germany

## Germany, Federal Republic of

Deutschen Gesellschaft fur Herpetologie und Terrarienkunde
Dr. W. Bohme, President
Zoologisches Forschungsinstitut A. Koenig
Adenauerallee 150–164
5300 Bonn 1, Federal Republic of Germany

Herpetofauna
Postfach 1110

Stuttgarter Strasse 35
7056 Weinstadt 1, Federal Republic of Germany

Interessen—Gemeinschaft Schildkrotenschutz
R. Windolf
Katharina-Eberhard Strasse 12–14
8013 Haar bei Munchen, Federal Republic of Germany

Isis Gesellschaft für Biologische Aquarien und Terrarienkunde
J. Woolmann
Schwanthalerstrasse 123
8000 München 2, Federal Republic of Germany

## India

Madras Snake Park Trust
Guindy Deer Park
Madras 600, 022, India

## Japan

Herpetological Society of Japan
Dr. R. C. Goris
Sugao 9480–7
Miyamae ku, Kawasaki-shi 213, Japan

The Japan Snake Institute
Dr. Y. Sawai
Yabuzuka-honmachi, Nittagun
Gunmma Prefecture 379–23, Japan

## Netherlands

Nederlandse Doelgroep Slangen (The Dutch Snake Society)
J. Kooij
Langervelderweg 137
2211 AG Noordwijkerhout, The Netherlands

Chelonian Documentation Center
J. H. de Pon
P.O.Box 125
8700 AC Bolsward, The Netherlands

Nederlandse Schildpadden Vereniging
Papelaan 18
2522 EJ Voorschoten, The Netherlands

Nederlandse Studiegroep Anolissen
F. van Leeuwen
2e Boerhavestraat 5hs
1091 AK Amsterdam, The Netherlands

Nederlandse Vereniging voor Herpetologie en Terrariumkunde
E. F. Elzenga
Burg. H. van Konijnenburglaan 46
3925 XB Scherpenzeel, The Netherlands

Societas Europaea Herpetologica
Dr. M. S. Hoogmoed
Rijksmuseum van Natuurlijke Historie
Postbus 9517
2300 RA Leiden, The Netherlands

# New Zealand

New Zealand Herpetological Society
A. J. Howard
66 Don Buck Road, Massey
Aukland 8, New Zealand

# Puerto Rico

Chelonia—Sociedad para el estudio de los Quelonios
J. L. Pinero
P.O.Box 22061, UPR Station
San Juan, 00931 Puerto Rico

# South Africa

Herpetological Association of Africa
Dr. W. R. Branch
Port Elizabeth Museum
P.O.Box 13147
Humewood 6013, Republic of South Africa

# Sweden

Swedish Herpetological Society
Department of Zoology
University of Goteborg
400 33 Göteborg, Sweden.

**Switzerland**

Schildkroten—Informationsdienst
H. H. D. Falk
Bachserstrasse 10
8174 Stadel b. Niederglatt/ZH, Switzerland

## United Kingdom

Association of the study of Reptilia and Amphibia
Cotswold Wildlife Park
Burford, Oxon OX8 4JW, England

British Chelonia Group
Miss F. McGrattan
10 Clyde Park, Redland
Bristol BS6 6RR, England

British Herpetological Society
Zoological Society of London
Regents Park
London NW1 4RY, England

International Herpetological Society
A. J. Mobbs
65 Broadstone Avenue, Walsall
West Midlands WS3 1JA, England

Southwestern Herpetological Society
F. B. Gibbons
59 St. Marychurch Road
Torquay, Devon TQ1 3HG, England

## United States of America

American Society of Ichthyologists and Herpetologists
National Marine Fisheries Service Systematics Laboratory
National Museum of Natural History
Washington, D.C. 20560, U.S.A.

Arizona Herpetological Association
1433 W. Huntington Drive
Tempe, Arizona 85282, U.S.A.

Arkansas Herpetological Society
P. Floyd
16, Lakeside Drive
Hensley, Arkansas 72065, U.S.A.

Bay Area Turtle and Tortoise Society
P.O.Box 17
2000 Allston Way
Berkeley, California 94701, U.S.A.

California Turtle and Tortoise Club
P.O.Box 90252
Los Angeles, California 90009, U.S.A.

Chicago Herpetological Society
Chicago Academy of Science
2001 North Clark Street,
Chicago, Illinois 60614, U.S.A.

Colorado Herpetological Society
P.O.Box 15281
Denver, Colorado, 80215, U.S.A.

Connecticut Herpetological Society
G. Whitney
Whitney Clinic
860 Oakwood Road
Orange, Connecticut 06477, U.S.A.

Dallas Herpetological Society
P.O.Box 153672
Irving, Texas 75015, U.S.A.

El Paso Herpetological Society
7505 Dempsey
El Paso, Texas 79925, U.S.A.

Greater Cincinnati Herpetological Society
Cincinnati Museum of Natural History
172 Gilbert Avenue
Cincinnati, Ohio, 45202, U.S.A.

Greater Dayton Herpetological Society
Dayton Museum of Natural History
2629 Ridge Avenue
Dayton, Ohio 45414, U.S.A.

Herpetologists' League
J. Lee
Department of Biology

University of Miami
Coral Gables, Florida 33124, U.S.A.

Kansas Herpetological Society
Museum of Natural History
University of Natural History
Lawrence, Kansas 66045, U.S.A.

Maryland Herpetological Society
Natural History Society of Maryland
2643 North Charles Street
Baltimore, Maryland 21218, U.S.A.

Massachusetts Herpetological Society
P.O.Box 1082
Boston, Massachusetts 02103, U.S.A.

Michigan Society of Herpetologists
T. Moran
214 W. Broad Street
Eaton Rapids, Michigan 48827, U.S.A.

Minnesota Herpetological Society
Bell Museum of Natural History
10 Church Street
Minneapolis, Minnesota 55455–0104, U.S.A.

Mississippi Herpetological Society
P.O.Box 8087
Jackson, Mississippi 39204, U.S.A.

Nebraska Herpetological Society
J. D. Fawcett
Department of Biology
University of Nebraska
Omaha, Nebraska 68182, U.S.A.

New Mexico Herpetological Society
Department of Biology
University of New Mexico
Albuquerque, New Mexico 87131, U.S.A.

New York Herpetological Society
P.O.Box 1245
Grand Central Station
New York, New York 10017, U.S.A.

New York Turtle and Tortoise Society
H. Bender
215 West 92nd Street
New York, New York 10025, U.S.A.

Northern California Herpetological Society
Box 1363
Davis, California 95616, U.S.A.

North Carolina Herpetological Society
North Carolina State Museum of Natural History
101 Halifax Street
Raleigh, North Carolina 27611, U.S.A.

Northern Ohio Association Herpetologists
Department of Biology
Case Western Reserve University
Cleveland, Ohio 44106, U.S.A.

Oklahoma Herpetological Society
Department of Biology
Oklahoma Baptist University
Shawnee, Oklahoma 74801, U.S.A.

Palm Beach County Herpetological Society
G. Longhurst
P.O.Box 125
Loxahatchee, Florida 33470, U.S.A.

Philadelphia Herpetological Society
J. Feuer
102 S.New Ardmore Avenue
Broomall, Pennsylvania 19008, U.S.A.

San Diego Herpetological Society
P.O.Box 4439
San Diego, California 92104–0439, U.S.A.

San Diego Turtle and Tortoise Society
6957 Tanglewood Road
San Diego, California 92111, U.S.A.

Society for the study of Amphibians and Reptiles
H. C. Seibert
Department of Zoology

Ohio University
Athens, Ohio 45701, U.S.A.

Southwestern Herpetological Society
P.O.Box 7469
Van Nuys, California 91409, U.S.A.

St. Louis Herpetological Society
P.O.Box 9216
St. Louis, Missouri 63117, U.S.A.

Toledo Herpetological Society
Toledo Zoological Society
2700 Broadway
Toledo, Ohio 43609, U.S.A.

Utah Herpetological Society
P.O.Box 9361
Salt Lake City, Utah 84109, U.S.A.

Virginia Herpetological Society
Lafayette Zoological Park
3500 Granby Street
Norfolk, Virginia 23504, U.S.A.

Wisconsin Herpetological Society
Milwaukee Public Museum
800 West Wells
Milwaukee, Wisconsin 53233, U.S.A.

# Bibliography

Abuys, A. (1985). Breeding results: *Corallus enhydris enhydris*. *Litteratura Serpentium* 5: 31.

Acharjyo, L. N. and Misra, R. (1976). Egg laying of the mugger (*Crocodylus palustris*) in captivity. *Journal of the Bombay Natural History Society* 73: 223.

Acharjyo, L. N. and Molapatra, S. (1980). Eggs of the water monitor (*Varanus salvator*) laid in captivity. *Indian For.* 106: 230.

Acharjyo, L. N. and Murthy, T. S. N. (1983). Studies on the king cobras of Orissa, India. *The Snake* 15: 22–31.

Adler. K. K. (1958). Observations on the Australian genera *Egernia* and *Tiliqua* in captivity. *Journal of the Ohio Herpetological Society* 1: 9–12.

Agrawal, H. P. (1979). Food and feeding habits of *Naja naja naja*. *Journal of Animal Morphology and Physiology* 26: 272–275.

Akester, J. (1979). Successful mating and reproduction by a Gaboon viper, *Bitis gabonica gabonica*, in captivity. *Arnoldia Rhodesia* 8(31): 1–5.

Akester, J. (1980). Breeding Gaboon vipers, *Bitis gabonica gabonica*, in captivity. In *The Care and Feeding of Captive Reptiles*, edited by Townson and others (1980): 63–68.

Akester, J. (1983). Male combat and reproductive behaviour in captive *Bitis caudalis* (A. Smith). *British Journal of Herpetology* 6: 329–333.

Alberico, M. S. (1978). Notes on reproduction in *Lampropeltis getulus* from southern New Mexico. *Bulletin of the Maryland Herpetological Society* 14: 264–265.

Alcala, A. C. and Brown, W. C. (1967). Population ecology of the tropical scincoid lizard *Emoia atrocostata*, in the Philippines. *Copeia*: 596–604.

Alcock, A. and Rogers, L. (1902). On the toxic properties of the saliva of certain "non-poisonous" colubrines. *Proceedings of the Royal Society* 70: 445–454.

Alho, C. J. R. and Padua, L. F. M. (1982). Reproductive parameters and nesting behavior of the Amazon turtle *Podocnemis expansa* (Testudinata: Pelomedusidae) in Brazil. *Canadian Journal of Zoology* 60: 97–103.

Allen, C. E. (1940). Behavior of *Micrurus fulvius frontalis*. *Copeia*: 51–52.

Allen, E. R. and Neill, W. T. (1950). The life history of the Everglades rat snake, *Elaphe obsoleta rossalleni*. *Herpetologica* 6: 109–112.

Allen, E. R. and Neill, W. T. (1957). The gecko-like habits of *Anolis lucius*, a Cuban anole. *Herpetologica* 13: 246–247.

Allen, S. (1982). Notes on a captive-born litter of the canebrake rattlesnake (*Crotalus horridus atricaudatus*). *Journal of the Venomous Animal Society of Canada* 3: 5–6.

Almandarz, E. (1969). Hatching and care of the bearded dragon, *Amphibolurus barbatus*, at Lincoln Park Zoo, Chicago. *International Zoo Yearbook* 9: 50–51.

Alpaugh, W. C. (1980). Earthworm (*Lumbricus terrestris*) consumption in captive garter snakes (*Thamnophis sirtalis*). *Herpetological Review* 11: 93.

Alvarez del Toro, M. (1969). Breeding the spectacled caiman, *Caiman crocodilus*, at Tuxtla Gutierrez Zoo. *International Zoo Yearbook* 9: 35–36.

Ananjeva, N. B. and Orlov, N. L. (1982). Feeding behaviour of snakes. *Vertebrata Hungarica* 21: 25–31.

Anderson, J. D. (1958). Egg laying and nesting in *Sceloporus scalaris* Slevini. *Herpetologica* 18: 211–215.

Andren, C. (1982). Effect of prey density on reproduction, foraging and other activities in the adder, *Vipera berus*. *Amphibia—Reptilia* 3: 81–96.

Andreotti, F. (1977). Breeding rainbow boas: observations of a pair of *Epicrates cenchris*. *Bulletin of the New York Herpetological Society* 13: 33–34.

Ankenman, G. (1981). Maintenance of the Okinawa habu (*Trimeresurus flavoviridis*) in captivity. *Journal of the Venomous Animal Society of Canada* 1: 5–6.

Ankenman, G. (1982). Observations on courtship and mating behaviour in the jumping viper (*Bothrops nummifer*). *Journal of the Venomous Animal Society of Canada* (2): 6–8.

Antonio, F. B. (1980). Mating behavior and reproduction of the Eyelash viper (*Bothrops schlegeli*) in captivity. *Herpetologica* 36: 231–233.

Applegate, R. (1984). Feeding baby snakes. *Northern California Herpetological Society Newsletter* 3(7): 3 pp.

Appleyard, D. C. (1978). Notes on the care and breeding of green lizards (*Lacerta viridis*). *British Herpetological Society Newsletter* 19: 12–14.

Appleyard, D. C. (1979a). Care of wall lizards (*Podarcis muralis*). *Herptile* 4(1): 33–34.

Appleyard, D. C. (1979b). Notes on the incubation of four clutches of green lizard (*Lacerta viridis*) eggs. *Herptile* 4(1): 35–38.

Armstrong, G. (1982). Notes on feeding and growth rates in juvenile *Chelodina longicollis*. *Herpetofauna* 13(2): 27.

Armstrong, M. (1979). Induced feeding of royal pythons. *Herptile* 4(3): 9–10.

Arndt, R. G. (1972). Additional records of *Clemmys muhlenbergi* in Delaware with notes on reproduction. *Bulletin of the Maryland Herpetological Society* 8: 1–5.

Arndt, R. G. (1977). Notes on the natural history of the bog turtle, *Clemmys muhlenbergi* (Schoepff), in Delaware. *Chesapeake Science* 18: 67–76.

Arnett, J. R. (1979). Breeding the Fiji banded iguana, *Brachylophus fasciatus*, at Knoxville Zoo. *International Zoo Yearbook* 19: 78–79.

Arnold, S. J. (1977). Polymorphism and geographic variation in the feeding behavior of the garter snake *Thamnophis elegans*. *Science* 197: 676–678.

Asana, J. (1931). The natural history of *Calotes versicolor*, the common blood sucker. *Journal of the Bombay Natural History Society* 34: 1041–1047.

Asplund, K. K. (1964). Reproductive cycles of the Iguanid lizards *Urosaurus ornatus* and *Uta stansburiana* in southeastern Arizona. *Journal of Morphology* 115: 27–33.

Asplund, K. K. (1974). Body size and habitat utilization in whiptail lizards (*Cnemidophorus*). *Copeia*: 695–703.

Assetto, R., Jr. (1978). Reproduction of the grey-banded kingsnake, *Lampropeltis mexicana alterna*. *Herpetological Review* 9: 56–57.

Auffenberg, W. (1966). On the courtship of *Gopherus polyphemus*. *Herpetologica* 22: 113–117.

Auffenberg, W. (1970). Social behavior of *Geochelone denticulata*. *Southwest Naturalist* 15: 50–58.

Auffenberg, W. (1978). Courtship and breeding behavior in *Geochelone radiata* (Testudines:Testudinidae). *Herpetologica* 34: 277–287.

Avery, R. A. (1962). Notes on the ecology of *Lacerta vivipara*. *British Journal of Herpetology* 3: 36–39.

Avery, R. A. (1966). Food and feeding habits of the common lizard (*Lacerta vivipara*) in the west of England. *Journal of Zoology, London* 149: 115–121.

Avery, R. A. (1971). Estimates of food consumption by the lizard *Lacerta vivipara* Jacquin. *Journal of animal ecology* 40: 351–365.

Avery, R. A. (1975a). Age structure and longevity of common lizard (*Lacerta vivipara*) populations. *Journal of Zoology, London* 176: 555–558.

Avery, R. A. (1975b). Clutch size and reproductive effort in the lizard *Lacerta vivipara* Jacquin. *Oecologia* (Berlin) 19: 165–170.

Avery, R. A. (1978). Activity patterns, thermoregulation and food consumption in two sympatric lizard species (*Podarcis muralis* and *P. sicula*) from central Italy. *Journal of Animal Ecology* 47: 143–158.

Avery, R. A. (1979). *Lizards—a study in thermoregulation*. E. Arnold, Institute of Biology, Studies in Biology no. 109.

Avery, R. A. (1981). Feeding ecology of the nocturnal gecko *Hemidactylus brookii* in Ghana. *Amphibia—Reptilia* 1: 269–276.

Avery, R. A. (1985). Thermoregulatory behaviour of reptiles in the field. In *Reptiles breeding behaviour and veterinary aspects*, edited by Townson, S. and Lawrence, K. (1985): 45–60.

Avery, R. A. and McArdle, B. H. (1973). The morning emergence of the common lizard *Lacerta vivipara* Jacquin. *British Journal of Herpetology* 5: 363–368.

Axtell, C. A. and Axtell, R. W. (1970). Hibernacula, birth and young of *Sceloporus grammicus disparilis*. *Southwestern Naturalist* 14: 363–366.

Axtell, R. W. (1960). Orientation by *Holbrookia maculata* (Lacertilia, Iguanidae) to solar and reflected heat. *Southwestern Naturalist* 5: 47–48.

Bacon, J. P. (1980). Some observations on the captive management of Galapagos tortoises. In Murphy, J. B. and Collins, J. T. (1980) (editors): 97–113.

Badir, N. (1968). The effect of population density on the embryonic mortality in the viviparous lizard *Chalcides ocellatus* (Forsk.). *Anat. Anz.* 122: 11–14.

Badir, N. and Hussein, M. F. (1965). Effect of temperature, food and illumination on the reproduction of *Chalcides ocellatus* (Forsk.) and *Scincus scincus* (Linn.). *Bulletin of the Faculty of Science*, Cairo University 39: 179–185.

Bailey, J. W. (1928). A revision of the lizards of the genus *Ctenosaura*. *Proceedings of the United States National Museum* 73(12): 1–55.

Bakhuis, W. L. (1982). Size and sexual differentiation in the lizard *Iguana iguana* on a semi-arid island. *Journal of Herpetology* 16: 322–325.

Ball, D. J. (1974). Handling and restraint of reptiles. *International Zoo Yearbook* 14: 138–140.

Ballinger, R. E. and Congdon, J. D. (1981). Population ecology and life history strategy of a montane lizard (*Sceloporus scalaris*) in southeastern Arizona. *Journal of Natural History* 15: 213–222.

Ballinger, R. E., Droge, D. L. and Jones, S. M. (1981). Reproduction in a Nabraska sandhills population of the northern prairie lizard *Sceloporus undulatus garmani*. *American Midland Naturalist* 106: 157–164.

Ballinger, R. E., Newlin, M. E. and Newlin, S. J. (1977). Age-specific shift in the diet of the crevice spiny lizard, *Sceloporus poinsetti* in southwestern New Mexico. *American Midland Naturalist* 97: 482–484.

Balvers, M. (1982). Breeding results: *Telescopus semiannulatus*. *Litteratura Serpentium* 2: 195.

Banks, C. B. (1983a). Reproduction in two species of captive brown snakes, genus *Pseudonaja*. *Herpetological Review* 14: 77–79.

Banks, C. B. (1983b). Breeding and growth of the plumed basilisk (*Basiliscus plumifrons*) at the Royal Melbourne Zoo. *British Herpetological Society, Bulletin* 8: 26–30.

Banta, B. H. (1961). Herbivorous feeding of *Phrynosoma platyrhinos* in southern Nevada. *Herpetologica* 17: 136–139.

Barbault, R. (1974). Structure et dynamique des populations naturelles du lézard *Mabuya buettneri* dans la savana de Lamto (Cote d'Ivoire). *Bulletin d'Écologie* 5: 105–121.

Barbault, R. (1976). Population dynamics and reproductive patterns of three African skinks. *Copeia*: 483–490.

Barbault, R. (1977). Étude comparative des cycles journaliers d'activité des lézards *Cophosaurus texanus, Cnemidophorus scalaris, Cnemidophorus tigris* dans le désert de Mapimi (Mexique). *Bulletin de Société Zoologique, France* 102: 159–168.

Barbour, R. W., Harvey, M. J. and Hardin, J. W. (1969). Home range, movements, and activity of the Eastern Worm snake, *Carphophis amoenus amoenus*. *Ecology* 50: 470–476.

Barden, A. (1943). Food of the basilisk lizard in Panama. *Copeia*: 118–121.

Bardulla, F. (1984). Breeding results: *Dasypeltis scabra*. *Litteratura Serpentium* 4: 121.

Barker, D. (1979). Basic techniques for handling large lizards and snakes. *Occasional Papers, Dallas Herpetological Society* 1979(1): 6–8.

Barker, D. G., Murphy, J. B. and Smith, K. W. (1979). Social behavior in a captive group of Indian Pythons, *Python molurus* (Serpentes, Boidae) with formation of a linear social hierarchy. *Copeia*: 466–471.

Barnett, B. (1979). Incubation of sand goanna (*Varanus gouldii*) eggs. *Herpetofauna* 11(1): 21–22.

Barnett, B. (1980). Captive breeding and a novel egg incubation technique of the childrens python (*Liasis childreni*). *Herpetofauna* 11(3): 15–18.

Barnett, B. (1982). Kweken in gevangenschap met *Liasis childreni*; een nieuwe incubatie techniek. *Lacerta* 40: 164–166.

Baron, J. P. (1976). Elevage et reproduction de *Crotalus viridis oreganus* (Holbrook) dans des conditions artificielles. *Bulletin de Société Zoologie, France* 101: 734.

Baron, J. P. (1980). Donneés sur l'écologie de *Vipera ursinii ursinii* au Mont Ventoux. *Bulletin de Société Herpetologique, France* 14, 26.

Barten, S. L. (1981). Reproduction of *Lampropeltis triangulum elapsoides* from Onslow County, North Carolina. *Herpetological Review* 12: 62.

Bartlett, R. D. (1981). Notes on the captive reproduction of Storr's monitor, *Varanus storri*. *Bulletin of the Chicago Herpetological Society* 16: 65–66.

Bartlett, R. D. (1982a) Initial observations on the captive reproduction of *Varanus storri* Mertens. *Herpetofauna* 13(2): 6–7.

Bartlett, R. D. (1982b). Notes on the burrowing boids of the genera *Eryx* and *Calabaria* in captivity. *Notes from Noah* 10(1): 2–4.

Bartlett, R. D. (1984). Notes on the captive reproduction of the Australian skink *Tiliqua nigrolutea*. *British Herpetological Society Bulletin* 10: 33–35.

Bartlett, R. D. (1985). Notes on the natural history and reproductive strategy of the Island Glass Lizard, *Ophisaurus compressus*. *British Herpetological Society Bulletin* 11: 19–21.

Barwick, R. E. (1959). The life history of the common New Zealand skink *Leiolopisma zelandica* (Gray, 1843). *Transactions of the Royal Society of New Zealand* 86: 331–380.

Batist, P. de. (1984). De reuzenmeelworm. *Terra* 20: 13–15.

Bauwens, D. and Verheyen, R. F. (1985). The timing of reproduction in the lizard *Lacerta vivipara*: differences between individual females. *Journal of Herpetology* 19: 353–364.

Beardsley, H. and Barten, S. (1983). A note on reproduction in a captive born indigo snake, *Drymarchon corais couperi*. *Bulletin of the Chicago Herpetological Society* 18: 15–18.

Beaver, R. A. (1976). Food habits of the western diamondback rattlesnake, *Crotalus atrox*, in Texas (Viperidae). *Southwest Naturalist* 20: 503–515.

Bech, R. (1982). Zur Haltung und Nachzucht von *Chamaeleo jacksonii* in Terrarium. *Aquar. Terrar.* 29: 99–103.

Bechtel, H. B. and Bechtel, E. (1958). Reproduction in captive corn snakes, *Elaphe guttata guttata*. *Copeia*: 148–149.

Beck, C. (1978). Breeding the West African dwarf crocodile, *Osteolaemus tetraspis tetraspis*, at Memphis Zoo. *International Zoo Yearbook* 18: 89–91.

Behler, J. L. and Brazaitis, P. (1974). Breeding the Egyptian cobra, *Naja haje*, at the New York Zoological Park. *International Zoo Yearbook* 14: 83–84.

Belluomini, H. E. and Veinert, T. (1967). Notes on breeding anacondas, *Eunectes murinus*, at Sao Paulo Zoo. *International Zoo Yearbook* 7: 181–182.

Bels, V. (1983). Analyse de la parade de *Pelomedusa subrufa subrufa* (LACEPEDE). *Amphibia—Reptilia* 4: 297–309.

Benefield, J. (1979). Hatching the Argentine snake-necked turtle *Hydromedusa tectifera* at San Antonio Zoo. *International Zoo Yearbook* 19: 55–58.

Bennefield, B. L. (1982). Captive breeding of the tropical leopard tortoise, *Geochelone pardalis babcocki*, in Zimbabwe. *Testudo* 2: 1–5.

Benson, P. A. (1983). A semi-aquatic vivarium. *Herptile* 8: 75–77.

Berger, H. (1978). *Chamaesaura anguina*—birth of live young in captivity. *Journal of the Herpetological Association of Africa* 19: 22–24.

Berger, J. (1983). The importance of using vitamin/mineral powder with lizards. *Northern California Herpetological Society Newsletter* 2(8): 5.

Berger, J. (1984a). Care sheet: Western Skink (*Eumeces skiltonianus*). *Northern California Herpetological Society Newsletter* 3(4): 7.

Berger, J. (1984b). Care sheet: Banded gecko (*Coleonyx variegatus*). *Northern California Herpetological Society Newsletter* 3(5): 7.

Berrie, A. (1981). Incubation period of the eggs of the pigmy chamaeleon *Rhampholeon brachyurus*. *Nyala* 7: 143–144.

Berry, K. H. (1974). The ecology and social behavior of the chuckwalla, *Sauromalus obesus* Baird. *University of California Publications, Zoology* 101: 1–60.

Berry, P. Y. and Lim, G. S. (1967). The breeding pattern of the puff-faced water snake, *Homalopsis buccata* Boulenger. *Copeia*: 307–313.

Best, T. L. and Gennaro, A. L. (1984). Feeding ecology of the lizard *Uta stansburiana* in southeastern New Mexico. *Journal of Herpetology* 18: 291–301.

Billiau, F. (1972a). Het leven en lijden van de groene leguaan, *Iguana iguana*. *Lacerta* 30: 35–39.

Billiau, F. (1972b). Voedselweigering en genezing van een woestijnvaraan (*Varanus griseus*). *Lacerta* 31: 30–32.

Biswas, S. (1976). On the feeding habits of the king cobra *Ophiophagus hannah* (Cantor) at Nandankanan Biological Park, Orissa. *Journal of the Bombay Natural History Society* 73: 225–226.

Blackwell, K. (1954a). Behaviour of the African snake *Psammophis sibilans* before and during egg laying. *British Journal of Herpetology* 1: 189.

Blackwell, K. (1954b). Some notes on the egg laying and retention of the spermatozoa by the African snake *Boaedon lineatus*. *British Journal of Herpetology* 1: 189–190.

Black, E. (1985). The captive breeding of *Physignathus* and the use of vitamin D3 with other species of lizards. *Herptile* 10: 51–58.

Blake, E. and Blake, R. (1978). Captive breeding of the Hermann's tortoise, *Testudo hermanni*. *Testudo* 1(1): 8–11.

Blanc, C. P. and Carpenter, C. C. (1969). Studies on the Iguanidae of Madagascar III. Social and reproductive behavior of *Chalarodon madagscariensis*. *Journal of Herpetology* 3: 125–134.

Blanc, P. (1979). Technique de fabrication et d'aménagement de terrariums pour lézards verts (*Lacerta viridis*). *Bulletin de Société Herpetologique, France* 10: 14.

Blanchard, F. N. (1931). Secondary sex characters of certain snakes. *Bulletin of the Antivenin Institute of America* 4: 95–104.

Blem, C. R. (1981). Reproduction of the eastern cottonmouth *Agkistrodon piscivorus piscivorus* (Serpentes: Viperidae) at the northern edge of its range. *Brimleyana* 5: 117–128.

Blody, D. A. (1983). Notes on the reproductive biology of the eyelash viper *Bothrops schlegeli* in captivity. *Herpetological Review* 14: 45–46.

Blok, J. (1971). Verslag over gedrag en voortplanting van *Anolis bimaculatus sabanus* in het terrarium. *Lacerta* 30: 3–6.

Blok, J. (1973). Belevenissen met een kleine agame van Formosa, *Japalura swinhonisii*. *Lacerta* 31: 102–104.

Bloomer, R. J. and Holub, R. J. (1977). The bog turtle, *Clemmys muhlenbergi*, a natural history. *Bulletin of the New York Herpetological Society* 13(2): 9–22.

Bloxam, Q. M. C. (1977). Maintenance and breeding of the Jamaican boa (*Epicrates subflavus* Stejneger, 1901) at the Jersey Zoological Park. *Dodo* 14: 69–73.

Bloxam, Q. M. C. (1980). Breeding and maintenance of the Plumed basilisk *Basiliscus plumifrons* at the Jersey Wildlife Preservation Trust. *Dodo* 17: 88–96.

Bloxam, Q. M. C. and Tonge, S. (1980). Maintenance and breeding of *Phelsuma guentheri* (Boulenger 1885). In Townson and others (editors) (1980): 51–62.

Bloxam, Q. M. C. and Vokins, M. (1978). Breeding and maintenance of *Phelsuma guentheri* (Boulenger 1885) at the Jersey Zoological Park. *Dodo* 15: 82–91.

Boerema, H. (1981). Kweekresultaten: *Trimeresurus gramineus*. *Litteratura Serpentium* 1: 157–158.

Boerema, H. (1985). Breeding results: *Elaphe guttata guttata*. *Litteratura Serpentium* 5: 32–33.

Bogdanov, O. P. and Zinjakova, M. P. (1980). Sur le rythme d'activité de *Vipera lebetina* dans les montagnes de Noura Tan. *Bulletin de Société Herpetologique, France* 15: 10.

Bogerd, M. (1981). Het met succes tot zelfstandig eten brengen van *Python regius*. *Litterature Serpentium* 1: 186–188.

Booth, J. and Peters, J. A. (1972). Behavioural studies on the green turtle (*Chelonia mydas*) in the sea. *Animal Behaviour* 20: 808–812.

Bostic, D. L. (1965). Home range of the teiid lizard *Cnemidophorus hyperythrus beldingi*. *Southwest Naturalist* 10: 278–281.

Bostic, D. L. (1966a). Food and feeding behavior of the teiid lizard *Cnemidophorus hyperythrus beldingi*. *Herpetologica* 22: 23–31.

Bostic, D. L. (1966b). A preliminary report of reproduction in the teiid lizard *Cnemidophorus hyperythrus beldingi*. *Herpetologica* 22: 81–90.

Botte, V., Angelini, F., Picariello, O. and Molino, R. (1976). The regulation of the reproductive cycle of the female lizard *Lacerta sicula sicula* Raf. *Monitore Zoologico Italiano (N. S.)* 10: 119–133.

Bowers, J. H. (1966). Food habits of the diamond-backed water snake *Natrix r. rhombifera* in Bowie and Red River counties, Texas. *Herpetologica* 22: 225–229.

Bowler, J. K. (1977). Longevity of reptiles and amphibians in North American collections. *Society for the Study of Amphibians and Reptiles, Miscellaneous Publications* 6: 1–32.

Bowser, D. (1979). An effective method to induce feeding in wild caught, adult blood pythons (*Python curtus*). *Notes from Noah* 6:(5): 4–6.

Bragg, A. N. (1960). Is *Heterodon* venomous? *Herpetologica* 16: 121–123.

Brain, C. K. (1961). *Chamaeleo dilepis*—a study of its biology and behavior. *Journal of the Herpetological Association of Rhodesia* 15: 15–20.

Branch, W. R. and Erasmus, H. (1976). Reproduction in Madagascar ground and tree boas, *Acrantophis madagascariensis* and *Sanzinia madagascariensis*. *International Zoo Yearbook* 16: 78–80.

Branch, W. R. and Erasmus, H. (1977). Reproduction in Madagascar ground and treee boas. *Journal of the Herpetological Association of Africa* 15: 6–18.

Branch, W. R. and Patterson, R. W. (1975). Notes on the development of embryos of the African rock python, *Python sebae* (Serpentes: Boidae). *Journal of Herpetology* 9: 243–248.

Branch, W. R. and Patterson, R. W. (1976). Notes on eggs and hatchlings of *Xenocalamus bicolor lineatus* Roux from South Africa. *Herpetological Review* 7: 116–117.

Brand, L. (1981). Ervaringen met de rode rattenslang, *Elaphe guttata guttata*. *Litteratura Serpentium* 1: 88–100.

Brand, L. (1982). Verzorging en kweek van de gele rattenslang (*Elaphe obsoleta quadrivittata*). *Litteratura Serpentium* 2: 102–109.

Branson, B. A. and Baker, E. C. (1974). An ecological study of the queen snake *Regina septemvittata* (Say) in Kentucky. *Tulane Studies Zool. Bot.* 18: 153–171.

Brattstrom, B. H. (1952). The food of the nightlizards, genus *Xantusia*. *Copeia*: 168–172.

Brattstrom, B. H. and Collins, R. (1972). Thermoregulation. *International Turtle and Tortoise Society Journal* 6: 15–19.

Brattstrom, B. H. and Schwenkmeyer, R. (1951). Notes on the natural history of the worm snake, *Leptotyphlops humilis*. *Herpetologica* 7: 193–196.

Brecke, B. J., Murphy, J. B. and Seifert, W. (1976). An inventory of reproductive and social behavior in captive Baird's ratsnakes, *Elaphe obsoleta bairdi* (Yarrow). *Herpetologica* 32: 389–395.

Breckenridge, W. J. (1943). The life history of the black-banded skink, *Eumeces septentrionalis septentrionalis* (Baird). *American Midland Naturalist* 29: 591–606.

Brederode, R. van (1982). Breeding results: *Corallus enhydris cookii*. *Litteratura Serpentium* 2: 45.

Broadley, D. G. (1959). The herpetology of Southern Rhodesia. Part 1, Snakes. *Bulletin of the Museum of Comparative Zoology* 121: 1–100.

Brodsky, O. (1969). Breeding the great house gecko, *Gekko gecko*, at Prague Zoo. *International Zoo Yearbook* 9: 37–39.

Brooks, G. R., Jr. (1967). Population ecology of the ground skink, *Lygosoma laterale* (Say). *Ecological Monographs* 37: 72–87.

Broucko, Z. K. (1981). Données sur la reproduction de la Tortue d'Asie centrale (*Testudo horsfieldi*) dans le sud du lac Baikal. *Bulletin de Société Herpetologique, France* 18: 19.

Brown, E. E. (1956). Nests and young of the six-lined racerunner, *Cnemidophorus sexlineatus* Linnaeus. *Journal of the Elisha Mitchell Science Society* 72: 30–40.

Brown, E. E. (1978). A note on the food and young in *Natrix rigida*. *Bulletin of the Maryland Herpetological Society* 14: 91–92.

Brown, K. M. and Sexton, O. J. (1973). Stimulation of reproductive activity of female *Anolis sagrei* by moisture. *Physiological Zoology* 46: 168–172.

Brown, W. S. (1974). Ecology of the aquatic turtle *Terrapene coahuila* (Chelonia: Emydidae) in Northern Mexico. *Bulletin of the Florida State Museum, Biological Sciences* 19: 1–67.

Brunner, J. C. (1978). Captive breeding of Colombian rainbow boas *Epicrates cenchris crassus*. *Bulletin of the Philadelphia Herpetological Society* 26: 3–12.

Brunner, J. C. (1979). Captive breeding of Colombian rainbow boas, *Epicrates cenchris crassus*. *Proceedings of the Second Annual Reptile Symposium* 39–47.

Brunner, J. C. (1981). Breeding the eastern indigo snake. *Notes from Noah* 9: 14–15.

Bruno, B. B. (1983). Techniques of captive maintenance for the southern pine snake (*Pituophis m. mugitus*). *Herp Notes* (El Paso Herpetological Society) 3(2): 4–6.

Bruton, M. N. (1977). Feeding, social behaviour and temperature preferences in *Agama atra* Daudin (Reptilia, Agamidae). *Zoologica Africana* 12: 183–199.

Bruyndonckx, H. (1981). Het dwangvoederen van Thamnophissen. *Litteratura Serpentium* 1: 173–176.

Bruyndonckx, H. (1984). Refrigerator hibernation. *Litteratura Serpentium* 4: 146–148.

Bryant, C. J. (1981a) Notes on force-feeding Florida king snake (*Lampropeltis getulus floridana*). *Herptile* 6(3): 34–35.

Bryant, C. J. (1981b). Breeding the gopher snake *Pituophis melanoleucus*. *Herptile* 6(4): 30–31.

Bryant, C. J. (1982a). Reproductive data—orange ratsnake (*Elaphe obsoleta rossalleni*). *Herptile* 7(2): 29.

Bryant, C. J. (1982b). The red-tailed racer *Goniosoma (Elaphe) oxycephala*. *Herptile* 7(3): 33–34.

Bulian, I. and Bulian, J. (1983). Haltung und Zucht von *Boiga trigonata*. *Herpetofauna* (Ludwigsburg) 5(27): 13–15.

Bumgardner, M. (1985). A review of green tree python (*Chondropython viridis*). Propagation and husbandry. *Northern California Herpetological Society Newsletter* 4(8): 4–7.

Burchfield, P. M. (1975a). Hatching the radiated tortoise, *Testudo radiata*, at Brownsville Zoo. *International Zoo Yearbook* 15: 90–92.

Burchfield, P. M. (1975b). Raising the fer-de-lance, *Bothrops atrox*, in captivity. *International Zoo Yearbook* 15: 173–174.
Burchfield, P. M. (1975c). Adaptation of adult eastern diamondback rattlesnakes, *Crotalus adamanteus*, to captivity. *International Zoo Yearbook* 15: 174–175.
Burchfield, P. M. (1975d). The bushmaster, *Lachesis muta*, in captivity. *International Zoo Yearbook* 15: 175–177.
Burchfield, P. M. (1977). Breeding the king cobra, *Ophiophagus hannah*, at Brownsville Zoo. *International Zoo Yearbook* 17: 136–140.
Burchfield, P. M. (1982). Additions to the natural history of the crotaline snake *Agkistrodon bilineatus taylori*. *Journal of Herpetology* 16: 376–382.
Burger, J. (1976). Behavior of hatchling diamondback terrapins (*Malaclemys terrapin*) in the field. *Copeia*: 742–748.
Burger, J. and Montevecchi, W. A. (1975). Nest site selection in the terrapin *Malaclemys terrapin*. *Copeia*: 113–119.
Burger, W. L. (1974). A case of mild envenomation by the mangrove snake, *Boiga dendrophila*. *The Snake* 6: 99–100.
Burghardt, G. (1964). Effects of prey size and movement on the feeding behavior of the lizards *Anolis carolinensis* and *Eumeces fasciatus*. *Copeia*: 576–578.
Burghardt, G. M. and Rand, A. S. (1982) (editors). *Iguanas of the World: Their behavior, ecology and conservation*. Noyes Publ., Park Ridge, New Jersey 472 pp.
Burkett, R. D. (1966). Natural history of Cottonmouth moccasin, *Agkistrodon piscivorus* (Reptilia). *University of Kansas Publications, Museum of Natural History* 17: 435–491.
Burkholder, G. L. and Tanner, W. W. (1974). Life history and ecology of the Great Basin sagebrush swift, *Sceloporus graciosus graciosus* Baird and Girard, 1852. *Brigham Young University Science Bulletin, Biological Series* 19(15): 1–14.
Burkholder, G. L. and Walker, J. M. (1973). Habitat and reproduction of the desert whiptail lizard, *Cnemidophorus tigris* Baird and Girard, in southwestern Idaho at the northern part of its range. *Herpetologica* 29: 76–83.
Burns, T. A. and Williams, K. L. (1972). Notes on the reproductive habits of *Malaclemys terrapin pileata*. *Journal of Herpetology* 6: 237–238
Burrage, B. R. (1964). The eggs and young of *Gerrhonotus multicarinatus nanus* Fitch. *Herpetologica* 20: 133.
Burrage, B. R. (1973). Comparative ecology and behaviour of *Chamaeleo pumilis pumilis* (Gmelin) and *C. namaquensis* A. Smith (Sauria: Chamaeleonidae). *Annals of the South African Museums* 61: 1–158.
Burrage, B. R. (1974). Population structure in *Agama atra* and *Cordylus cordylus cordylus* in the vicinity of De Kelders, C. P. *Annals of the South African Museums* 66: 1–23.
Bury, R. B. and Balgooyen, T. G. (1976). Temperature selectivity in the legless lizard *Anniella pulchra*. *Copeia*: 152–155.
Busack, S. D. (1976). Activity cycles and body temperatures of *Acanthodactylus erythrurus*. *Copeia*: 826–830.
Busack, S. D. and Jaksic, F. M. (1982). Autecological observations of *Acanthodactylus erythrurus* (Sauria: Lacertidae) in southern Spain. *Amphibia—Reptilia* 3: 237–255.
Buskirk, J. (1982). *Platysternon megacephalum*: some observations on a captive pair. *Turtle Power* 11(7): 1–2.
Bustard, H. R. (1963). Notes on the eyed gecko (*Pachydactylus geitje*) with special reference to incubation. *Copeia*: 433–434.
Bustard, H. R. (1964). Reproduction in the Australian rain forest skinks *Siaphos equalis* and *Sphenomorphus tryoni*. *Copeia*: 715–716.
Bustard, H. R. (1965a). Observations on Australian geckos. *Herpetologica* 21: 294–302.
Bustard, H. R. (1965b). Observations on the life history and behavior of *Chamaeleo hohnelii* (Steindachner). *Copeia*: 401–410.
Bustard, H. R. (1966). Notes on the eggs, incubation and young of the Bearded

Dragon, *Amphibolurus barbatus barbatus* (Cuvier). *British Journal of Herpetology* 3: 252–259.

Bustard, H. R. (1967a). Reproduction in the Australian gekkonid genus *Oedura* Gray 1842. *Herpetologica* 23: 276–284.

Bustard, H. R. (1967b). Activity cycle and thermoregulation in the Australian gecko *Gehyra variegata*. *Copeia*: 753–758.

Bustard, H. R. (1968a). Temperature dependent activity in the Australian gecko *Diplodactylus vittatus*. *Copeia*: 606–612.

Bustard, H. R. (1968b). The ecology of the Australian gecko *Heteronotia binoei* in northern New South Wales. *Journal of Zoology, London* 156: 483–497.

Bustard, H. R. (1969). The ecology of the Australian geckos *Diplodactylus williamsi* and *Gehyra australis* in the northern New South Wales. *Koninkl. Nederl. Akademie van wetenschappen, Amsterdam* C72: 451–477.

Bustard, H. R. (1970a). The role of behavior in the natural regulation of numbers in the gekkonid lizard *Gehyra variegata*. *Ecology* 51: 724–728.

Bustard, H.R . (1970b). Activity cycle of the tropical house gecko *Hemidactylus frenatus*. *Copeia* 173–176.

Bustard, H. R. (1980). Captive breeding of crocodiles. In Townson and others (1980) (editors): 1–20.

Butler, R. (1985). The captive care and breeding of *Thamnophis elegans terrestris*. *Herptile* 10: 34–38.

Cagle, F. R. (1940). Eggs and natural nests of *Eumeces fasciatus*. *American Midland Naturalist* 23: 227–233.

Cagle, F. R. (1950). The life history of the slider turtle *Pseudemys scripta troosti* (Holbrook). *Ecological Monographs* 21: 31–54.

Cahill, L. W. (1971). Observations on a captive beak-nosed snake, *Scaphiophis albopunctatus*, at the University of Ife Zoo. *International Zoo Yearbook* 11: 233–234.

Cahn, A. R. (1926). The breeding habits of the Texas horned toad, *Phrynosoma cornutum*. *American Natural History* 50: 546–550.

Cairncross, B.L. and Greig, J. C. (1977). Note on variable incubation period within a clutch of eggs of the leopard tortoise (*Geochelone pardalis*) (Chelonia, Cryptodira, Testudinidae). *Zoologica Africana* 12: 255–256.

Campbell, H. and Simmons, R. S. (1961). Notes on the eggs and young of *Eumeces callicephalus* Bocourt. *Herpetologica* 17: 212–213.

Campbell, H. W. and Thompson, F. G. (1978). Observations on a captive Mona Island boa, *Epicrates monensis monensis* Zenneck. *Bulletin of the Maryland Herpetological Society* 14: 98–99.

Campbell, J. A. (1972a). Observations on Central American river turtles, *Dermatemys mawi*, at Fort Worth Zoo. *International Zoo Yearbook* 12: 202–204.

Campbell, J. A. (1972b). Reproduction in captive Trans-Pecos ratsnakes, *Elaphe subocularis*. *Herpetological Review* 4: 129–130.

Campbell, J. A. (1973). A captive hatching of *Micrurus fulvius tenere* (Serpentes: Elapidae). *Journal of Herpetology* 7: 312–315.

Campbell, J. A. and Murphy, J. B. (1977). Miscellaneous notes on the reproductive biology of reptiles.1. Two colubrid snake species from the Malagasy Republic, *Leioheterodon madagascariensis* and *Madagascariophis colubrina* (Reptilia, Serpentes, Colubridae). *Journal of Herpetology* 11: 228–230.

Campbell, J. A. and Quinn, H. R. (1975). Reproduction in a pair of Asiatic cobras, *Naja naja* (Serpentes, Elapidae). *Journal of Herpetology* 9: 229–233.

Capel-Williams, G. and Patten, D. (1978). The diet of adult and juvenile *Agama bibroni* (Reptilia: Lacertilia) and a study of the jaw mechanism in the two age groups. *Journal of Zoology, London* 185: 309–318.

Capezzone, L. (1979). Méthode et construction de terrariums en bois pour Reptiles et Batraciens. *Bulletin de Société Herpetologique, France* 10: 14.

Carey, W. M. (1966). Observations on the ground iguana *Cyclura macleayi caymanensis* on Cayman Brac, British West Indies. *Herpetologica* 22: 265–268.

Carl, G. (1978). Notes on worm eating in the prairie ringneck snake, *Diadophis punctatus arnyi*. *Bulletin of the Maryland Herpetological Society* 14: 95–97.

Carl, G. (1981). Reproduction in the captive brazos water snake *Nerodia harteri*. *Texas Journal of Science* 33: 77–78.

Carl, G. and Jones, J. P. (1979). The eggs and hatchlings of *Sauromalus hispidus* (Reptilia, Lacertilia, Iguanidae). *Journal of Herpetology* 13: 293–296.

Carl, G., Peterson, K. H. and Hubbard, R. M. (1982a). Reproduction in captive Uracoan rattlesnakes, *Crotalus vegrandis*. *Herpetological Review* 13: 42–43.

Carl, G., Peterson, K. H. and Hubbard, R. M. (1982b). Reproduction in captive Aruba Island rattlesnakes, *Crotalus unicolor*. *Herpetological Review* 13: 89–90.

Carpenter, C. C. (1952). Comparative ecology of the common garter snake (*Thamnophis s. sirtalis*), the ribbon snake (*Thamnophis s. sauritus*) and Butler's garter snake (*Thamnophis butleri*) in mixed populations. *Ecological Monographs* 22: 235–258.

Carpenter, C. C. (1960a). Aggressive behavior and social dominance in the six-lined racerunner (*Cnemidophorus sexlineatus*). *Animal Behavior* 8: 61–66.

Carpenter, C. C. (1960b). Parturition and behavior at birth of Yarrow's spiny lizard (*Sceloporus jarrovi*). *Herpetologica* 16: 137–138.

Carpenter, C. C. (1960c). A large brood of western pigmy rattlesnakes. *Herpetologica* 16: 142–143.

Carpenter, C. C. (1961a). Patterns of social behavior of Merriam's canyon lizard (*Sceloporus m. merriami*—Iguanidae). *Southwestern Naturalist* 6: 138–148.

Carpenter, C. C. (1961b). Patterns of social behavior in the desert iguana, *Dipsosaurus dorsalis*. *Copeia*: 396–405.

Case, T. J. (1972). Thermoregulation and evaporative cooling in the chuckwalla, *Sauromalus obesus*. *Copeia*: 145–150.

Case, T. J. (1976). Seasonal aspects of thermoregulatory behavior in the chuckwalla, *Sauromalus obesus* (Reptilia, Lacertilia, Iguanidae). *Journal of Herpetology* 10: 85–95.

Chajek, T., Rubinger, D., Alkan, M., Melmed, R. N. and Gunders, A. E. (1974). Anaphylactoid reaction and tissue damage following bites by *Atractaspis engaddensis*. *Transactions of the Royal Society of Tropical Medicine and Hygiene* 68: 333–337.

Chapman, D. S. (1968). The symptomatology, pathology, and treatment of the bites of venomous snakes of central and southern Africa. In, Bucherl, W., Buckley, E. E. and Deulofeu, V. (editors), *Venomous animals and their venoms* 1: 468–527.

Chapman, G. (1979). Captive breeding of orange or Everglades ratsnakes (*Elaphe obsoleta rossaleni*) for the second consecutive year. *Herptile* 4(2): 19–22.

Chapman, G. (1983). Notes on *Elaphe carinata*. *Herptile* 8: 106–108.

Chapon, N., Burnichon, H. and Joubert, F. (1976). Reproduction en captivité de trois Boides: le Boa constrictor (*Boa constrictor* L.), le Boa arc-en-ciel (*Epicrates cenchria*) et l'Anaconda (*Eunectes murinus*). *Bulletin de Société Zoologie, France* 101: 30.

Charles, N., Field, R. and Shine, R. (1985). Notes on the reproductive biology of Australian pythons, genera *Aspidites*, *Liasis* and *Morelia*. *Herpetological Review* 16: 45–48.

Charles, N., Watts, A. and Shine, R. (1983). Captive reproduction in an Australian elapid snake *Pseudechis colletti*. *Herpetological Review* 14: 16–18.

Charles, N., Whitaker, P. and Shine, R. (1980). Oviparity and captive breeding in the spotted blacksnake *Pseudechis guttatus* (Serpentes: Elapidae). *Australian Zoology* 20: 361–364.

Cheng, H. Y. and Lin, J. I. (1977). Comparative reproductive biology of the lizards *Japalura swinhonis formosensis*, *Takydromus septentrionalis* and *Hemidactylus frenatus* in Taiwan. *Bulletin of the Institute of Zoology, Academy Senica* 16: 107–122.

Chetwynd, J. (1983). Notes on the maintenance of the African agama *Agama agama* in captivity. *Herptile* 8: 35–37.

Cheylan, M. (1981). Biologie et écologie de la Tortue d'Hermann, *Testudo hermanni* Gmelin 1789. *Bulletin de la Société Herpetologique de France* 19: 48.

Cheylan, M. (1982). Densité, structure des populations et rhythmes d'activité de la Tortue d'Hermann, *Testudo hermanni robertmertensi* dans le sud-est de la France. *Bulletin de la Société Herptologique de France* 22: 54.

Childress, J. R. (1970). Observations on the reproductive cycle of *Agama stellio picea*. *Herpetologica* 26: 149–155.

Chiras, S. (1982). Captive reproduction of the children's python, *Liasis childreni*. *Herpetological Review* 13: 14–15.

Chiszar, D., Scudder, K., Smith, H. M. and Radcliffe, C. W. (1975). Observations of courtship behavior in the western Messasauga (*Sistrurus catenatus tergeminus*). *Herpetologica* 32: 337–338.

Chondropoulos, B. P. and Lykakis, J. J. (1983). Ecology of the Balkan wall lizard *Podarcis taurica ionica* (Sauria: Lacertidae) from Greece. *Copeia*: 991–1001.

Christian, T. (1978). Notes on the incubation of olive python (*Liasis olivaceus*) eggs. *Herpetofauna* 9: 26.

Christiansen, J. L. (1971). Reproduction of *Cnemidophorus inornatus* and *Cnemidophorus neomexicanus* (Sauria, Teiidae) in northern New Mexico. *American Museum Novitate* 2442: 1–48.

Church, G. (1962). The reproductive cycles of the Javanese House geckos, *Cosymbotus platyurus*, *Hemidactylus frenatus* and *Peropus mutilatus*. *Copeia*: 262–269.

Claessen, H. (1979). Reproduction eggs: factors associated with incubation and hatching and suggestion for laboratory rearing. *Journal of Herpetology* 13: 512–515.

Claessen, H. (1982a). Pneumonia in snakes. *Litteratura Serpentium* 2: 89–93.

Claessen, H. (1982b). Vitaminen. *Litteratura Serpentium* 2: 139–147.

Claessen, H. (1983). Brief instruction on medicine for terrarium animals. *Litteratura Serpentium* 3: 32–40.

Claffey, O. and Johnson, B. (1982). Captive reproduction of the sheltopusik (*Ophisaurus apodus*). *Animal Keepers Forum* 9: 329–332.

Clark, D. L., Gillingham, J. C. and Rebischke, A. (1984). Notes on the combat behaviour of the Californian kingsnake *Lampropeltis getulus californiae* in captivity. *British Journal of Herpetology* 6: 380–382.

Clark, D. R. (1964). Reproduction and sexual dimorphism in a population of the rough earth snake *Virginia striatula* (Linnaeus). *The Texas Journal of Science* 16: 265–295.

Clark, D. R. (1967). Notes on sexual dimorphism in tail-length in American snakes. *Transactions of the Kansas Academy of Science* 69: 226–232.

Clark, D. R. (1968). Experiments into selection of soil type, soil moisture level and temperature by five species of small snakes. *Transactions of the Kansas Academy of Science* 70: 490–496.

Clark, D. R. (1970). Ecological study of the worm snake *Carphophis vermis* (Kennicott). *University of Kansas Publications, Museum of Natural History* 19: 85–194.

Clark, D. R. (1976). Ecological observations on a Texas population of six-lined racerunners, *Cnemidophorus sexlineatus* (Reptilia, Lacertilia, Teiidae). *Journal of Herpetology* 10: 133–138.

Clark, D. R. and Lieb, C. S. (1973). Notes on reproduction in the night snake (*Hypsiglena torquata*). *The Southwestern Naturalist* 18: 241–255.

Clarke, R. F. (1954). Eggs and egg-laying of *Lampropeltis c. calligaster* (Harlan). *Herpetologica* 10: 15–16.

Clarke, R. F. (1965). An ethological study of the iguanid genera *Callisaurus, Cophosaurus* and *Holbrookia*. *Emporia State Research Studies* 13: 1–66.

Clausen, H. J. (1936). Observations on the brown snake *Storeria dekayi* (Holbrook), with special reference to the habits and birth of young. *Copeia*: 98–102.

Cloudsley-Thompson, J. L. (1970). On the biology of the desert tortoise *Testudo sulcata* in Sudan. *Journal of Zoology, London* 160: 17–33.

Cloudsley-Thompson, J. L. (1971a). Courtship of *Pelomedusa galeata*. *British Journal of Herpetology* 4: 237.
Cloudsley-Thompson, J. L. (1971b). *The temperature and water relations of Reptiles*. Merrow, Watford, vi, 159 pp.
Cloudsley-Thompson, J. L. (1972a). Temperature regulation in desert reptiles. In Maloiy, G. M. O. (editor), *Comparative Physiology of Desert Animals. Symposia of the Zoological Society of London* 31: 39–59.
Cloudsley-Thompson, J. L. (1972b). Site tenure and selection in the African gecko *Tarentola annularis* (Geoffroy). *British Journal of Herpetology* 4: 286–292.
Cloudsley-Thompson, J. L. (1981). Bionomics of the rainbow lizard *Agama agama* (L.) in eastern Nigeria during the dry season. *Journal of Arid Environments* 4: 235–245.
Coakley, J. and Klemens, M. (1983). Two generations of captive-hatched leopard tortoises *Geochelone pardalis babcocki*. *Herpetological Review* 14: 43–44.
Cohen, J. H. (1977). Breeding report: *Terrapene c. carolina*. *Chelonia* 3(3): 5.
Coles, R. W. (1984). Breeding the leopard tortoise (*Geochelone pardalis*) in captivity. In *Proceedings of the International Herpetological Society Symposium*: 16–32.
Coles, R. W. (1985). Reproductive date: the leopard tortoise (*Geochelone pardalis*). *Herptile* 10: 28–29.
Collins, P. W. P. (1980). The captive breeding of Mediterranean tortoises in Britain. In Townson and others (1980): 21–36.
Compton, A. W. (1981). Courtship and nesting behaviour of the freshwater crocodile *Crocodylus johnstoni*, under controlled conditions. *Australian Wildlife Research* 8: 443–450.
Cook, D. G. (1984). A case of envenomation by the Neotropical colubrid snake *Stenorrhina freminvillei*. *Toxicon* 22: 823–827.
Cooper, J. E., Arnold, L. S. and Henderson, G. (1983). A developmental abnormality in the Round Island Skink *Leiolopisma telfairii*. *Journal of the Jersey Wildlife Preservation Trust* 19: 78–81.
Cooper, J. E., Hutchison, M. F., Jackson, O. F. and Maurice, R. J. (1985) (editors). *Manual of exotic pets*. B.S.A.V.A., London.
Cooper, J. E. and Jackson, O. F. (1981) (editors). *Diseases of the Reptilia*. 2 vols. Academic Press, London.
Cooper, W. E. (1971). Display behavior of hatchling *Anolis carolinensis*. *Herpetologica* 27: 498–500.
Cooper, W. E. (1979). Variability and predictability of courtship in *Anolis carolinensis* (Reptilia, Lacertilia, Iguanidae). *Journal of Herpetology* 13: 233–243.
Cooper, W. E., Caffrey, C. and Vitt, L. J. (1985). Diel activity patterns in the banded gecko *Coleonyx variegatus*. *Journal of Herpetology* 19: 308–311.
Coote, J. (1978a). Captive husbandry and reproduction facilities for the three striped mud terrapin *Kinosternon baurii baurii*. *Testudo* 1(1): 17–19.
Coote, J. (1978b). The eggs and young of the eastern indigo. *Herptile* 3(3): 17–19.
Coote, J. (1979). Reproductive data: the green cat snake *Boiga Cyanea*. *Herptile* 4(3): 16.
Coote, J. (1981). Second generation captive breeding of the prairie kingsnake *Lampropeltis calligaster calligaster* (Harlan). In *Proceedings of the sixth Symposium of the Association of British Wild Animal Keepers*: 8–10.
Coote, J. (1983). The three-striped mud turtle and its captive reproduction. *Herptile* 8: 14–20.
Coote, J. (1984a). Second generation captive breeding of the Californian mountain kingsnake (*Lampropeltis zonata multicincta*). In *Proceedings of the International Herpetological Society Symposium*: 2–6.
Coote, J. (1984b). Snake husbandry equipment. *Litteratura Serpentium* 4: 149–159.
Coote, J. (1985). Breeding colubrid snakes, mainly *Lampropeltis*. In Townson, S. and Lawrence, K. (editors) (1985): 5–17.

Coote, J. G. and Riches, R. J. (1978). Captive reproduction in North American colubrids of the genera *Lampropeltis* and *Elaphe*. *Report of the Cotswold Herpetological Symposium*: 6–15.

Corkill, N., Ionides, C. J. P. and Pitman, C. R. S. (1959). Biting and poisoning by the mole vipers of the genus *Atractaspis*. *Transactions of the Royal Society of Tropical Medicine and Hygiene* 53: 95.

Corkill, N. L. and Kirk, R. (1954). Poisoning by the Sudan mole viper *Atractaspis microlepidota* Gunther. *Transactions of the Royal Society of tropical Medicine and Hygiene* 48: 376.

Cowie, A. F. (1976) (editor). *A manual of the care and treatment of children's and exotic pets*. B.S.A.V.A., London.

Cowles, R. B. (1930). The life history of *Varanus niloticus* as observed in Natal, South Africa. *Journal of Entomology and Zoology* 22: 3–31.

Cowles, R. B. (1944). Parturition in the Yucca night lizard. *Copeia* 98–100.

Cox, W. A., Nowak, M. C. and Marion, K. R. (1980). Observations on courtship and mating behavior in the musk turtle, *Sternotherus minor*. *Journal of Herpetology* 14: 200–204.

Cranston, T. (1985). Notes on natural history and husbandry of the grey-banded kingsnake. *Northern California Herpetological Society Newsletter* 4(1): 4 pp.

Crenshaw, J. W., Jr. (1955). The life history of the southern spiny lizard, *Sceloporus undulatus undulatus* Latreille. *American Midland Naturalist* 54: 257–298.

Crewes, D. and Garrick, L. D. (1980). Methods of inducing reproduction in captive reptiles. In Murphy, J. B. and Collins, J. T. (1980) (editors): 49–70.

Crimmins, M. L. (1937). A case of *Oxybelis* poisoning in man. *Copeia*: 233.

Crooks, B. (1983). The care and breeding of *Sauromalus obesus obesus* in captivity. *British Herpetological Society Bulletin* 7: 68–71.

Curry-Lindahl, K. (1979). Thermal ecology of the tree agama *Agama atricollis* in Zaire with a review of heat tolerance in reptiles. *Journal of Zoology, London* 188: 185–220.

D'Abreu, E. A. (1913). Effect of a bite from Schneider's water snake, *Hypsyrhina enhydris*. *Journal of the Bombay natural history society* 22: 203.

Daele, F. van (1980). Geslaagde kweek van *Mabuya brevicollis* in het terrarium. *Lacerta* 38: 85–87.

Daniel, P. M. (1960). Growth and cyclic behavior in the West African lizard *Agama agama africana*. *Copeia*: 94–97.

Daniel, P. M. (1961). Notes on the life history of *Agama agama africana* (Hallowell) in Liberia. *Special Publications, Ohio Herpetological Society* 3: 1–5.

David, R. (1970). Breeding the mugger crocodile and water monitor, *Crocodylus palustris* and *Varanus salvator* at Ahmedabad Zoo. *International Zoo Yearbook*. 10: 116–117.

Davies, R. (1983). The Lacertid lizards (Part one). *Herptile* 8: 91–96.

Davies, R. (1984a). The Lacertid lizards (Part two). *Herptile* 9: 14–19.

Davies, R. (1984b). The Lacertid lizards (Part three). *Herptile* 9: 66–70.

Davies, R. (1984c). The Lacertid lizards (Part four). *Herptile* 9: 126–130.

Davis, D. D. (1953). Behavior of the lizard *Corythophanes cristatus*. *Fieldiana Zoology* 35: 1–8.

Davis, J. and Ford, R. G. (1983). Home range in the western fence lizard (*Sceloporus occidentalis occidentalis*). *Copeia*: 933–940.

Davis, J. and Verbeek, N. A. M. (1972). Habitat preferences and the distribution of *Uta stansburiana* and *Sceloporus occidentalis* in coastal California. *Copeia*: 643–649.

Davis, J. D. and Jackson, C. G. (1970). Copulatory behavior in the red-eared turtle *Pseudemys scripta elegans*. *Herpetologica* 26: 238–239.

Davis, J. D. and Jackson, C. G. (1973). Notes on the courtship of a captive male *Chrysemys scripta taylori*. *Herpetologica* 29: 62–64.

Davis, S. (1979). Husbandry and breeding of the red-footed tortoise *Geochelone carbonaria* at the National Zoological Park, Washignton. *International Zoo Yearbook* 19: 50–53.

Davis, W. F. (1976). How to maintain desert iguanas (*Dipsosaurus dorsalis*) in captivity. *British Herpetological Society Newsletter* 14: 13–14.

Day, K. (1980). Notes on the birth of the pygmy spiny tailed skink, *Egernia depressa* (Gunther) in captivity. *Herpetofauna* 11(2): 29.

Demeter, B. J. (1976). Observations on the care, breeding and behavior of the giant day gecko, *Phelsuma madagascariensis*, at the National Zoological Park, Washington, *International Zoo Yearbook* 16: 130–133.

Denardo, D. (1985). Captive reproduction of the banded gecko (*Coleonyx variegatus*). *Northern California Herpetological Society Newsletter* 4(3): 2 pp.

Dennis, J. (1980). Reproductive data: the barred grass snake (*Natrix natrix helvetica*). *Herptile* 5(4): 26–27.

Dennis, J. (1982). Reproductive data: Viperine snake *Natrix maura*. *Herptile* 7(3): 28.

Deschanel, J. P. (1978). Reproduction of anacondas, *Eunectes murinus*, at Lyons Zoo. *International Zoo Yearbook* 18: 98–99.

De Silva, A. (1977). Some observations on the development of *Elaphe helena* (Daudin) eggs. *Hamadryad* 2(2): 8–9.

De Silva, A. (1983). Reproductive habits of *Trimeresurus trigonocephalus* (Sonnini et Latreille). *The Snake* 15: 16–21.

De Silva, A. and Toriba, M. (1984). Reproductive habits of *Hypnale hypnale* (Merrem) in Sri Lanka. *The Snake* 16: 135–138.

Dial, B. E. (1978). Aspects of the behavioral ecology of two Chihuahuan desert geckos (Reptilia, Lacertilia, Gekkonidae). *Journal of Herpetology* 12: 209–216.

Ditmars, R. L. (1931). *Snakes of the World* Macmillan, N.Y. 207 pages, 84 plates.

Ditmars, R. L. (1933). *Reptiles of the World*. Macmillan, N.Y. 321 pages, 89 plates.

Dloogatch, M. A. and Zaremba, T. A. (1981). Captive propagation of the scarlet kingsnake, *Lampropeltis triangulum elapsoides*. *Bulletin of the Chicago Herpetological Society* 16: 81–85.

Dmi'el, R. (1967). Studies on reproduction, growth, and feeding in the snake *Spalerosophis cliffordi* (Colubridae). *Copeia*: 332–346.

Dobbs, J. S. (1967). The feeding of dead food to a king cobra, *Ophiophagus hannah*. *International Zoo Yearbook* 7: 229.

Douglas, N. H. (1965). Observations on the predaceous and cannibalistic feeding habits of *Eumeces laticeps* Schneider. *Herpetologica* 21: 308–309.

Douglas, R. (1981). Notes on the reproduction of the common horned adder (*Bitis caudalis*) in the central Namib Desert. *Journal of the Herpetological Association of Africa* 25: 5–6.

Douglass, J. F. (1978). Refugia of juvenile gopher tortoises, *Gopherus polyphemus* (Reptilia, Testudines, Testudinidae). *Journal of Herpetology* 12, 413–415.

Douglass, J. F. and Layne, J. N. (1978). Activity and thermoregulation of the gopher tortoise (*Gopherus polyphemus*) in southern Florida. *Herpetologica* 34: 359–374.

Drummond, H. and Burghardt, G. M. (1983). Nocturnal and diurnal nest emergence in green iguanas. *Journal of Herpetology* 17: 290–292.

Duellman, W. E. (1960). Variation, distribution and ecology of the Mexican teiid lizard *Cnemidophorus calidipes*. *Copeia*: 97–101.

Duellman, W. E. and Duellman, A. S. (1959). Variation, distribution and ecology of the iguanid lizard *Enyaliosaurus clarki* of Michoacan, Mexico. *Occasional Papers of the Museum of Zoology, University of Michigan* 598: 1–10.

Duellman, W. E. and Schwartz, A. (1958). Amphibians and reptiles of southern Florida. *Bulletin of the Florida State Museum* 3: 181–324.

Dumont, M. (1979). Elevage et reproduction de *Natrix maura*. *Bulletin de la Société Herpetologie, France* 12: 7.

Dunn, E. R. (1937). Hybrids and intergrades. *Copeia*: 1–4.

Dunn, R. W. (1976). Breeding the elongate tortoise, *Testudo elongata*, at Melbourne Zoo. *International Zoo Yearbook* 16: 73–74.

Dunn, R. W. (1977). Notes on the breeding of Johnstone's crocodile, *Crocodylus johnsoni*, at Melbourne Zoo. *International Zoo Yearbook* 17: 130–131.

Dunn, R. W. (1979a). Breeding children's python, *Liasis childreni*, at Melbourne Zoo. *International Zoo Yearbook* 19: 89–90.

Dunn, R. W. (1979b). Breeding African pythons, *Python sebae*, at Melbourne Zoo. *International Zoo Yearbook* 19: 91–92.

Dunn, R. W. (1981). Further observations on the captive reproduction of Johnstone's crocodile. *International Zoo Yearbook* 21: 82–83.

Echelle, A. A., Echelle, A. F. and Fitch, H. S. (1972). Observations of fish-eating and maintenance behavior in two species of *Basiliscus*. *Copeia*: 387–389.

Edmondson, C. R. (1976). Hatching royal pythons (*Python regius*) eggs. *Journal of the Southwestern Herpetological Society* 1(3): 14–16.

Edmondson, C. R. (1979). Breeding Florida indigo snakes—*Drymarchon corais couperi*. *Southwestern Herpetological Society Bulletin* 2: 2–3.

Eerden, J. L. A. van der (1985). Successful breeding of Texas rat snake (*Elaphe obsoleta lindheimeri*). *Litteratura Serpentium* 5: 163–165.

Erasmus, H. and Branch, W. (1982). Reproduction in the Madagascan snake *Madagascariophis colubrina* (Schlegel) (Colubridae: Lycodontinae). *Journal of the Herpetological Association of Africa* 27: 9–10.

Ernst, C. H. (1970). Reproduction in *Clemmys guttata*. *Herpetologica* 26: 228–232.

Ernst, C. H. (1976). Ecology of the spotted turtle, *Clemmys guttata* (Reptilia, Testudines, Testudinidae) in southeastern Pennsylvania. *Journal of Herpetology* 10: 25–33.

Ernst, C. H. (1981). Courtship of the African helmeted turtle (*Pelomedusa subrufa*). *British Journal of Herpetology* 6: 141–142.

Ernst, C. H. (1982). Environmental temperatures and activities in wild spotted turtles, *Clemmys guttata*. *Journal of Herpetology* 16: 112–120.

Evans, L. T. (1951). Field study of the social behavior of the black lizard, *Ctenosaura pectinata*. *American Museum Novitate 1493*: 1–26.

Evans, L. T. (1953). The courtship pattern of the box turtle, *Terrapene c.carolina*. *Herpetologica* 9: 189–192.

Fauci, J. (1981). Breeding and rearing of captive Solomon Island ground boas, *Candoia carinata paulseni*. *Herpetological Review* 12: 60–61.

Feldman, M. L. (1983). Effects of rotation on the viability of turtle eggs. *Herpetological Review* 14: 76–77.

Ferguson, G. W. (1970). Mating behaviour of the side-blotched lizards of the genus *Uta* (Sauria:Iguanidae). *Animal Behaviour* 18: 65–72.

Ferner, J. W. (1976). Notes on natural history and behavior of *Scelopotus undulatus erythrocheilus* in Colorado. *American Midland Naturalist* 96: 291–302.

Ferner, J. W. (1979). A review of marking techniques for amphibians and reptiles. *Society for the study of Amphibians and Reptiles Publication* 9: 1–41.

Fertard, B. (1978). Le caméléon commun en terrarium. *Bulletin de la Société de Herpetologie de France* 8: 5.

Fertard, B. (1982). Reproduction de *Boaedon lineatum*. *Bulletin de la Société de Herpetologie de France* 24: 22.

Field, R. (1980). The pink-tongued skink (*Tiliqua gerrardii*) in captivity. *Herpetofauna* 11(2): 6–10.

Finnegan, D. (1984). Hibernation and hibernaculum construction. *Northern California Herpetological Society Newsletter* 3(9): 4 pp.

Fitch, H. S. (1954). Life history and ecology of the five-lined skink, *Eumeces fasciatus*. *Publications of the Museum of Natural History, University of Kansas* 8: 1–156.

Fitch, H. S. (1955). Habits and adaptations of the Great Plains skink (*Eumeces obsoletus*). *Ecological Monographs* 25: 59–83.

Fitch, H. S. (1956). An ecological study of the collared lizard (*Crotaphytus collaris*. *University of Kansas Publications, Museum of Natural History* 8: 213–274.

Fitch, H. S. (1958). Natural history of the six-lined racerunner (*Cnemidophorus sexlineatus*). *University of Kansas Publications, Museum of Natural History* 11: 11–62.

Fitch, H. S. (1960). Criteria for determining sex and breeding maturity in snakes. *Herpetologica* 16: 49–51.

Fitch, H. S. (1963a). Natural History of the racer *Coluber constrictor*. *University of Kansas Publications, Museum of Natural History* 15: 351–468.

Fitch, H. S. (1963b). Natural history of the black snake (*Elaphe o. obsoleta*) in Kansas. *Copeia*: 649–658.

Fitch, H. S. (1965). An ecological study of the garter snake *Thamnophis sirtalis*. *University of Kansas Publications, Museum of Natural History* 15: 493–564.

Fitch, H. S. (1970). Reproductive cycles in lizards and snakes. *University of Kansas Museum of Natural History Miscellaneous Publications* 52: 1–247.

Fitch, H. S. (1972). Ecology of *Anolis tropidolepis* in Costa Rican cloud forest. *Herpetologica* 28: 10–21.

Fitch, H. S. and Achen, P. L. von (1977). Spatial relationships and seasonality in the skinks *Eumeces fasciatus* and *Scincella laterale* in northeastern Kansas. *Herpetologica* 33: 303–313.

Fitch, H. S. and Fleet, R. R. (1970). Natural history of the milk snake (*Lampropeltis triangulum*) in northeastern Kansas. *Herpetologica* 26: 387–396.

Fitch, H. S. and Henderson, R. W. (1976). A field study of the rock anoles (Reptilia, Lacertilia, Iguanidae) of southern Mexico. *Journal of Herpetology* 10: 303–311.

Fitch, H. S. and Henderson, R. W. (1977). Age and sex differences, reproduction and conservation of *Iguana iguana*. *Contributions in Biology and Geology, Milwaukee Public Museum* 13: 1–21.

Fitch, H. S. and Twining, H. (1946). Feeding habits of the Pacific rattlesnake. *Copeia*: 64–71.

Fitzsimons, D. C. and Smith, H. M. (1958). Another rear-fanged South African snake lethal to humans. *Herpetologica* 14: 198–202.

Fitzsimons, F. W. (1919). *The snakes of South Africa, their venom and the treatment of snake bite*. Maskew Miller, Cape Town.

Fitzsimons, V. F. M. (1962). *Snakes of Southern Africa*. Purnell, Cape Town.

Fleet, R. R. and Fitch, H. S. (1974). Food habits of *Basiliscus basiliscus* in Costa Rica. *Journal of Herpetology* 8: 260–262.

Fleet, R. R. and Kroll, J. C. (1978). Litter size and parturition behavior in *Sistrurus miliarius streckeri*. *Herpetological Review* 9: 11.

Foekema, G. M. M. (1970). Een kennismaking met *Cylindrophis rufus* (Serpentes: Aniliidae). *Lacerta* 28: 59–61.

Foekema, G. M. M. (1974). Enkele notities over *Corallus enhydris* (slanke boomboa), met een verslag over verzorging en gedrag van drie *Corallus enhydris cookii* in een huiskamerterrarium. *Lacerta* 32: 151–164.

Foekema, G. M. M. (1975). Ontwikkeling en voortplanting van *Sanzinia madagascariensis* in een huiskamerterrarium. *Lacerta* 33: 71–82.

Force, E. R. (1931). Habits and birth of young of the lined snake, *Tropidoclonion lineatum* (Hallowell). *Copeia*: 51–53.

Ford, N. B. (1974). Growth and food consumption in the yellow rat snake, *Elaphe obsoleta quadrivittata*. *Herpetologica* 30: 102–104.

Ford, N. B. and Ball, R. (1977). Clutch size and size of young in the Mexican garter snake *Thamnophis melanogaster* (Reptilia, Serpentes, Colubridae). *Herpetological Review* 8: 118.

Ford, N. B. and Killebrew, D. W. (1983). Reproductive tactics and female body size in Butler's garter snake, *Thamnophis butleri*. *Journal of Herpetology* 17: 271–275.

Fouquette, M. J., Jr. (1968). Observations on the natural history of microteiid lizards from the Venezuelan Andes. *Copeia*: 881–884.

Franz, R. (1977). Observations on the food, feeding behavior, and parasites of the striped swamp snake, *Regina alleni*. *Herpetologica* 33: 91–94.

Franz, R. and Gicca, D. F. (1982). Observations on the Haitian snake *Antillophis parvifrons alleni*. *Journal of Herpetology* 16: 419–421.

Freed, P. S. and Freed, M. G. (1983). An additional restraint technique for venomous snakes. *Herpetological Review* 14: 114.

Fretey, J. (1976). Reproduction de *Kinosternon scorpoides scorpoides* (Linne) (Testudinata, Kinosternidae). *Bulletin de la Société de Zoologie, France* 101: 732–733.

Friend, J. and Friend, C. (1983). Reproductive data: banded water snakes (*Nerodia fasciata fasciata*). *Herptile* 8: 152.

Friend, J. and Friend, C. (1984). Reproductive data: the yellow ratsnake (*Elaphe obsoleta quadrivittata*). *Herptile* 9: 7.

Froese, A. D. (1978). Habitat preferences of the common snapping turtle, *Chelydra s.serpentina* (Reptilia, Testudines, Chelydridae). *Journal of Herpetology* 12: 53–58.

Frost, J. S. (1982). A time-efficient, low cost method for the laboratory rearing of frogs. *Herpetological Review* 13: 73–77.

Frye, F. L. (1973). *Husbandry, medicine and surgery in captive reptiles*. V. M. Publ. Inc., Kansas.

Frye, F. L. (1981). *Biomedical and surgical aspects of captive reptile husbandry*. V. M. Publ. Inc., Kansas.

Fukada, H. (1965). Breeding habits of some Japanese reptiles. *Bulletin of the Kyoto Gakugei University* B27: 65–82.

Fukada, H. (1976). Food habits of the snake *Elaphe climacophora* in the fields. *Japanese Journal of Herpetology* 6: 116.

Fukada, H. (1978). Growth and maturity of the Japanese rat snake, *Elaphe climacophora* (Reptilia, Serpentes, Colubridae). *Journal of Herpetology* 12: 269–274.

Fukuoka, N. (1975). Egg hatching of the snake, *Elaphe quadrivirgata* at 25°C. *Japanese Journal of Herpetology* 6: 6–7.

Fyfe, G. and Harvey, C. (1981). Some observations on the woma (*Aspidites ramsayi*) in captivity. *Herpetofauna* 13: 23–25.

Gaal, R. J. (1983). Breeding results: *Corallus enhydris enhydris*. *Litteratura Serpentium* 3: 41.

Gadow, H. (1901). *Amphibia and Reptiles. The Cambridge Natural History* 8: xiii + 668 pp.

Galbraith, D. A. and Brooks, R. J. (1984). A simple restraining device for large turtles. *Herpetological Review* 14: 115.

Gallo, J. F., Jr. and Reese, K. (1978). Notes on the hatching of eggs and description of the hatchlings of the reticulated gecko, *Coleonyx reticulatus* Davis & Dixon (Lacertilia: Eublepharidae). *Southwest Naturalist* 23: 308–309.

Gannon, V. P. J. and Secoy, D. M. (1984). Growth and reproductive rate of a northern population of the prairie rattlesnake, *Crotalus v.viridis*. *Journal of Herpetology* 18: 13–19.

Gans, C. and Dawson, W. R. (1976) (editors). *Biology of the Reptilia. Physiology A*. Vol. 5: xv + 556 pp. Academic Press, London.

Gans, C., Gillingham, J. C. and Clark, D. L. (1984). Courtship, mating and male combat in Tuatara, *Sphenodon punctatus*. *Journal of Herpetology* 18: 194–197.

Gans, C. and Pough, F. H. (1982) (editors). *Biology of the Reptilia. Physiology C*. Vol. 12: xv + 536 pp. Academic Press, London.

Garthwaite, D. B. (1984). Geckos: their care and breeding with emphasis on the breeding of live food for these and other lizards. In *Proceedings of the International Herpetological Society Symposium*: 33–46.

Gartlan, J. S. and Struhsaker, T. T. (1971). Notes on the habits of the Calabar ground python (*Calabaria reinhardtii* Schlegel) in Cameroon, West Africa. *British Journal of Herpetology* 4: 201–202.

Gaten, P. van der (1982). Een geslaagde kweek met *Python molurus bivittatus*. *Litteratura Serpentium* 2: 26–33.

Gibbons, J. W. (1969). Ecology and population dynamics of the chicken turtle *Deirochelys reticularia*. *Copeia*: 669–676.

Gibbons, J. W. (1972). Reproduction, growth, and sexual dimorphism in the canebrake rattlesnake (*Crotalus horridus atricaudatus*). *Copeia*: 222–226.

Gibbons, J. W. (1977). Ecological and life history aspects of the cooter, *Chrysemys floridana* (Le Conte). *Herpetologica* 33: 29–33.

Gibbons, J. W., Coker, J. W. and Murphy, T. M., Jr. (1977). Selected aspects of the life history of the rainbow snake (*Farancia erythrogramma*). *Herpetologica* 33: 276–281.

Gillingham, J. C. (1974). Reproductive behavior of the western fox snake, *Elaphe v.vulpina* (Baird and Girard). *Herpetologica* 30: 309–313.

Gillingham, J. C. (1977). Further analysis of the reproductive behavior of the western fox snake, *Elaphe v.vulpina*. *Herpetologica* 33: 349–352.

Gillingham, J. C. (1979). Reproductive behavior of the rat snakes of eastern North America, genus *Elaphe*. *Copeia*: 319–331.

Gillingham, J. C., Carpenter, C. C., Brecke, B. J. and Murphy, J. B. (1977). Courtship and copulatory behavior of the Mexican milk snake, *Lampropeltis triangulum sinaloae* (Colubridae). *Southwest Naturalist* 22: 187–194.

Gillingham, J. C. and Chambers, J. A. (1980). Observations on the reproductive behaviour of the eastern indigo snake, *Drymarchon corais couperi*, in captivity. *British Journal of Herpetology* 6: 99–100.

Gillingham, J. C., Clark, D. L. and Ten Eyck, G. R. (1983). Venomous snake immobilization: a new technique. *Herpetological Review* 14: 40.

Gilpin, H. G. B. (1969a) Breeding *Chalcides ocellatus tilingugu*. *Aquarist and Pondkeeper* 34: 44–45.

Gilpin, H. G. B. (1969b) Keeping and breeding *Lacerta vivipara*. *Aquarist and Pondkeeper* 34: 68–69.

Gilpin, H. G. B. (1972). Breeding *Hemidactylus turcicus*. *Aquarist and Pondkeeper* 36: 337–346.

Goedings, M. Th. J. (1972). Bouw en inrichting van een tropisch terrarium. *Lacerta* 30: 128–131.

Goldberg, S. R. (1974). Reproduction in mountain and lowland populations of the lizard *Sceloporus occidentalis*. *Copeia*: 176–182.

Goldberg, S. R. (1976). Reproduction in a mountain population of the coastal whiptail lizard, *Cnemidophorus tigris multiscutatus*. *Copeia* 260–266.

Goldberg, S. R. (1977). Reproduction in a mountain population of the side-blotched lizard *Uta stansburiana* (Reptilia, Lacertilia, Iguanidae). *Journal of Herpetology* 11: 31–35.

Goldberg, S. R. and Robinson, M. D. (1979). Reproduction in two Namib Desert lacertid lizards (*Aporosaura anchietae* and *Meroles cuneirostris*). *Herpetologica* 35: 169–175.

Gonzales, R. B. (1974). Behavioral notes on captive sail-tailed lizards (*Hydrosaurus pustulosus*: Agamidae). *Silliman Journal* 21: 129–138.

Goode, M. (1979). Notes on captive reproduction in *Echis colorata* (Serpentes: Viperidae). *Herpetological Review* 10: 94.

Gooding, A. (1982). Notes on breeding the naked fingered gecko *Cyrtodactylus kotschyi*. *Herptile* 7(3): 29–30.

Gorman, G. C. and Harwood, R. (1977). Notes on population density, vagility, and activity patterns of the Puerto Rican grass lizard *Anolis pulchellus* (Reptilia, Lacertilia, Iguanidae). *Journal of Herpetology* 11: 363–368.

Gorman, G. C. and Licht, P. (1975). Differences between the reproductive cycles of sympatric *Anolis* lizards on Trinidad. *Copeia*: 332–337.

Granger, A. M. (1982a). Notes on the captive breeding of the desert rosy boa (*Lichanura trivirgata gracia*). *Herptile* 7(3): 5–7.

Granger, A. M. (1982b). Notes on the captive breeding of the desert rosy boa (*Lichanura trivirgata gracia*). *British Herpetological Society Bulletin* 5: 33–34.

Gray, R. L. (1984a). Care sheet: *Phrynosoma*. *Northern California Herpetological Society Newsletter* 3(2): 5–6.

Gray, R. L. (1984b). The egg incubator. *Northern California Herpetological Society Newsletter* 3(4): 8.

Gray, R. L. (1985). Outdoor enclosures: a better way. *Northern California Herpetological Society Newsletter* 4(2): 2 pp.

Green, B. and King, D. (1978). Home range and activity patterns of the sand goanna, *Varanus gouldii* (Reptilia: Varanidae). *Australian Wildlife Research* 5: 417–424.

Greenberg, B. (1943). Social behavior of the western banded gecko, *Coleonyx variegatus*. *Physiological Zoology* 16: 110–122.

Greenberg, B. and Noble, G. K. (1944). Social behavior of the American chamaeleon (*Anolis carolinensis* Voigt). *Physiological Zoology* 17: 392–439.

Greenberg, N. (1976). Thermoregulatory aspects of behavior in the blue spiny lizard *Sceloporus cyanogenys* (Sauria: Iguanidae). *Behaviour* 59: 1–21.

Greene, H. W. (1970). Reproduction in a Mexican Xantusiid lizard, *Lepidophyma tuxtlae*. *Journal of Herpetology* 4: 85–87.

Gregory, P. T. (1983). Identification of sex of small snakes in the field. *Herpetological Review* 14: 42–43.

Grenot, Cl. (1978). Ecophysiologie du lézard saharien, *Uromastix acanthinurus* Bell 1825 (Agamidae, herbivore). *Bulletin de la Société de Herpetologie, France* 5: 25.

Griffiths, R. A. (1984). The influence of light and temperature on diel activity rhythms in the sand boa *Eryx conicus*. *Journal of Herpetology* 18: 374–380.

Grogan, W. L. (1974). Effects of accidental envenomation from the saliva of the eastern hognose snake, *Heterodon platyrhinos*. *Herpetologica* 30: 248–249.

Groves, F. (1973). Reproduction and venom in Blanding's tree snake, *Boiga blandingi*. *International Zoo Yearbook* 13: 106–108.

Groves, J. D. (1974). Reproduction in the mangrove snake, *Boiga dendrophila*, at Baltimore Zoo. *International Zoo Yearbook* 14: 82.

Groves, J. D. (1976). A note on the eggs and young of the smooth green snake, *Ophedrys vernalis*, in Maryland. *Bulletin of the Maryland Herpetological Society* 12: 131–132.

Groves, J. D. (1978). Observations on the reproduction of the emerald tree boa *Corallus caninus*. *Herpetological Review* 9: 100–102.

Groves, J. D. (1980). Observations and comments on the post-parturient behaviour of some tropical boas of the genus *Epicrates*. *British Journal of Herpetology* 6: 89–91.

Groves, J. D. and Altimari, W. (1977). Keratophagy in the slender vine snake, *Uromacer oxyrhynchus*. *Herpetological Review* 8: 124.

Groves, J. D. and Altimari, W. (1979). First breeding of the St. Lucia serpent *Bothrops caribbaea* in captivity. *International Zoo Yearbook* 19: 101–102.

Groves, J. D. and Mellendick, J. R. (1973). Breeding the Madagascan boa, *Sanzinia madagascariensis* at Baltimore Zoo. *International Zoo Yearbook* 13: 106.

Grubb, P. (1971). Comparative notes on the behavior of *Geochelone sulcata*. *Herpetologica* 27: 328–333.

Grundy, A. P. (1982). A note on breeding the European pond terrapin. *Herptile* 7(4): 28–29.

Gudynas, E. (1981). Some notes from Uruguay on the behavior, ecology and conservation of the macroteiid lizard *Tupinambis teguixin*. *Bulletin of the Chicago Herpetological Society* 16: 29–39.

Gudynas, E. and Gambarotta, J. C. (1980). Notes on the ecology of the gekkonid lizard *Homonota uruguayensis*. *Association for the Study of Reptiles and Amphibians Journal* 1(3): 13–26.

Guillette, L. J. (1983). Notes concerning reproduction of the montane skink *Eumeces copei*. *Journal of Herpetology* 17: 144–148.

Haan, C. C. de (1981). La reproduction en aquaterrarium de la Cistude d'Europe (*Emys orbicularis*). *Bulletin de la Société de Herpetologie, France* 19: 17.

Haast, W. E. (1969). Hatching rhinoceros iguanas, *Cyclura cornuta*, at the Miami Serpentarium. *International Zoo Yearbook* 9: 49.

Hain, M. L. (1965). Ecology of the lizard *Uta mearnsi* in a desert canyon. *Copeia*: 78–81.

Hairston, N. G. (1957). Observations on the behavior of *Draco volans* in the Philippines. *Copeia*: 262–265.

Hall, B. J. (1978). Notes on the husbandry, behavior and breeding of captive tegu lizards, *Tupinambis teguixin*. *International Zoo Yearbook* 18: 91–95.

Hall, R. J. (1971). Ecology of a population of the Great Plains skink (*Eumeces obsoletus*). *University of Kansas Science Bulletin* 49: 359–387.

Hamilton, W. J. III, and Coetzee, C. G. (1969). Thermoregulatory behaviour of the vegetarian lizard *Angolosaurus skoogi* on the vegetationless northern Namib Desert dunes. *Scientific Papers of the Namib Desert Research Station* 47: 95–103.

Hammerson, G. A. (1978). Observations on the reproduction, courtship and aggressive behavior of the striped racer, *Masticophis lateralis euryxanthus* (Reptilia, Serpentes, Colubridae). *Journal of Herpetology* 12: 253–255.

Hanlon, R. W. (1964). Reproductive activity of the Bahaman boa (*Epicrates striatus*). *Herpetologica* 20: 143–144.

Hara, K. (1975). Hatchings of *Gekko tawaensis*. *Japanese Journal of Herpetology* 6: 13.

Hara, K. and Kikuchi, F. (1978). Breeding the west African dwarf crocodile, *Osteolaemus tetraspis tetraspis*, at Ueno Zoo, Tokyo. *International Zoo Yearbook* 18: 84–87.

Harding, J. H. (1981). Observations on the African helmeted turtle, *Pelomedusa subrufa*, in captivity with comments on breeding behavior. *Bulletin of the Chicago Herpetological Society* 16: 86–94.

Harding, K. A. (1977). The use of ketamine anaesthesia to milk two tropical rattlesnakes (*Crotalus durissus terrificus*). *The Veterinary Record* 100: 289–290.

Hardy, D. R. (1962). Ecology and behavior of the six-lined racerunner *Cnemidophorus sexlineatus*. *University of Kansas Science Bulletin* 43: 3–73.

Hardy, L. M. and McDiarmid, R. L. (1969). The amphibians and reptiles of Sinaloa, Mexico. *University of Kansas Publications, Museum of Natural History* 18: 39–52.

Harris, V. A. (1964). *The life of the rainbow lizard*. Hutchison, London. 174 pp.

Hartmann, P. and Steiner, B. (1984a). Breeding results: *Boaedon fuliginosus*. *Litteratura Serpentium* 4: 79.

Hartmann, P. and Steiner, B. (1984b). Breeding results: *Elaphe guttata guttata*. *Litteratura Serpentium* 4: 79–80.

Hartmann, P. and Steiner, B. (1984c). Breeding results: *Bitis arietans*. *Litteratura Serpentium* 4: 80.

Hartmann, P. and Steiner, B. (1984d). Breeding results: *Trimeresurus albolabris*. *Litteratura Serpentium* 4: 80.

Hawes, B. (1974). Observations on the feeding habits of the royal python, *Python regius*. *Journal of the South Western Herpetological Society* 1(2): 5–6.

Hayes, W. K. and Hayes, F. E. (1985). Human envenomation from the bite of the Eastern Garter snake, *Thamnophis s.sirtalis* (Serpentes: Colubridae). *Toxicon* 23: 719–721.

Healy, W. (1953). Notes on the feeding habits of *Thamnophis s.sirtalis* in captivity. *Herpetologica* 9: 163.

Heatwole, H. (1976). *Reptile ecology. University of Queensland Press*, 178 pp.
Heatwole, H. and Banuchi, I. B. (1966) Envenomation by the colubrid snake *Alsophis portoricensis. Herpetologica* 22: 132–134.
Hegeman, G. (1961). Enzymatic constitution of *Alsophis* saliva and its biological implications. *Breviora* 134: 1–8.
Heijnen, G. (1982). Breeding results: *Thamnophis sirtalis sirtalis. Litteratura Serpentium* 2: 194.
Heijnen, G. (1983). Breeding results: *Thamnophis sirtalis. Litteratura Serpentium* 3: 42.
Henderson, R. W. (1972). Notes on the reproduction of a giant anole, *Anolis biporcatus* (Sauria, Iguanidae). *Journal of Herpetology* 6: 239–240.
Henderson, R. W. (1974). Aspects of the ecology of the Neotropical vine snake, *Oxybelis aeneus* (Wagler). *Herpetologica* 30: 19–24.
Henderson, R. W. and Binder, M. H. (1980). The ecology and behavior of vine snakes (*Ahaetulla, Oxybelis, Thelotornis, Uromacer*): A review. *Contributions in Biology and Geology, Milwaukee Public Museum* 37: 1–38.
Henderson, R. W., Binder, M. H., Sajdak, R. A. and Buday, J. A. (1980). Aggregating behavior and exploitation of subterranean habitat by gravid eastern milksnakes (*Lampropeltis t.triangulum*). *Contributions in Biology and Geology, Milwaukee Public Museum* 32: 1–9.
Henderson, R. W. and Horn, H. W. (1983). The diet of the snake *Uromacer frenatus dorsalis* on Ile de la Gonave, Haiti. *Journal of Herpetology* 17: 409–412.
Henderson, R. W. and Nickerson, M. A. (1976). Observations on the behavioral ecology of three species of *Imantodes* (Reptilia, Serpentes, Colubridae). *Journal of Herpetology* 10: 205–210.
Henderson, R.W. and Nickerson, M. A. (1977). Observations on the feeding behaviour and movements of the snakes *Oxybelis aeneus* and *O. fulgidus. British Journal of Herpetology* 5: 663–667.
Henley, G. B. (1981). A new technique for recognition of snakes. *Herpetological Review* 12: 56.
Herman, D. W. (1979a). Captive reproduction in the Scarlet kingsnake, *Lampropeltis triangulum elapsoides* (Holbrook). *Herpetological Review* 10: 115.
Herman, D. W. (1979b). Breeding of the Jaliscan milk snake, *Lampropeltis triangulum arcifera*, at Atlanta Zoo. *International Zoo Yearbook* 19: 96–97.
Hertz, P.E. (1974). Thermal passivity of a tropical forest lizard, *Anolis polylepis. Journal of Herpetology* 8: 323–327.
Heuclin, D. (1979). Description de terrariums intérieurs et extérieurs. *Bulletin de la Société de Herpetologie, France* 10: 18.
Heuclin, D. (1982). Quelques réflexions pour le maintien des serpents vénimeux en captivité. *Bulletin de la Société de Herpetologie de France* 21: 40.
Hidalgo, H. (1982). Courtship and mating behavior in *Rhinoclemmys pulcherrima incisa* (Testudines: Emydidae: Batagurinae). *Transactions of the Kansas Academy of Sciences* 85: 82–95.
Hikita, T. (1976). Reproduction of the Japanese skink (*Eumeces latiscutatus*) in Kyoto. *Japanese Journal of Herpetology* 6: 115–116.
Hine, M. L. (1978). Reproduction of the leopard tortoise in captivity. *British Herpetological Society Newsletter* 18: 8–11.
Hine, M. L. (1982). Notes on the marginated tortoise (Testudo marginata) in Greece and in captivity. *British Herpetological Society Bulletin* 5: 35–38.
Hine, R. A. (1980). Care and captive breeding of the northern pine snake *Pituophis m. melanoleucus. British Herpetological Society Bulletin* 2: 33–36.
Hine, R. A. (1984). Breeding results: *Drymarchon corais couperi. Litteratura Serpentium* 4: 192–193.
Hingley, K. (1982). Notes on keeping the scarlet king snake *Lampropeltis triangulum elapsoides. Herptile* 7(2): 18.

Hingley, K. (1983a). Reproductive data: the golden skink *Mabuya multifasciata*. *Herptile* 8: 49–50.
Hingley, K. (1983b). Observations on *Python regius*, the royal python in captivity. *Herptile* 8: 70–74.
Hingley, K. (1983c). The treatment of scale rot using hydrogen peroxide and gentian violet. *Litteratura Serpentium* 3: 164–165.
Hingley, K. (1985). Maintenance and captive reproduction of the leopard gecko (*Eublepharis macularis*). *Herptile* 10: 123–128.
Hirth, H. F. (1963). Some aspects of the natural history of *Iguana iguana* on a tropical beach. *Ecology* 44: 613–615.
Hoddenbach, G. A. (1966). Reproduction in western Texas *Cnemidophorus sexlineatus* (Sauria: Teiidae). *Copeia*: 110–113.
Hoessle, C. (1969). Simple incubators for reptile eggs at St. Louis Zoological Park. *International Zoo Yearbook* 9: 13–14.
Hoff, G. L., Frye, F. L. and Jacobson, E. (1984) (editors). *Diseases of amphibians and reptiles*. Plenum Press, London.
Hoffman, E. G. (1963). Reproduction and raising of jewel lizard, *Lacerta lepida lepida*. *Bulletin of the Philadelphia Herpetological Society* 11: 53–55.
Hollander, P. (1979). Breeding report: *Chondropython viridis*. *Notes from Noah* 7: 6–7.
Holstrom, W.F. (1980). Observations on the reproduction of the common anaconda *Eunectes murinus*, at the New York Zoological Park. *Herpetological Review* 11: 32–33.
Honegger, R. E. (1975). Beitrag zur Kenntnis des Wickelskinks *Corucia zebrata*. *Salamandra* 11: 27–32.
Honegger, R. E. (1985). Additional notes on the breeding and captive management of the prehensile-tailed skink (*Corucia zebrata*). *Herpetological Review* 16: 21–23.
Howard, C. J. (1976). Notes on the adder (*Vipera berus berus*) in captivity. *Journal of the South Western Herpetological Society* 1(3): 8.
Howard, C. J. (1980a). Reproductive data—the plated lizard (*Gerrhosaurus major*). *Herptile* 5(3): 16.
Howard, C. J. (1980b). Breeding the flat-tailed day gecko *Phelsuma laticauda* at Twycross Zoo. *International Zoo Yearbook* 20: 193–196.
Howard, C. J. (1980c). Notes on the maintenance and breeding of the common iguana (*Iguana iguana iguana*) at Twycross Zoo. In Townson and others (1980) (editors), 47–50.
Howard, C. J. (1982). Observations on the water dragon *Physignathus cocincinus* in captivity. *Herptile* 7(4): 3–5.
Howard, C. J. (1983). Reproductive data: common boa (*Constrictor constrictor*). *Herptile* 8: 153.
Howard, C. J. (1984). Points to look for when sexing lizards. *Herptile* 9(2): 44–49.
Howard, C. J. (1985a). Notes on breeding the eyed lizard (*Lacerta lepida*). *Herptile* 10: 18–23.
Howard, C. J. (1985b). Husbandry and breeding of the Honduran Milk Snake (*Lampropeltis triangulum hondurensis*) at Twycross Zoo. *Herptile* 10: 81–84.
Hubbard, R. M. (1980). Captive propagation in the lancehead rattlesnake *Crotalus polystictus*. *Herpetological Review* 11: 33–34.
Hübers, R. and Fricke-Hübers, M. (1983). *Agkistrodon haly caraganus* (Eichwald 1831) in Terrarium. *Herpetofauna* (Ludwigsburg) 5(26): 25–27.
Hudnall, J. A. (1982). New methods for measuring and tagging snakes. *Herpetological Review* 13: 97–98.
Hudson, P. (1981). Observations on egg laying by the marbled gecko, *Phyllodactylus marmoratus* (Fitzinger). *Herpetofauna* 13: 32–33.
Huey, R. B. (1974). Winter thermal ecology of the iguanid lizard *Tropidurus peruvianus*. *Copeia*: 149–155.

Huff, T. A. (1976). Breeding the Cuban boa *Epicrates angulifer* at the Reptile Breeding Foundation. *International Zoo Yearbook* 16: 81–82.

Huff, T. A. (1978). Breeding the Puerto Rican boa *Epicrates inornatus* at the Reptile Breeding Foundation. *International Zoo Yearbook* 18: 96–97.

Huff, T. A. (1979). Breeding the Jamaican boa, *Epicrates subflavus*, in captivity: a five-year review. *A.A.Z.P.A. Reg. Conference Proceedings, Wheeling, West Virginia*: 339–345.

Huff, T. A. (1980). Captive propagation of the subfamily Boinae with emphasis on the genus *Epicrates*. In Murphy and Collins (1980) (editors): 125–134.

Huff, T. A. (1983). The husbandry and propagation of the Madagascar ground boa *Acrantophis dumerili* in captivity with notes on the other Malagasy boids. *A.S.R.A. Journal* 2(1): 38–53.

Huffman, T. N. (1974). Reproduction of a gaboon viper, *Bitis gabonica gabonica*, in captivity. *Arnoldia Rhodesia* 6(39): 1–7.

Hunt, L. E. and Ottley, J. R. (1982). Reproduction and feeding in *Eridiphas slevini* (Serpentes: Colubridae). *Herpetological Review* 13: 8–9.

Hunt, R. H. (1969). Breeding the spectacled caiman, *Caiman c.crocodilus* at Atlanta Zoo. *International Zoo Yearbook* 9: 36–37.

Hunt, R. H. (1973). Breeding the Morelet's crocodile, *Crocodylus moreletti*, at Atlanta Zoo. *International Zoo Yearbook* 13: 103–105.

Hunt, R. H. (1980). Propagation of Morelet's crocodile. In Murphy and Collins (1980) (editors): 161–165.

Husband, G. (1979). Notes on a nest and hatchlings of *Varanus acanthurus*. *Herpetofauna* 11(1): 29–30.

Inskeep, R. (1984a). A note on the captive breeding of the box turtle *Cuora amboinensis* (Daudin, 1802). *British Journal of Herpetology* 6: 383–384.

Inskeep, R. (1984b). Second breeding of *Cuora amboinensis* (Daudin 1802). *British Herpetological Society Bulletin* 9: 28.

Ionides, C. J. P. (1965). *A Hunter's Story*. W. H. Allen, London. 222 pp.

Ippen, R., Schroder, H. D. and Elze, K. (1985) (editors). *Handbuch der Zootierkrankheitein Band 1: Reptilien*. Akademie Verlag, Berlin.

Iverson, J. B. (1979). Reproduction and growth of the mud turtle, *Kinosternon subrubrum* (Reptilia, Testudines, Kinosternidae) in Arkansas. *Journal of Herpetology* 13: 105–111.

Iverson, J. B. (1980a). Behavior and ecology of the rock iguana *Cyclura carinata*. *Bulletin of the Florida State Museum, Biological Sciences* 24: 175–358.

Iverson, J. B. (1980b). The reproductive biology of *Gopherus polyphemus* (Chelonia: Testudinidae). *American Midland Naturalist* 103: 353–359.

Jackson, D. R. and Franz, R. (1981). Ecology of the eastern coral snake (*Micrurus fulvius*) in northern peninsular Florida. *Herpetologica* 37: 213–228.

Jackson, D. R. and Telford, S. R., Jr. (1975). Food habits and predatory role of the Japanese Lacertid *Takydromus tachydromoides*. *Copeia*: 343–351.

Jackson, J. R. and Telford, S. R., Jr. (1974). Reproductive ecology of the Florida scrub lizard *Sceloporus woodi*. *Copeia*: 689–694.

Jackson, O. F. (1980). Weight and measurement data on tortoises (*Testudo graeca* and *T.hermanni*) and their relationship to health. *Journal of Small Animal Practice* 21: 409–416.

Jacobsen, N. H. G. (1972). Some notes on the biology and behavior of the Transval girdled lizard (*Cordylus vittifer*) in captivity. *Journal of the Herpetological Association of Africa* 9: 35–37.

Jaksic, F. M. and Schwenk, K. (1983). Natural history observations on *Liolaemus magellanicus*, the southernmost lizard in the world. *Herpetologica* 39: 457–461.

James, F. C. and Porter, W. P. (1979). Behavior- micro-climate relationships in the African rainbow lizard *Agama agama*. *Copeia*: 585–593.

Janssen, P. (1981). *Vipera ammodytes* in de natuur en in gevangenschap. *Litteratura Serpentium* 1: 78–87.

Janssen, P. (1982). Breeding results: *Trimeresurus popeorum*. *Litteratura Serpentium* 2: 256.

Jardine, D. R. (1981). First successful captive propagation of Schneider's smooth-fronted caiman, *Paleosuchus trigonatus*. *Herpetological Review* 12: 58–60.

Jarvis, P. (1981). Husbandry—keeping a pair of golden tegus (*Tupinambis nigropunctatus*). *Rephiberary* 50: 3.

Jarvis, P. and Jarvis, P. (1980). Reproductive cycle of a pair of common boas. *A.S.R.A. Journal* 1(3): 9–12.

Jauch, H. (1984). Haltung und Nachzucht nordamerikanischer Kettennattern (*Lampropeltis getulus*) in Terrarium. *Elaphe*: 45–47.

Jenssen, T. A. (1970). The ethoecology of *Anolis nebulosus* (Sauria, Iguanidae). *Journal of Herpetology* 4: 1–38.

Jenvey, J. (1982). Observations on *Testudo marginata* in captivity. *British Herpetological Society Bulletin* 5: 39–43.

Joanen, T. and McNease, L. (1980). Reproductive biology of the American alligator in southwest Louisiana. In Murphy and Collins (1980) (editors): 153–159.

Johnson, C. (1960). Reproductive cycle in females of the Greater Earless Lizard, *Holbrookia texana*. *Copeia*: 297–300.

Johnson, C. R. (1965). The diet of the Pacific fence lizard *Sceloporus occidentalis occidentalis* (Baird and Girard) from northern California. *Herpetologica* 21: 114–117.

Johnston, G. R. (1979). The eggs, incubation and young of the bearded dragon *Amphibolurus vitticeps* Ahl. *Herpetofauna* 11(1): 5–8.

Jones, J. P. (1978). Photoperiod and reptile reproduction. *Herpetological Review* 9: 95–100.

Judd, F. W. and Ross, R. K. (1978). Year-to-year variation in clutch size of island and mainland populations of *Holbrookia propinqua* (Reptilia, Lacertilia, Iguanidae). *Journal of Herpetology* 12: 203–207.

Kamb, A. (1978). Unusual feeding behavior in the red milk snake, *Lampropeltis triangulum syspila*. *Transactions of the Kansas Academy of Sciences* 81: 273.

Kardon, A. (1979). A note on captive reproduction in three Mexican milk snakes, *Lampropeltis triangulum polyzona*, *L.t. nelsoni* and *L.t.sinaloae*. *International Zoo Yearbook* 19: 94–96.

Kassing, E. F. (1961). A life history study of the Great Plains ground snake (*Sonora episcopa episcopa* Kennicott). *Texas Journal of Science* 13: 185–203.

Katuska, C. J. (1982). Husbandry and management of the genus *Python*. *Bulletin of Connecticut Herpetological Society* 9: 20–30.

Kauffeld, C. (1953). Methods of feeding captive snakes. *Herpetologica* 9: 129–131.

Kauffeld, C. (1969). The effect of altitude, ultraviolet light, and humidity on captive reptiles. *InternationalZoo Yearbook* 9: 8–9.

Kay, F. R., Miller, B. W. and Miller, C. L. (1970). Food habits and reproduction of *Callisaurus draconoides* in Death Valley, California. *Herpetologica* 26: 431–436.

Keenlyne, K. D. (1972). Sexual differences in feeding habits of *Crotalus horridus horridus*. *Journal of Herpetology* 6: 234–237.

Kennedy, J. P. (1956). Food habits of the rusty lizard *Sceloporus olivaceus* Smith. *Texas Journal of Science* 8: 328–349.

Kennedy, J. P. (1968). Observations on the ecology and behavior of *Cnemidophorus guttatus* and *Cnemidophorus deppei* (Sauria, Teiidae) in southern Veracruz. *Journal of Herpetology* 2: 87–96.

Kennerson, K. J. (1980). Notes on hatchling *Chelodina longicollis* (Shaw). *Herpetofauna* 11(2): 27–28.

Kieve, R. J. (1979). Growth rate of a black rat snake (*Elaphe o.obsoleta*). *Bulletin of the Philadelphia Herpetological Society* 25: 8.

King, D. and Green, B. (1979). Notes on diet and reproduction of the sand goanna, *Varanus gouldii rosenbergi*. *Copeia*: 64–70.

King, M. (1977). Reproduction in the Australian gekko *Phyllodactylus marmoratus* (Gray). *Herpetologica* 33: 7–13.

King, M. B. and Duvall, D. (1984). Noose tube: a lightweight, sturdy, and portable snake restraining apparatus for field and laboratory use. *Herpetological Review* 15: 109.

Kivit, R. (1983). Breeding results: *Boa Constrictor constrictor*. *Litteratura Serpentium* 3: 131.

Kivit, R. and Kivit, P. (1981). Breeding results: *Boa constrictor constrictor*. *Litteratura Serpentium* 1: 247.

Klemmer, K. (1967). Observations on the seasnake *Laticauda laticaudata* in captivity. *International Zoo Yearbook* 7: 229. 231.

Koba, K. (1971). Natural history of the Habu, *Trimeresurus flavoviridis* (Hallowell). *The Snake* 3: 75–96.

Koba, K. and Morimoto, H. (1978). The nighttime habitat of *Trimeresurus flavoviridis* (Serpentes: Viperidae) on Amami-oshima and Kume-jima of the Nansei Islands, Japan. *Bulletin of Ginkyo College of Medicine and Technology* 3: 17–20.

Kono, H. and Sawai, Y. (1975). Systematic poisoning from the bite of *Rhabdophis tigrinus*. *The Snake* 7: 38–39.

Koore, J. van der (1985a). Breeding results: *Elaphe obsoleta quadrivittata*. *Litteratura Serpentium* 5: 33–34.

Koore, J. van der (1985b). Breeding results: *Epicrates cenchria maurus*. *Litteratura Serpentium* 5: 76–77.

Koppel, J. (1979). Diverses observations en terrarium sur la vie communautaire de *Natrix natrix* et *Natrix maure*. *Bulletin de la Société Herpetologique de France* 12: 11.

Kozak, M. and Simecek, J. (1977). Some knowledge on keeping *Coronella austriaca* in captivity. *Fauna Bohemiae Septentrionalis* 2: 65–68. (In Czech; English summary).

Kragh, L. (1982). Keeping *Kinixys belliana*. *Testudo* 2: 31–32.

Kronen, D. (1980). Notes on the eggs and hatchlings of the longnose snake, *Rhinocheilus lecontei*, including the occurrence of a semi-striped pattern. *Bulletin of the Chicago Herpetological Society* 15: 54–56.

Krzystyniak, S. (1984a). Hatching and rearing the Egyptian cobra. (*Naja haje annulifera*). *Herptile* 9: 4–5.

Krzystyniak, S. (1984b). Notes on the angulate tortoise, *Chersina angulata* (Schweig-ger). *Herptile* 9: 36–41.

Lambert, M. R. K. (1984). Amphibians and reptiles. In Cloudsley-Thompson, J. L. (editor), *Sahara Desert (Key Environments)*: 205–227. Pergamon Press, Oxford.

Lamers, H. (1984). Breeding results: *Eryx colubrinus loveridgei*. *Litteratura Serpentium* 4: 78.

Lamers, H. (1985). Breeding results: *Epicrates cenchria maurus*. *Litteratura Serpentium* 5: 118.

Lancon, M. and Lancon, M. (1981). Reproduction et élevage en Charente d'*Emys orbicularis* et de *Testudo hermanni robertmertensi*. *Bulletin de la Société de Herpetologique of France* 19: 25.

Landreth, H. F. (1973). Orientation and behavior of the rattlesnake *Crotalus atrox*. *Copeia*: 26–31.

Lang, R. de (1970). Ultravioletlampen in het terrarium. *Lacerta* 28: 67–72.

Lang, R. de (1984). *Python curtus*, difficulty in feeding? *Litteratura Serpentium* 4: 4–5.

Langebaek, R. (1979). Observations on the behaviour of captive *Phelsuma guentheri* during the breeding season at the Jersey Wildlife Preservation Trust. *Dodo* 16: 75–83.

Langerwerf, B. A. W. A. (1974). Ervaringen met de aardhagedis *Blanus cinereus* Vandelli. *Lacerta* 32: 106–107.

Langerwerf, B. A. W. A. (1977a). De Marokkaanse parelhagedis, *Lacerta lepida pater*, in het terrarium. *Lacerta* 35: 63–65.

Langerwerf, B. A. W. A. (1977b). De kweek van de tweede generatie *Lacerta lepida pater. Lacerta* 35: 75–76.

Langerwerf, B. A. W. A. (1977c). De hardoen, *Agama stellio*, in het terrarium. *Lacerta* 35: 84–86.

Langerwerf, B. A. W. A. (1980a). The Caucasian green lizard *Lacerta strigata* Eichwald 1831, with notes on its reproduction in captivity. *British Herpetological Society Bulletin* 1: 23–26.

Langerwerf, B. A. W. A. (1980b). The Armenian wall lizard, *Lacerta armeniaca* Mehely 1909, with notes on its care and reproduction in captivity. *British Herpetological Society Bulletin* 2: 26–28.

Langerwerf, B. A. W. A. (1980c). The successful breeding of lizards from temperate regions. In Townson and others (editors): 37–46.

Langerwerf, B. A. W. A. (1981a). *Agama stellio*, with observations on its care and breeding in captivity. *British Herpetological Society Bulletin* 3: 32–35.

Langerwerf, B. A. W. A. (1981b). The southern alligator lizard, *Gerrhonotus multicarinatus* Blainville 1935: its care and breeding in captivity. *British Herpetological Society Bulletin* 4: 21–25.

Langerwerf, B. A. W. A. (1983). Notes on the Mosor rock lizard, *Lacerta mosorensis* Kolombatovic 1886, and its reproduction in captivity. *British Herpetological Society Bulletin* 6: 20–22.

Langerwerf, B. A. W. A. (1984). The Taygetos lizard, *Lacerta graeca* Bedriaga 1886, and its reproduction in captivity. *British Herpetological Society Bulletin* 9: 25–27.

Lardie, R. L. (1965). Eggs and young of *Rhinocheilus lecontei tessellatus. Copeia*: 366.

Lardie, R. L. (1975). Additional observations on courtship and mating in the yellow mud turtle, *Kinosternon flavescens flavescens. Journal of Herpetology* 9: 223–227.

Lardie, R. L. (1978). Additional observations on courtship and mating in the Plains yellow mud turtle, *Kinosternon flavescens flavescens. Bulletin of the Oklahoma Herpetological Society* 3: 70–72.

Lardie, R. L. (1979). Eggs and young of the Plains yellow mud turtle. *Bulletin of the Oklahoma Herpetological Society* 4: 24–32.

Laszlo, J. (1969). Observations on two new artificial lights for reptile displays. *International Zoo Yearbook* 9: 12–13.

Laszlo, J. (1975). Probing as a practical method of sex recognition in snakes. *International Zoo Yearbook* 15: 178–179.

Laszlo, J. (1977). Practical methods of inducing mating in snakes using extended day lengths and darkness. *A.A.Z.P.A. Reg. Conference Proceedings*: 204–210.

Laurens, B. L. (1976). *Sceloporus malachiticus* Cope 1864. *Lacerta* 34: 142–145.

Leach, E. (1978). Techniques for breeding corn snakes. *Notes from Noah* 5(7): 11–13.

LeBuff, C. R. (1953). Observations on the eggs and young of *Drymarchon corais couperi. Herpetologica* 9: 166.

Lee, J. C. (1974). The diel activity cycle of the lizard *Xantusia henshawi. Copeia*: 934–940.

Legler, J. M. (1954). Nesting habits of the western painted turtle, *Chrysemys picta bellii* (Gray). *Herpetologica* 10: 137–144.

Legler, J. M. (1960). Natural history of the ornate box turtle, *Terrapene ornata ornata* Agassizi. *University of Kansas Publications, Museum of Natural History* 11: 527–699.

Legler, J. M. (1978). Observations on behavior and ecology in an Australian turtle, *Chelodina expansa* (Testudines, Chelidae). *Canadian Journal of Zoology* 56: 2449–2453.

Lehmann, C. and Lehmann, K. (1985). Husbandry and breeding of the ball python *Python regius* in the terrarium. *Litteratura Serpentium* 5: 64–68.

Lehmann, M. (1982). *Pseudocerastes persicus fieldi* (Schmidt) in Terrarium. *Herpetofauna* (Ludwigsburg) 4(21): 20–22.

Leloup, P. (1962). The egg-laying of *Naja melanoleuca*. *Herpetologica* 18: 71.
Leloup, P. (1964). Observations sur la reproduction du *Dendroaspis jamesoni kaimosae* (Loveridge). *Bulletin Soc. Roy. Zool. Anvers* 33: 13–27.
Lemke, T. O. (1978). Predation upon bats by *Epicrates cenchris cenchris* in Colombia. *Herpetological Review* 9: 47.
Leuck, B. E. (1985). Comparative social behavior of bisexual and unisexual whiptail lizards (*Cnemidophorus*). *Journal of Herpetology* 19: 492–506.
Levinson, S. R., Evans, M. H. and Groves, F. (1976). A neurotoxic component of the venom from Blanding's tree snake (*Boiga blandingi*). *Toxicon* 14: 307–312.
Licht, P. and Moberly, W. R. (1965). Thermal requirements for embryonic development in the tropical lizard *Iguana iguana*. *Copeia*: 515–517.
Lieberman, A. (1980). Nesting of the basilisk lizard (*Basiliscus basiliscus*). *Journal of Herpetology* 14: 103–105.
Lillywhite, H. B. (1985). Trailing movements and sexual behavior in *Coluber constrictor*. *Journal of Herpetology* 19: 306–308.
Littleford, R. A. and Keller, W. F. (1946). Observations on captive pilot black snakes and common water snakes. *Copeia*: 160–167.
Logan, T. (1969). Experiments with Gro-lux light and its effect on reptiles. *International Zoo Yearbook* 9: 9–11.
Logan, T. (1972). A method of heating reptile terraria. *International Zoo Yearbook* 12: 91–93.
Logan, T. (1973). Observations on the ball python (*Python regius*) in captivity at Houston Zoological Gardens. *Journal of the Herpetological Association of Africa* 10: 5–8.
Lopez-Jurado, L. F., Ruiz, M. and Gallego, J. (1982). Primeros datos sobre la duracion del periodo de incubacion de los huevos de *Tarentola mauritanica* en Cordoba (sur de España). *Amphibia-Reptilia* 3: 65–70.
Louw, G. N. and Holm, E. (1972). Physiological, morphological and behavioural adaptations of the ultrapsammophilous Namib Desert lizard *Aporosaura anchietae* (Bocage). *Madoqua (ser.II)* 1: 67–85.
Loveridge, A. (1956). On a third collection of reptiles and amphibians taken in Tanganyika by C. J. P. Ionides, Esq. *Journal of the Tanganyika Society*: 1–19.
Lowe, C. H., Jr. (1954). Normal field movements and growth rates of marked regal horned lizards (*Phrynosoma solare*). *Ecology* 35: 420–421.
Luckenbach, R. A. (1982). Ecology and management of the desert tortoise (*Gopherus agasizii*) in California. In Bury, R. B. (editor), *North American tortoises: Conservation and Ecology*: 1–37. Washington, D. C.
Maddocks, M. (1975). A study of the yellow faced whip snake (*Demansia psammophis*) in the field and in captivity. *Herpetofauna* 7(2): 12–13.
Madsen, T. and Osterkamp, M. (1982). Notes on the biology of the fish-eating snake *Lycodonomorphus bicolor* in Lake Tanganyika. *Journal of Herpetology* 16: 185–188.
Mahmoud, I. Y. (1967). Courtship behavior and sexual maturity in four species of Kinosternid turtles. *Copeia*: 314–319.
Mahrdt, C. R. (1976). Courtship and copulatory behavior of *Cnemidophorus tigris tigris*. (Sauria: Teiidae). *Southwest Naturalist* 21: 252–254.
Mamonov, G. (1976). Vergiftungen durch den Biss der ungiftigen Natter *Coluber ravergieri* in Russland (USSR). *Dt.Aquar. Terr. Z.* 29: 299–250.
Manders, J. H. M. (1985). Breeding results: *Thamnophis sirtalis parietalis*. *Litteratura Serpentium* 5: 79–80.
Mantel, P. (1984). Broedzorg bij *Lacerta lepida pater*(Marokkaanse parelhagedis) in het terrarium. *Lacerta* 42: 217–220.
Marais, J. (1980). *Macrelaps microlepidotis* breeding records. *Journal of the Herpetological Association of Africa* 24: 39.
Marais, J. (1984). Notes on the giant girdled lizard *Cordylus giganteus* A. Smith. *British Herpetological Society Bulletin* 10: 30–33.

Marcellini, D. L. (1971). Activity patterns of the gecko *Hemidactylus frenatus*. *Copeia*: 631–635.

Marcellini, D. L. and Davis, S. W. (1982). Effects of handling on reptile egg hatching. *Herpetological Review* 13: 43–44.

Marcellini, D. L. and Mackey, J. P. (1970). Habitat preferences of the lizards *Sceloporus occidentalis* and *S.graciosus* (Lacertilia, Iguanidae). *Herpetologica* 26: 51–56.

Marcus, L. C. (1981). *Veterinary biology and medicine of captive amphibians and reptiles*. Lea & Febiger, Philadelphia.

Marcus, L. F. (1976a). Notes on breeding behavior in a captive pair of Sonora Mountain kingsnakes (*Lampropeltis pyromelana*). *Bulletin of the Maryland Herpetological Society* 12: 23–24.

Marcus, L. F. (1976b). A reproductive record for the New Mexican ridge-nosed rattlesnake (*Crotalus willardi obscurus*). *Bulletin of the Maryland Herpetological Society* 12: 126–128.

Marion, K. R. and Sexton, O. J. (1971). The reproductive cycle of the lizard *Sceloporus malachiticus* in Costa Rica. *Copeia*: 517–526.

Markx, T. (1985). Breeding results: *Epoicrates striatus striatus*. *Litteratura Serpentium* 5: 78–79.

Marle, R. van (1982). Breeding results: *Thamnophis sirtalis parietalis*. *Litteratura Serpentium* 2: 94–95.

Marshall, A. J. and Hook, R. (1960). The breeding biology of equatorial vertebrates: reproduction of the lizard *Agama agama* Boulenger at Lat. 0°01'N. *Proceedings of the Zoological Society, London* 134: 197–205.

Martin, C. and Martin, M. (1984a). Reproductive data: Indian python *Python molurus bivittatus*. *Herptile* 9: 11.

Martin, C. and Martin, M. (1984b). Reproductive data: boa constrictor (*Constrictor c.constrictor*). *Herptile* 9: 76.

Maslin, T. P. and Walker, J. M. (1973). Variation, distribution and behavior of the lizard *Cnemidophorus parvisocius* Zweifel (Lacertilia: Teiidae). *Herpetologica* 29: 128–143.

Mattison, C. (1981). Notes on the care and breeding of the wall lizards, genus *Podarcis*, and related species. In *Proceedings of Symposium 6 of the Association of British Wild Animal Keepers*: 11–15.

Mautz, W. J. and Case, T. J. (1974). A diurnal activity cycle in the granite night lizard, *Xantusia henshawi*. *Copeia*: 243–251.

Mayer, J. (1977). The raising of northern prairie lizard hatchlings (*Sceloporus undulatus garmani*). *Colorado Herpetology* 3: 4–5.

Mayhew, W. W. (1963a). Some food preferences of captive *Sauromalus obesus*. *Herpetologica* 19: 10–16.

Mayhew, W. W. (1963b). Reproduction in the granite spiny lizard *Sceloporus orcutti*. *Copeia*: 144–152.

Mayhew, W. W. (1966a). Reproduction in the psammophilous lizard *Uma scoparia*. *Copeia*: 114–122.

Mayhew, W. W. (1966b). Reproduction in the arenicolous lizard *Uma notata*. *Ecology* 47: 9–18.

Mayhew, W. W. (1968). Biology of desert amphibians and reptiles. In Brown, G. W., Jr. (editor) *Desert Biology* 1: 196–356. Academic Press, N.Y.

McCoy, C. J. (1967). Natural history notes on *Crotaphytus wislizeni* (Reptilia: Iguanidae) in Colorado. *American Midland Naturalist* 77: 138–146.

McCoy, M. (1980). *Reptiles of the Solomon Islands*. Wau Ecology Institute 7: 80 pp.

McGinnis, S. M. and Brown, C. W. (1968). Thermal behavior of the green iguana, *Iguana iguana*. *Herpetologica* 22: 189–198.

McGurty, B. M. (1982). Hatching snake eggs: substrate considerations. *San Diego Herpetological Society Newsletter* 4: 4–5.

McIntyre, D. C. (1977). Reproductive habits of captive Trans-Pecos rat snakes (*Elaphe subocularis*). *Journal of the Northern Ohio Association of Herpetology* 3: 20–22.

McKinstry, D. M. (1983). Morphologic evidence of toxic saliva in colubrid snakes: a checklist of world genera. *Herpetological Review* 14: 12–15.

McLain, J. M. (1982). Reproduction in captive Kenya sand boas, *Eryx colubrinus loverdigei*. *Proceedings of the 5th Reptile Symposium on Captive Propagation and Husbandry*: 76–82.

Meade, G. P. (1937). Breeding habits of *Farancia abacura* in captivity. *Copeia*: 12–15.

Medica, P. A. and Arndt, R. G. (1976). Opportunistic feeding in *Sceloporus horridus* from Jalisco, Mexico. *Great Basin Naturalist* 36: 108–110.

Medica, P. A. and Turner, F. B. (1976). Reproduction by *Uta stansburiana* (Reptilia, Lacertilia, Iguanidae) in southern Nevada. *Journal of Herpetology* 10: 123–128.

Meek, R. (1983). Notes on incubation of the eggs of the grass snake *Natrix natrix natrix*. *British Herpetological Society Bulletin* 6: 36–38.

Meerman, J. (1981). Breeding results: *Thamnophis sauritus proximus*. *Litteratura Serpentium* 1: 249–250.

Meeuwen, H. M. van (1974). Eeen opmerkelijk dreiggedrag van *Lacerta lepida pater* Lataste. *Lacerta* 32: 166–167.

Mehrtens, J. M. (1962). A successful technique for exhibiting Amphisbaenids. *International Zoo Yearbook* 4: 123.

Mendelssohn, H. (1980). Observations on a captive colony of *Iguana iguana*. In Murphy, J. B. and Collins, J. T. (editors): 119–123.

Meritt, D. A., Jr. (1980). The wood turtle, *Clemys insculpta* (Le Conte) natural history, behavior and food habits. *Bulletin of the Chicago Herpetological Society* 15: 6–9.

Merzec, G. (1980). Captive propagation of the Japanese pit viper *Agkistrodon blomhoffi blomhoffi*. *Japanese Journal of Herpetology* 8: 90–94.

Miller, M. R. (1951). Some aspects of the life history of the Yucca night lizard, *Xantusia vigilis*. *Copeia*: 114–120.

Miller, M. R. (1954). Further observations on reproduction in the lizard *Xantusia vigilis*. *Copeia*: 38–40.

Miller, R. and Grall, G. (1978). Reproductive data on *Lampropeltis triangulum temporalis* from Maryland. *Bulletin of the Maryland Herpetological Society* 14: 36–38.

Millichamp, N. J. (1981). Nutritional diseases of captive reptiles. In *Proceedings of Symposium 6 of the Association of British Wild Animal Keepers*: 21–32.

Milstead, W. W. (1965). Notes on the eggs and young of the lizards *Gerrhonotus multicarinatus webbi* and *G.M.namus*. *Copeia*: 512–514.

Minakami, K. and Nakamoto, E. (1980). Hatching and early development of habu, *Trimeresurus flaviviridis*. *The Snake* 12: 11–14.

Minnich, J. E. and Shoemaker, V. H. (1970). Diet, behavior and water turnover in the desert iguana *Dipsosaurus dorsalis*. *American Midland Naturalist* 84: 496–509.

Minobe, H. (1927). Notes on the food habits of *Takydromus tachydromoides* (Schlegel). *Proceedings of the Imperial Academy of Japan* 3: 547–549.

Minton, S. A. (1966). A contribution to the herpetology of West Pakistan. *Bulletin of the American Museum of Natural History* 134: 27–184.

Mishima, S., Sawai, Y., Yamasato, S. and Sawai, K. (1977). Studies on a natural monument, Shirohebi (albino *Elaphe climacophora*) on the Iwakuni in Japan. 3. Observations on copulation, egg-laying and hatching of the Shirochebi (1). *The Snake* 9: 14–26.

Mishima, S., Sawai, Y. Yamasato, S., Toriba, M. and Sawai, K. (1976). Studies on natural monument, Shirohebi (albino *Elaphe climacophora*) on the Iwakuni in Japan. 1. Study on the captive breeding of the snakes, young shirohebi. *The Snake* 8: 69–77.

Mishima, S., Sawai, Y., Yamasato, S., Toriba, M., and Sawai, K. (1977). Studies on a natural monument, Shirohebi (albino *Elaphe climacophora*) on the Iwakuni in Japan.

2. Study on the captive breeding of the snakes, young Shirohebi (2). *The Snake* 8: 121–144.

Mitchell, J. C. (1976). Notes on reproduction in *Storeria dekayi* and *Virginia striatula* from Virginia and North Carolina. *Bulletin of the Maryland Herpetological Society* 12: 133–135.

Mitchell, J. C. (1985). Female reproductive cycle and life history attributes in a Virginia population of painted turtles, *Chrysemys picta*. *Journal of Herpetology* 19: 218–226.

Mittermeier, R. A., Rhodin, A. G. J., Medem, F., Soini, P., Hoogmoed, M. S. and Carrillo de Espinoza, N. (1978). Distribution of the South American Chelid turtle *Phrynops gibbus*, with observations on habitat and reproduction. *Herpetologica* 34: 94–100.

Mittleman, M. B. and Goris, R. C. (1974). Envenomation from the bite of the Japanese colubrid snake, *Rhabdophis tigrinus* (Boie). *Herpetologica* 30: 113–119.

Mittleman, M. B. and Goris, R. C. (1978) Death caused by the bite of the Japanese colubrid snake *Rhabdophis tigrinus* (Boie). *Journal of Herpetology* 12: 109.

Mobbs, A. J. (1979). Breeding the Kuhl's gecko *Ptychozoon kuhli*. *Herptile* 4(3): 19–23.

Mobbs, A. J. (1980). The Streak Gecko *Gonatodes vittatus*. *Herptile* 5(1): 24–26.

Mobbs, A. J. (1981a). *Lygodactylus* (day geckos) —their care and breeding. *Herptile* 6(1): 20–23.

Mobbs, A. J. (1981b). *Phelsuma* (day geckos), their care and breeding. In *Proceedings of Symposium 6 of the Association of British Wild Animal Keepers*: 3–7.

Moehn, L. D. (1974). The effect of quality of light on agonistic behavior of iguanid and agamid lizards. *Journal of Herpetology* 8: 175–183.

Moehn, L. D. (1976). The effect of sunlight on a despotism in the desert collared lizard, *Crotaphytus insularis* (Reptilia, Lacertilia, Iguanidae). *Journal of Herpetology* 10: 259–261.

Moll, D. (1976). Food and feeding strategies of the Ouachita map turtle (*Graptemys pseudogeographics ouachitensis*). *American Midland Naturalist* 96: 478–482.

Moll, E. O. and Legler, J. M. (1971). The life history of a neotropical slider turtle *Pseudemys scripta* (Schoepff) in Panama. *Bulletin of the Los Angeles County Museum of Natural History* 1: 1–102.

Montanucci, R. R. (1965). Observations on the San Joaquin leopard lizard, *Crotaphytus wislizenii silus* Stejneger. *Herpetologica* 21: 270–283.

Moore, R. G. (1978). Seasonal and daily activity patterns and thermoregulation in the southwestern speckled rattlesnake (*Crotalus mitchelli pyrrhus*) and the Colorado desert sidewinder (*Crotalus cerastes laterorepens*). *Copeia*: 439–442.

Morafka, D. J. and Banta, B. H. (1973). The distribution and microhabitat of *Xantusia vigilis* (Reptilia: Lacertilia) in the Pinnacles National Monument, San Benito and Monterey Counties, California. *Journal of Herpetology* 7: 97–108.

Morgan, D. R. (1984). The captive maintenance and reproduction of the Trans-Pecos ratsnake (*Elaphe subocularis*) at the Transvaal Snake Park. *Herptile* 9: 118–121.

Moriguchi, H. and Naito, S. (1982). Activities and food habits of *Amphiesma vibakari* (Boie) and *Rhabdophis tigrinus* (Boie). *The Snake* 14: 136–142.

Moss, P. (1985). Breeding yellow ratsnakes (*Elaphe obsoleta quadrivittata*). *Herptile* 10: 13–14.

Mount, R. H. (1963). The natural history of the red-tailed skink, *Eumeces egregius* Baird. *American Midland Naturalist* 70: 356–385.

Mowbray, L. S. (1966). A note on breeding South American tortoises, *Testudo denticulata*, at Bermuda Zoo. *International Zoo Yearbook* 6: 216.

Mudde, P. M. (1980a). Vliegende gekko's (*Ptychozoon* spec.) in het terrarium en in de kas. *Lacerta* 38: 54–55.

Mudde, P. M. (1980b). *Basiliscus vittatus* in een terrarium. *Lacerta* 38: 66–68.

Mueller, H. (1971). Ecological and ethological studies on *Cnemidophorus lemniscatus* L. (Reptilia: Teiidae) in Colombia. *Forma Functio* 4: 189–224.

Mueller, H. (1972). Ecological and ethological studies on *Iguana iguana* L. (Reptilia: Iguanidae) in Colombia. *Zool. Beitr.* 18: 109–131.

Munnig Schmidt, C. H. (1971). Waarnemingen bij het broeden van *Python sebae*. *Lacerta* 29: 105–106.

Munnig Schmidt, C. H. (1973). Verslag van een geslaagde kweek met de afrikaanse python (*Python sebae*). *Lacerta* 31: 91–101.

Murphy, J. B. (1971a). Notes on the care of the ridge-tailed monitor, *Varanus acanthurus brachyurus* at Dallas Zoo. *International Zoo Yearbook* 11: 230–231.

Murphy, J. B. (1971b). A method of immobilizing venomous snakes at Dallas Zoo. *International Zoo Yearbook* 11: 233.

Murphy, J. B. (1975). A brief outline of suggested treatments for diseases of captive reptiles. *S.S.A.R. Miscellaneous Publication* 4: 1–13.

Murphy, J. B. and Armstrong, B. L. (1978). Maintenance of rattlesnakes in captivity. *Special Publication, Museum of Natural History, University of Kansas* 3: 1–40.

Murphy, J. B., Barker, D. G. and Tyron, B. W. (1978). Miscellaneous notes on the reproductive biology of Reptiles 2. Eleven species of the family Boidae, genera *Candoia, Corallus, Epicrates* and *Python*. *Journal of Herpetology* 12: 385–390.

Murphy, J. B. and Collins, J. T. (1980) (editors). *Reproductive biology and diseases of captive reptiles. S.S.A.R. Contributions to Herpetology* 1: 1–277.

Murphy, J. B. and Guese, R. K. (1977). Reproduction in the Hispaniolan boa, *Epicrates fordii fordii*, at Dallas Zoo. *International Zoo Yearbook* 17: 132–133.

Murphy, J.B., Tryon, B. W. and Brecke, B. J. (1978). An inventory of reproduction and social behavior in captive grey-banded kingsnakes, *Lampropeltis mexicana alterna* (Brown). *Herpetologica* 34: 84–93.

Murthy, T. S. N. (1980). Some ecological observations on the Uropeltid snakes of South Indian hills. *The Snake* 12: 56–59.

Murthy, T. S. N. and Arockiasamy, R. A. A. (1977). Observations on the spiny-tailed lizard, *Uromastix hardwicki* Gray in captivity. *Geobios* 4: 167–168.

Murthy, T. S. N. and Sharma, B. D. (1975). The feeding habits of the cliff racer, *Coluber rhodorhachis* (Jan). *Journal of the Bombay Natural History Society* 75: 233.

Mushinsky, H. R. (1984). Observations of the feeding habits of the short-tailed snake, *Stilosoma extenuatum*, in captivity. *Herpetological Review* 15: 67–68.

Mushinsky, H. P., Hebrard, J. J. and Walley, M. G. (1980). The role of temperature on the behavioral and ecological associations of sympatric water snakes. *Copeia*: 744–754.

Muth, A. (1977). Eggs and hatchlings of captive *Dipsosaurus dorsalis*. *Copeia*: 189–190.

Myers, C. W. (1965). Biology of the ringneck snake, *Diadophis punctatus*, in Florida. *Bulletin of the Florida State Museum* 10: 43–90.

Nägele, V. (1984a). Breeding results: *Boaedon fuliginosus fuliginosus*. *Litteratura Serpentium* 4: 122.

Nägele, V. (1984b). Breeding results: *Elaphe obsoleta spiloides*. *Litteratura Serpentium* 4: 193.

Nägele, V. (1984c). Breeding results: *Elaphe guttata guttata*. *Litteratura Serpentium* 4: 193–194.

Nägele, V. (1984d). Breeding results: *Boiga dendrophila*. *Litteratura Serpentium* 4: 194–195.

Nägele, V. (1985). *Lamprophis fuliginosus* Boie, 1827, the brown housesnake. *Litteratura Serpentium* 5: 88–95.

Nagy, K. A. (1973). Behavior, diet and reproduction in a desert lizard, *Sauromalus obesus*. *Copeia*: 93–102.

Naulleau, G. (1970). La reproduction de *Vipera aspis* en captivité dans des conditions artificielles. *Journal of Herpetology* 4: 113–121.

Naulleau, G. (1973). Rearing the asp viper, *Vipera aspis*, in captivity. *International Zoo Yearbook* 13: 108–111.

Naulleau, G. (1977). Biologie et reproduction de la Vipère de Russel (*Vipera russelli*

Shaw 1797) en captivité. *Bulletin de la Société de Zoologie de France* 102: 492.

Naulleau, G. (1983). The effects of temperature on digestion in *Vipera aspis*. *Journal of Herpetology* 17: 166–170.

Naulleau, G. and Brule, B. van den (1980). Captive reproduction of *Vipera russelli* (Shaw 1797). *Herpetological Review* 11: 110–112.

Neill, W. T. (1949). Two cases of snake bite in New Guinea. *Copeia*: 228–229.

Neill, W. T. (1954). Evidence of venom in snakes of the genera *Alsophis* and *Rhadinea*. *Copeia*: 59–60.

Neill, W. T. and Allen, R. (1962). Parturient anaconda, *Eunectes gigas* Latreille, eating own abortive eggs and foetal membranes. *Quarterly Journal of the Florida Academy of Sciences* 25: 73–75.

Neitman, K. (1980). Captive reproduction in Sonoran black kingsnakes (*Lampropeltis getulus nigritus*). *Herpetological Review* 11: 78–79.

Nelson, D. H. and Gibbons, J. W. (1972). Ecology, abundance and seasonal activity of the scarlet snake, *Cemophora coccinea*. *Copeia*: 582–584.

Nemuras, K. (1967). Notes on the natural history of *Clemmys muhlenbergi*. *Bulletin of the Maryland Herpetological Society* 3: 80–96.

Neumann, D. (1978). De verzorging van de zwartkoppython *Aspidites melanocephalus* in het terrarium. *Lacerta* 36: 186–188.

Nichols, J. T. (1939). Data on size, growth and age in the box turtle, *Terrapene carolina*. *Copeia*: 14–20.

Nichols, T. J. (1982). Courtship and copulatory behavior of captive eastern hognose snakes, *Heterodon platyrhinos*. *Herpetological Review* 13: 16–17.

Nickerson, M. A. and Henderson, R. W. (1976). A case of envenomation by the South American colubrid *Philodryas olfersii*. *Herpetologica* 32: 197–198.

Niekisch, M. (1981). *Chamaesaura anguina* im Terrarium. *Herpetofauna* (Ludwigsburg) 3(13): 9–10.

Nijhof, E. (1984). Breeding results: *Elaphe obsoleta obsoleta*. *Litteratura Serpentium* 4: 27.

Nolan, M. (1981). Notes on the care and captive breeding of the Sinaloan milk snake (*Lampropeltis triangulum sinaloae*). *British Herpetological Society Bulletin* 4: 40–44.

Norrie, S. (1981). Notes on breeding Lilford's wall lizard (*Podarcis lilfordi*) in captivity. *British Herpetological Society Bulletin* 4: 27–29.

Norrie, S. (1982). The chain kingsnake *Lampropeltis getulus getulus*. *Herptile* 7(2): 26–28.

Norris, K. S. (1949). Observations on the habits of the horned lizard *Phrynosoma m'callii*. *Copeia*: 176–180.

Norris, K. S. (1953). The ecology of the desert iguana *Dipsosaurus dorsalis*. *Ecology* 34: 265–287.

Norris, P. (1983). Keeping *Cyclemys dentata* in captivity. *Herptile* 8: 56–57.

Nowlinski, B. (1977). Voortplanting van de Cubaanse boa, *Epicrates angulifer*, in het Terrarium. *Lacerta* 35: 144–147.

Nussbaum, R. A. and Diller, L. V. (1976). The life history of the side-blotched lizard, *Uta stansburiana* Baird and Girard, in north-central Oregon. *Northwest Science* 50: 243–260.

Ober, L. D. (1970). Reproduction in the anguid lizard *Diploglossus curtissi aporus* Schwartz. *Herpetologica* 26: 275.

Olexa, A. (1969). Breeding the common musk turtle, *Sternotherus odoratus*, at Prague Zoo. *International Zoo Yearbook* 9: 28–29.

Oliver, J. A. (1956). Reproduction in the king cobra, *Ophiophagus hannah* Cantor. *Zoologica* 41: 145–152.

Oliver, P. (1984). Unusual food items for iguanas. *Herptile* 9: 23.

Olliff, N. J. (1980). Observations of the Malayan box terrapin (*Cuora amboinensis*) in captivity. *Testudo* 1: 62–69.

Oosten, R. van (1981). Breeding results: *Elaphe guttata guttata*. *Litteratura Serpentium* 1: 249.

Oosten, R. van (1982a). Breeding results: *Trimeresurus albolabris. Litteratura Serpentium* 2: 195–196.

Oosten, R. van (1982b). The keeping and breeding of *Trimeresurus albolabris* (Bamboo viper). *Litteratura Serpentium* 2: 210–213.

Oretga, A. and Barbault, R. (1984). Reproductive cycles in the mesquite lizard *Sceloporus grammicus. Journal of Herpetology* 18: 168–175.

Osborne, S. (1985). The captive breeding of colubrid snakes. *Litteratura Serpentium* 5: 42–57.

Osman, H. (1967). A note on the breeding behavior of the Komodo dragon, *Varanus komodoensis*, at Jogjakarta Zoo. *International Zoo Yearbook* 7: 181.

Ottley, J. R. and Jacobsen, E. E. (1983). Pattern and coloration of juvenile *Elaphe rosaliae* with notes on natural history. *Journal of Herpetology* 17: 189–191.

Palmer, W. M. (1961). Notes on eggs and young of the scarlet kingsnake, *Lampropeltis doliata doliata. Herpetologica* 17: 65.

Palmer, W. M. and Braswell, A. L. (1976). Communal egg laying and hatchlings of the rough green snake, *Opheodrys aestivus* (Linnaeus) (Reptilia, Serpentes, Colubridae). *Journal of Herpetology* 10: 257–259.

Palmer, W. M. and Tregembo, G. (1970). Notes on the natural history of the scarlet snake, *Camophora coccinea copei* Jan in North Carolina. *Herpetologica* 26: 300–302.

Palmer, W. M. and Williamson, G. M. (1971). Observations on the natural history of the Carolina pigmy rattlesnake, *Sistrurus miliarius miliarius* Linnaeus. *Journal of the Elisha Mitchell Science Society* 87: 20–25.

Pandha, S. K. and Thapliyal, J. P. (1967). Egg- laying and development in the garden lizard, *Calotes versicolor. Copeia*: 121–125.

Papenfuss, T. J. (1982). The ecology and systematics of the Amphisbaenian genus *Bipes. Occasional Papers of the California Academy of Sciences* 136: 1–42.

Parker, D. R. (1981). Captive care and behavior of the southern alligator lizard (*Gerrhonotus multicarinatus*). *Journal Noah* 7: 33–37.

Parker, W. S. (1973). Natural history notes on the Iguanid lizard *Urosaurus ornatus. Journal of Herpetology* 7: 21–26.

Parker, W. S. (1974). Home range, growth and population density of *Uta stansburiana* in Arizona. *Journal of Herpetology* 8: 135–139.

Parker, W. S. and Brown, W. S. (1974). Notes on the ecology of regal ringneck snakes (*Diadophis punctatus regalis*) in northern Utah. *Journal of Herpetology* 8: 262–263.

Parker, W. S. and Brown, W. S. (1980). Comparative ecology of two colubrid snakes, *Masticophis t. taeniatus* and *Pituophis melanoleucus stejnegeri*, in northern Utah. *Milwaukee Public Museum Publications, Biology and Geology* 6: 1–104.

Parker, W. S. and Pianka, E. R. (1974). Further ecological observations on the western banded gecko, *Coleonyx variegatus. Copeia*: 528–531.

Parker, W. S. and Pianka, E. R. (1975). Comparative ecology of populations of the lizard *Uta stansburiana. Copeia*: 615–632.

Parker, W. S. and Pianka, E. R. (1976). Ecological observations on the leopard lizard (*Crotaphytus wislizeni*) in different parts of its range. *Herpetologica* 32: 95–114.

Pashley, A. I. (1981). Some observations on the care and captive breeding of Brook's gecko (*Hemidactylus brooki*). *Herptile* 6(2): 18–22.

Patterson, J. W. (1983). Frequency of reproduction, clutch size and clutch energy in the lizard *Anguis fragilis. Amphibia—Reptilia* 4: 195–203.

Patterson, R. W. (1974). Hatching the African python, *Python sebae*, in captivity. *International Zoo Yearbook* 14: 81–82.

Patterson, R. W. (1978). Hatching of Anchieta's dwarf python, *Python anchietae. International Zoo Yearbook* 18: 99–101.

Pawley, R. (1966). Observations on the care and nutrition of a captive group of marine iguanas, *Amblyrhynchus cristatus. International Zoo Yearbook* 6: 107–115.

Pawley, R. (1969a). Further notes on a captive colony of marine iguanas, *Amblyrhynchus cristatus*, at Brookfield Zoo. Chicago. *International Zoo Yearbook* 9: 41–44.

Pawley, R. (1969b). Observations on a prolonged food refusal period of an adult fer-de-lance, *Bothrops atrox asper. International Zoo Yearbook*9: 58–59.

Pawley, R. (1971). A convenient system for housing "off-exhibit" reptiles in Brookfield Zoo, Chicago. *British Journal of Herpetology* 4: 210–213.

Pawley, R. (1972). Notes on reproduction and behavior of the green crested basilisk, *Basiliscus plumifrons. International Zoo Yearbook* 12: 141–144.

Pearson, J. (1984). Tank design for ground pythons. *Herptile* 9: 109.

Pearson, O. P. (1954). Habits of the lizard *Liolaemus multiformis multiformis* at high altitudes in southern Peru. *Copeia*: 111–116.

Peels, G. (1981). *Boige dendrophila melanota*, de mangrove nacht-boomslang. *Litteratura Serpentium* 1: 132–138.

Peels, G. (1982). Ervaringen met de Amour rattenslang, *Elaphe schrenkii schrenkii. Litteratura Serpentium* 2: 19–25.

Pelt, J. van (1983). Breeding results: *Elaphe obsoleta obsoleta. Litteratura Serpentium* 3: 41–42.

Pendlebury, G. B. (1974). Stomach and intestine contents of *Corallus enhydris*: a comparison of island and mainland specimens. *Journal of Herpetology* 8: 241–244.

Perez-Higareda, G. (1981a). Nesting and incubation times in *Corytophanes hernandezi* (Lacertilia: Iguanidae). *Bulletin of the Maryland Herpetological Society* 17: 71–73.

Perez-Higareda, G. (1981b). *Sceloporus* and *Eumeces* in the diet of *Ameiva undulata amphigramma* (Lacertilia: Teiidae). *Bulletin of the Maryland Herpetological Society* 17: 78–79.

Perez-Higareda, G. (1981c). Oviposition of *Kinosternon l.leucostomum* in captivity (Testudines: Kinosternidae). *Bulletin of the Maryland Herpetological Society* 17: 80–82.

Peters, U. (1969). Some observations on the captive breeding of the Madagascan tortoise, *Testudo radiata*, at Sydney Zoo. *International Zoo Yearbook* 9: 29.

Peters, U. (1979). Second generation breeding of the cantil, *Agkistrodon bilineatus*, at Taronga Zoo. *International Zoo Yearbook* 19: 100–101.

Peterson, K. H. (1982). Reproduction in captive *Heloderma suspectum. Herpetological Review* 13: 122–124.

Petzold, H. G. (1962). Successful breeding of *Liocephalus carinatus* Gray. *International Zoo Yearbook* 4: 97–98.

Petzold, H. G. (1967). Some remarks on the breeding biology and the keeping of *Tretanorhinus variabilis*, a water snake of Cuba. *Herpetologica* 23: 242–246.

Petzold, H. G. (1969). Observations on the reproductive biology of the American ringed snake, *Leptodeira annulata*, at East Berlin zoo. *International Zoo Yearbook* 9: 54–56.

Pewtress, R. (1983). Hatching of the Cape file snake (*Mehelya capensis*) in captivity. *Herptile* 8: 115–117.

Phelps, T. (1981). *Poisonous snakes*. Blanford Press, Poole, U.K.

Phillips, C. M. (1983). Some reproductive notes on the green lizard (*Lacerta viridis*). *Herptile* 8: 99–101.

Pianka, E. R. (1970). Comparative autecology of the lizard *Cnemidophorus tigris* in different parts of its geographic range. *Ecology* 51: 703–720.

Pianka, E. R. (1971a). Comparative ecology of two lizards. *Copeia*: 129–138.

Pianka, E. R. (1971b). Ecology of the Agamid lizard *Amphibolurus isolepis* in Western Australia. *Copeia*: 527–536.

Pianka, E. R. and Parker, W. S. (1972). Ecology of the Iguanid lizard *Callisaurus draconoides. Copeia*: 493–508.

Pianka, E. R. and Parker, W. S. (1975). Ecology of horned lizards: A review with special reference to *Phrynosoma platyrhinos. Copeia*: 141–162.

Pianka, E. R. and Pianka, H. D. (1970). The ecology of *Moloch horridus* (Lacertilia: Agamidae) in Western Australia. *Copeia* 90–103.

Pickering, D. (1982). Captive maintenance and breeding of the common snake-necked turtle *Chelodina longicollis* at the Oklahoma City Zoo. In *Proceedings of the 4th Annual Reptile Symposium on captive propagation and husbandry* (Louisiana, 1980): 47–49.

Pickering, J. C. (1982). Building and heating of snake tanks. *Herptile* 7(1): 12–14.

Pillich, G. (1984). Die Zucht der Schwarzen Baumschlange *Thrasops jacksonii*. *Herpetofauna* (Ludwigsburg), 6(30): 14–16.

Platt, D. R. (1969). Natural history of the hog-nose snakes *Heterodon platyrhinos* and *Heterodon nasicus*. *University of Kansas Publications, Museum of Natural History* 18: 253–420.

Plummer, M. V. (1976). Some aspects of nesting success in the turtle *Trionyx muticus*. *Herpetologica* 32: 353–359.

Plummer, M. V. (1977a). Notes on the courtship and mating behavior of the soft-shell turtle, *Trionyx muticus* (Reptilia, Testudines, Trionychidae). *Journal of Herpetology* 11: 90–92.

Plummer, M. V. (1977b). Activity, habitat and population structure in the turtle *Trionyx muticus*. *Copeia*: 431–440.

Plummer, M. V. (1977c). Reproduction and growth in the turtle *Trionyx muticus*. *Copeia*: 440–447.

Plummer, M. V. (1981). Habitat utilization, diet and movements of a temperate arboreal snake (*Opheodrys aestivus*). *Journal of Herpetology* 15: 425–432.

Poel-Hellinga, E. M. C. (1974). Ervaringen met het houden van jonge kameleons. *Lacerta* 32: 71–73.

Poel-Hellinga, E. M. C. (1977). Nogmaals: *Chamaeleo jacksoni*. *Lacerta* 35: 47–49.

Polder, J. J. W. (1969). Feeding king cobras, *Ophiophagus hannah*, at Rotterdam Zoo. *International Zoo Yearbook* 9: 56.

Pols, J. J. van der (1980). Kweekresultaten: *Corallus enhydris enhydris*. *Litteratura Serpentium* 1: 28.

Pols, J. J. van der (1981a). Eetgedrag van *Calabaria reinhardtii*. *Litteratura Serpentium* 1: 183–185.

Pols, J. J. van der (1981b). Verzorging en kweek van *Corallus enhydris enhydris*. *Litteratura Serpentium* 1: 238–246.

Pols, J. J. van der (1982). Breeding results: *Corallus enhydris enhydris*. *Litteratura Serpentium* 2: 306.

Pooley, A. C. (1962). The Nile crocodile *Crocodylus niloticus*. Notes on the incubation period and growth rates of juveniles. *Lammergeyer* 2: 1–55.

Pooley, A. C. (1969). Preliminary studies on the breeding of the Nile crocodile, *Crocodylus niloticus*, in Zululand. *Lammergeyer* 10: 22–44.

Pope, C. H. (1958). Fatal bite of captive African rear-fanged snake (*Dispholidus*). *Copeia*: 280–282.

Porter, K. R. (1972). *Herpetology*. W. B. Saunders Co., 524 pp.

Pough, F. H. (1970). The burrowing ecology of the sand lizard *Uma notata*. *Copeia*: 145–157.

Pough, F. H., Morafka, D. J. and Hillman, P. E. (1978). The ecology and burrowing behavior of the Chihuahuan fringe-footed lizard, *Uma exsul*. *Copeia*: 81–86.

Pozio, E. (1983). The biology of freeliving and captive *Elaphe situla*. *Litteratura Serpentium* 3: 50–60.

Praedicow, G. (1984). De Chinese pauwoogschildpad (*Sacalia bealei*), een zeldzaam terrariumdier. *Lacerta* 42: 207–211.

Prestt, I. (1971). An ecological study of the viper *Vipera berus* in southern Britain. *Journal of Zoology, London* 164: 373–418.

Prieto, A. A. (1975). Reproductive cycle of the northern ringneck snake, *Diadophis punctatus edwardsi* (Merrem) in New Jersey. *Bulletin of the New Jersey Academy of Science* 20: 14–17.

Prieto, A. A. and Ryan, M. J. (1978). Some observations of the social behavior of the Arizona chuckwalla, *Sauromalus obesus tumidus* (Reptilia, Lacertilia, Iguanidae). *Journal of Herpetology* 12: 327–336.

Prieto, A. A. and Sorenson, M. W. (1975). Food preference of the Arizona chuckwalla (*Sauromalus obesus tumidus*). *Bulletin of the New Jersey Academy of Science* 20: 8–11.

Prieto, A. A. and Sorenson, M. W. (1977). Reproduction in the Arizona chuckwalla *Sauromalus obesus tumidus* (Shaw). *American Midland Naturalist* 98: 463–469.

Pritchard, P. C. H. (1979). *Encyclopedia of turtles*. TFH Publ., N.J. 895 pp.

Punzo, F. (1974). Comparative analysis of the feeding habits of two species of Arizona blind snakes, *Leptotyphlops h. humilis* and *Leptotyphlops d. dulcis*. *Journal of Herpetology* 8: 153–156.

Punzo, F. (1975). Studies on the feeding behavior, diet, nesting habits and temperature relationships of *Chelydra serpentina osceda* (Chelonia: Chelydridae). *Journal of Herpetology* 9: 207–210.

Quartero, H. W. P. (1982). Breeding results: *Thamnophis radix*. *Litteratura Serpentium* 2: 43.

Quayle, A. (1983). Notes on the diet of Erhard's wall lizard, *Podarcis erhardii*. *British Journal of Herpetology* 6: 309–310.

Quinn, H. (1977. Further notes on reproduction in *Crotalus willardi* (Reptilia, Serpentes, Crotalidae). *Bulletin of the Maryland Herpetological Society* 13: 111.

Quinn, H. and Hulsey, T. G. (1978). Growth of the cobra *Naja naja* (Serpentes: Elapidae). *Herpetological Review* 9: 138–139.

Quinn, H. R. (1979). Reproduction and growth of the Texas coral snake (*Micrurus fulvius tenere*). *Copeia* 453–463.

Quinn, H. R. and Neitman, K. (1978). Reproduction in the snake *Boiga cynodon* (Reptilia, Serpentes, Colubridae). *Journal of Herpetology* 12: 255–256.

Radcliffe, C. W. (1975). A method for force-feeding snakes. *Herpetological Review* 6: 18.

Radcliffe, C. W. and Chiszar, D. (1983). Clear plastic hiding boxes as a husbandry device for nervous snakes. *Herpetological Review* 14: 18.

Rand, A. S. (1972). The temperatures of iguana nests and their relation to incubation optima and to nesting sites and season. *Herpetologica* 28: 252–253.

Raney, E. C. and Lachner, E. A. (1942). Summer food of *Chrysemys picta marginata*, in Chautauqua Lake, New York. *Copeia*: 83–85.

Rankin, P. (1978). Notes on the biology of the skink *Sphenomorphus pardalis* (Macleay) including a captive breeding record. *Herpetofauna* 10: 4–7.

Raut, S. K. and Ghose, K. C. (1984). Nesting and egg laying behavior of the garden lizard (*Calotes versicolor*). *Herpetological Review* 15: 108.

Reagan, D. P. (1974). Habitat selection in the three-toed box turtle, *Terrapene carolina triunguis*. *Copeia*: 512–527.

Regal, P. J. (1980). Temperature and light requirements of captive reptiles. In Murphy and Collins (1980) (editors): 79–89.

Reinchenbach-Klinke, H. and Elkan, E. (1965). *The principal diseases of Lower Vertebrates*. Academic Press, 600 pp.

Reichling, S. (1982). Reproduction in captive black pine snakes *Pituophis melanoleucus lodingi*. *Herpetological Review* 13: 41.

Reid, A. (1984). Observatitons on breeding the green iguana *Iguana iguana*. *Herptile* 9: 56–59.

Reid, D. (1983). An account of reproduction in the Great Plains rat snake (*Elaphe guttata emoryi*). *Litteratura Serpentium* 3: 61–65.

Reid, D. B. (1981). The problems of reptile cage design for public display. In *Proceedings of Symposium 6 of the Association of British Wild Animal Keepers*: 16–20.

Reijst, N. R. (1980). Het houden en kweken van Thamnophissan. Deel 1. *Litteratura Serpentium* 1: 6–8.

Reijst, N. R. (1981). Het houden en kweken van Thamnophissen. Deel 2. *Litteratura Serpentium* 1: 45–52.

Reinert, H. K. (1981). Reproduction by the massasauga (*Sistrurus catenatus catenatus*). *American Midland Naturalist* 105: 393–394.
Reinert, H. K. and Kodrich, W. R. (1982). Movements and habitat utilization by the massasauga, *Sistrurus catenatus catenatus*. *Journal of Herpetology* 16: 162–171.
Renkema, H. (1981). Breeding results: *Corallus enhydris cookii*. *Litteratura Serpentium* 1: 248–249.
Reynolds, F. A. and Solberg, A. N. (1942). Notes on the life history of the mud snake. *Copeia*: 25–26.
Richards, J. (1978). Some notes on live food for reptiles and amphibians. *South Western Herpetological Society Bulletin* 1: 13–24.
Riches, R. J. (1976). *Breeding snakes in captivity*. Pet Reference Series no. 3. Palmetto Publ. Co. Florida.
Riches, R. J. (1978). Feeding hatchling *Elaphe* and *Lampropeltis*. *Herptile* 3(1): 17–19.
Riches, R. J. (1979). The Californian red-sided garter snake (*Thamnophis sirtalis infernalis*). *Herptile* 4(4): 23–25.
Riches, R. J. (1981). Maintaining ocellated skinks (*Chalcides ocellatus tiligugu*). *Herptile* 6(2): 8–9.
Riel, C. A. P. van (1976a). Voortplanting van *Thrasops jacksonii jacksonii* in het terrarium. *Lacerta* 34: 62–64.
Riel, C. A. P. van (1976b). Voortplanting in het terrarium van *Ptyas mucosus*. *Lacerta* 34: 104–107.
Riel, C. A. P. van (1977). Voortplanting van *Elaphe guttata* in een binnenterrarium met met behulp van een lange lichtperiode. *Lacerta* 35: 106–112.
Riel, C. A. P. van (1982a). Verzorging en kweek van *Epicrates striatus striatus*. *Litteratura Serpentium* 2: 54–60.
Riel, C. A. P. van (1982b). Breeding results: *Morelia spilotes variegata*. *Litteratura Serpentium* 2: 254.
Riel, C. A. P. van (1982c). Breeding results: *Elaphe guttata guttata*. *Litteratura Serpentium* 2: 254–255.
Riel, C. A. P. van (1982d). Breeding results: *Lampropeltis triangulum elapsoides*. *Litteratura Serpentium* 2: 255.
Riel, C. A. P. van (1984a). Breeding results: *Corallus caninus*. *Litteratura Serpentium* 4: 26.
Riel, C. A. P. van (1984b). *Morelia spilotes variegata* (Gray, 1842). *Litteratura Serpentium* 4: 57–62.
Riel, C. A. P. van (1984c). Reproduction of *Corallus caninus* Linnaeus 1758 in captivity. *Litteratura Serpentium* 4: 173–181.
Ripa, D. (1983a). Breeding results: *Bothrops nasutus*. *Litteratura Serpentium* 3: 42–43.
Ripa, D. (1983b). Breeding results: *Vipera ammodytes ammodytes*. *Litteratura Serpentium* 3: 43.
Risdon, D. H. S. (1982). A cheap and easy method of breeding mealworms. *Herptile* 7(2): 40.
Robinson, K. M. and Murphy, G. C. (1978). The reproductive cycle of the eastern spiny softshell turtle (*Trionyx spiniferus spiniferus*). *Herpetologica* 34: 137–140.
Robinson, M. D. and Cunningham, A. B. (1978). Comparative diet of two Namib Desert sand lizards (Lacertidae). *Madoqua* 11: 41–53.
Robinson, M. D. and Hughes, D. A. (1978). Observations on the natural history of Peringuey's adder, *Bitis peringueyi* (Boulenger) (Reptilia: Viperidae). *Annals of the Transvaal Museum* 31: 189–196.
Romer, J. D. (1979). Captive care and breeding of a little known Chinese snake *Elaphe porphyracea nigrofasciata*. *International Zoo Yearbook* 19: 92–94.
Rose, B. R. (1976). Habitat and prey selection of *Sceloporus occidentalis* and *Sceloporus graciosus*. *Ecology* 57: 531–541.
Rose, C. A. (1982). The house gecko (*Gehyra mutilata*: egg retention, artificial incubation and rearing of hatchlings. *Herptile* 7(1): 31–37.

Rösler, H. (1981). Erfolg und Mißerfolg bei der Vermehrung von *Hemitheconyx caudicinctus* (DUMERIL 1851) in Gefangenschaft. *Elaphe*: 49–54.

Rösler, H. (1983a). *Sphaerodactylus cinereus* (WAGLER 1830), ein Kugelfingergecko aus Kuba. *Elaphe*: 2–6.

Rösler, H. (1983b). Die gelungene Vermehrung einer australischen Gecko- Art, *Gehyra australis* (GRAY 1842). *Elaphe*: 49–51.

Ross, R. (1973). Successful mating and hatching of Children's Python, *Liasis childreni*. *H.I.S.S., N.J.* 1: 181–182.

Ross, R. (1978). *The python breeding manual*. Institute of Herpetological Research, 51 pp.

Ross, R. (1980). The breeding of pythons (subfamily Pythoninae) in captivity. In Murphy and Collins (1980) (editors): 135–139.

Ross, R. (1983). Reproduction of the Children's python (*Liasis childreni*) in a terrarium. *Litteratura Serpentium* 3: 18–21.

Ross, R. and Larman, R. (1977). Captive breeding in two species of python, *Liasis albertsii* and *L. mackloti*. *International Zoo Yearbook* 17: 133–136.

Rosselot, B. (1980). Une expérience d'élevage d'un Vipéridé africain, *Bitis arietans* (Merrem). *Bulletin de la Société Herpetologique de France* 14: 22.

Routman, E. J. and Hulse, A. C. (1984). Ecology and reproduction of a parthenogenetic lizard *Cnemidophorus sonorae*. *Journal of Herpetology* 18: 381–386.

Rowlands, R. P. V. (1978). Notes on the maintenance of a captive breeding group of the gecko *Hoplodactylus pacificus*. *Herpetofauna* 10: 18–19.

Rowlands, R. P. V. (1979). Notes on the green tree gecko *Naultinus elegans* including captive breeding records. *Herpetofauna* 11(1): 8–9.

Ruby, D. E. (1977). Winter activity in Yarrow's spiny lizard, *Sceloporus jarrovi*. *Herpetologica* 33: 322–333.

Ruby, D. E. (1978). Seasonal changes in the territorial behavior of the Iguanid lizard *Sceloporus jarrovi*. *Copeia*: 430–438.

Rudloff, H. W. (1982). Die Nachzucht von *Kinosternon leucostomum*. *Elaphe*: 19–23.

Ruibal, R. and Philibosian, R. (1974). The population ecology of the lizard *Anolis acutus*. *Ecology* 55: 525–537.

Ruibal, R., Philibosian, R. and Adkins, J. L. (1972). Reproductive cycle and growth in the lizard *Anolis acutus*. *Copeia*: 509–518.

Sanborn, S. R. (1972). Food habits of *Sauromalus obesus obesus* on the Nevada Test Site. *Journal of Herpetology* 6: 142–144.

Sautereau, L. (1980). Notes on the reproduction and rearing of the spiny footed lizard *Acanthodactylus erythrurus erythrurus* (Schinz 1833) Sauria: Lacertidae. *Herptile* 5(4): 16–21.

Sautereau, L. (1982). Notes on breeding the Caucasian green lizard, *Lacerta strigata* (Eichwald 1831) in an indoor terrarium. *Herptile* 7(1): 5–8.

Sautereau, L. and Bitter, P. de (1980). Notes sur l'élevage et la reproduction en captivité du varan de Timor. (Sauria—Varanidae). *Bulletin de la Société Herpetologique de France*: 4–9.

Sautereau, L. and Langerwerf, B. (1981). Notes sur l'élevage et la reproduction en captivité de *Lacerta danfordi anatolica* (WERNER, 1902). *Bulletin de la Société Herpetologique de France*: 10–16.

Savage, S. B. (1973). The housing and force-feeding of emerald tree boas, *Corallus caninus*. *International Zoo Yearbook* 13: 156–157.

Sayers, D. (1982). The eastern diamondback (*Crotalus adamanteus*) as a captive. *Journal of the Venomous Animal Society of Canada* 3: 3–4.

Saylor Done, B. and Heatwole, H. (1977). Social behavior of some Australian skinks. *Copeia*: 419–430.

Schaefer, W. H. (1934). Diagnosis of sex in snakes. *Copeia*: 181.

Schall, J. J. (1974). Population structure of the Aruban whiptail lizard, *Cnemidophorus arubensis*, in varied habitats. *Herpetologica* 30: 38–44.

arubensis, in varied habitats. *Herpetologica* 30: 38–44.

Schenone, H. and Reyes, H. (1965). Animais ponzonosos de Chile. *Bolm Chile Parasit.* 20: 104–109.

Schilt, J. van der (1981a). Kweekresultaten: *Boa constrictor constrictor. Litteratura Serpentium* 1: 158.

Schilt, J. van der (1981b). Verzorging en kweek van *Boa constrictor constrictor. Litteratura Serpentium* 1: 166–172.

Schley, K. (1976). Observations on the birth of Jackson's chamaeleons. *Notes from Noah* 4(3): 2.

Schmidt, D. (1983). Die Strahlennatter—*Elaphe radiata* (SCHLEGEL). *Elaphe*: 33–36.

Schouten, J. (1984). Breeding results: *Chondropython viridis. Litteratura Serpentium* 4: 25–26.

Schouten, J. (1985). Experiences in keeping and breeding the green tree python, *Chondropython viridis* (Schlegel, 1872), negative and positive results. *Litteratura Serpentium* 5: 122–156.

Schuett, G. W. (1978). Reproduction in captive broad-banded copperheads *Agkistrodon contortrix laticinctus. Natl. Assoc. Sound Wildlife Prog. Newsletter* 2(1): 40–42.

Sclater, P. L. (1862). Notes on the incubation of *Python sebae. Proceedings of the Zoological Society, London*: 365–368.

Scott, N. J., Wilson, D. E., Jones, C. and Andrews, R. M. (1976). The choice of perch dimensions by lizards of the genus *Anolis* (Reptilia, Lacertilia, Iguanidae). *Journal of Herpetology* 10: 75–84.

Seib, R. L. (1980). Human envenomation from the bite of an aglyphous false coral snake, *Pliocercus elapoides* (Serpentes: Colubridae). *Toxicon* 18: 399.

Selcer, K. W. and Judd, F. W. (1982). Variation in the reproductive ecology of *Holbrookia propinqua* (Sauria: Iguanidae). *Texas Journal of Science* 34: 125–135.

Sexton, O. J., Bauman, J. and Ortleb, E. (1972). Seasonal food habits of *Anolis limifrons. Ecology* 53: 182–186.

Sexton, O. J. and Claypool, L. (1978). Nest sites of a northern population of an oviparous snake, *Opheodrys vernalis* (Serpentes: Colubridae). *Journal of Natural History* 12: 365–370.

Sexton, O. J. and Marion, K. R. (1974). Duration of incubation of *Sceloporus undulatus* eggs at constant temperature. *Physiological Zoology* 47: 91–98.

Shaw, C. E. (1954). Captive bred *Cyclura macleayi macleayi. Herpetologica* 10: 73–78.

Shaw, C. E. (1960). Notes on the eggs, incubation and young of *Chamaeleo basiliscus. British Journal of Herpetology* 2: 182–185.

Shaw, C. E. (1961). Breeding the Galapagos tortoise (*Testudo elephantopus*). *International Zoo Yearbook* 3: 102–104.

Shaw, C. E. (1969). Breeding the rhinoceros iguana, *Cyclura cornuta cornuta*, at San Diego Zoo. *International Zoo Yearbook* 9: 45–48.

Sheargold, T. (1979). Notes on the reproduction of children's python, *Liasis childreni* (Gray 1842). *Herpetofauna* 10(2): 2–4.

Sherbrooke, W. C. (1975). Reproductive cycle of a tropical teiid lizard, *Neusticurus ecpleopus* Cope, in Peru. *Biotropica* 7: 194–207.

Shine, R. (1980a). Reproduction, feeding and growth in the Australian burrowing snake *Vermicella annulata. Journal of Herpetology* 14: 71–77.

Shine, R. (1980b). Ecology of eastern Australian whipsnakes of the genus *Demansia. Journal of Herpetology* 14: 381–389.

Shine, R. (1980c). Ecology of the Australian death adder *Acanthophis antarcticus* (Elapidae): evidence for convergence with the Viperidae. *Herpetologica* 36: 281–289.

Shine, R. (1980d). Comparative ecology of three Australian snake species of the genus *Cacophis* (Serpentes: Elapidae). *Copeia*: 831–838.

Shine, R. (1981). Ecology of Australian elapid snakes of the genera *Furina* and

Glyphodon. Journal of Herpetology 15: 219–224.

Shine, R. (1982). Ecology of the Australian elapid snake Echiopsis curta. Journal of Herpetology 16: 388–393.

Shine, R. (1983). Food habits and reproductive biology of Australian elapid snakes of the genus Denisonia. Journal of Herpetology 17: 171–175.

Shine, R. (1984). Reproductive biology and food habits of the Australian elapid snakes of the genus Cryptophis. Journal of Herpetology 18: 33–39.

Shine, R. and Charles, N. (1982). Ecology of the Australian elapid snake Tropidechis carinatus. Journal of Herpetology 16: 383–387.

Shine, R. and Covacevich, J. (1983). Ecology of highly venomous snakes: the Australian genus Oxyuranus (Elapidae). Journal of Herpetology 17: 60–69.

Sigg, H. (1984). Anspruchsvolle Schönheit-Anforderungen von Elaphe situla an Lebensraum und Terrarium. Herpetofauna (Ludwigsburg) 6(29): 11–20.

Sigmund, W. R. (1984). Female preference for Anolis carolinensis males as a function of dewlap color and background coloration. Journal of Herpetology 17: 137–143.

Simbotwe, M. P. (1980). Reproductive biology of the skinks Mabuya striata and Mabuya quinquetaeniata in Zambia. Herpetologica 36: 99–104.

Simmons, J. E. (1977). Reproduction of the Chinese red snake, Dinodon rufozonatum (Cantor) in captivity. Herpetological Review 8: 32.

Simon, C. A. (1975). The influence of food abundance on territory size in the iguanid lizard Sceloporus jarrovi. Ecology 56: 993–998.

Simon, C. A. (1976). Size selection of prey by the lizard Sceloporus jarrovi. American Midland Naturalist 96: 236–241.

Sims, K. J. and Singh, I. (1978). Breeding the west African dwarf crocodile, Osteolaemus tetraspis tetraspis, at Kuala Lumpur Zoo, with observations on nest construction. International Zoo Yearbook 18: 83–84.

Slavens, F. L. (1984). Inventory of live reptiles and amphibians in captivity, 1984. Seattle, Washington, 313 pp.

Smith, H. M. (1972). The Sonoran subspecies of the lizard Ctenosaura hemilopha. Great Basin Naturalist 32: 104–111.

Smith, H. M. and Taylor, E. H. (1950). An annotated checklist and key to the reptiles of Mexico exclusive of the snakes. Bulletin of the United States National Museum: 119: 1–243.

Smith, J. and Schwaner, T. D. (1981). Notes on reproduction by captive Amphibolurus nullarbor (Sauria: Agamidae). Transactions of the Royal Society of South Australia 105: 215–216.

Smith, M. A. (1935). The fauna of British India. Reptilia and Amphibia II. Sauria. 440 pp.

Smits, A. W. (1985). Behavioral and dietary responses to aridity in the chuckwalla, Sauromalus hispidus. Journal of Herpetology 19: 441–449.

Smyth, M. and Smith, M. J. (1974). Aspects of the natural history of three Australian skinks, Morethia boulengeri, Menetia greyii and Lerista bougainvillii. Journal of Herpetology 8: 329–335.

Somma, C. A. and Brooks, G. R. (1976). Reproduction in Anolis oculatus, Ameiva fuscata and Mabuya mabouya from Dominica. Copeia: 249–256.

Spawls, S. (1980). Notes on the reproduction of Psammophis elegans. British Herpetological Society Bulletin 2: 37.

Spellerberg, I. F. and Phelps, T. E. (1977). Biology, general ecology and behaviour of the snake Coronella austriaca Laurenti. Biological Journal of the Linnean Society 9: 133–164.

Spence, J. M. (1966). Observations on the Damara Chameleon Microsaura damarana Boulenger. Annals of the Cape Province Museums 5: 145–148.

Spoczynska, J. O. I. (1974). A zoo on your window-ledge. F. Muller, London, 224 pp.

Sprackland, R. G. (1976). Notes on Dumeril's monitor lizard, Varanus dumerili (Schlegel). Sarawak Museum Journal 24: 287–291.

Spruyt, G. (1984). Ervaringen met de Luipaardgecko. Terra 20: 2–4.

Staedeli, J. H. (1964). Eggs and young of the vermillion-lined ground snake *Sonora semiannulata linearis. Copeia*: 581–582.

Stafford, P. J. (1980). The short-tailed or blood python (*Python curtus*). *Herptile* 5(4): 5–8.

Stafford, P. J. (1982). Further observations of the blood python (*Python curtus*) in captivity including an effective method of induced feeding. *Herptile* 7(1): 21–22.

Stamps, J. A. (1973). Displays and social organization in female *Anolis aeneus. Copeia*: 264–272.

Stamps, J. A. (1976a). Rainfall, activity and social behavior in the lizard *Anolis aeneus. Animal Behavior* 24: 603–608.

Stamps, J. A. (1976b). Egg retention, rainfall and egg laying in a tropical lizard, *Anolis aeneus. Copeia*: 759–764.

Stamps, J. A. (1977). Rainfall, moisture and dry season growth rates in *Anolis aeneus. Copeia*: 415–419.

Stamps, J. A. and Crews, D. P. (1976). Seasonal changes in reproduction and social behavior in the lizard *Anolis aeneus. Copeia*: 467–476.

Staton, M. A. and Dixon, J. R. (1977). Breeding biology of the spectacled caiman, *Caiman crocodilus crocodilus* in the Venezuelan Llanos. *U.S. Fisheries and Wildlife Service, Wildlife Research Report* 5: 1–21.

Steehouder, A. M. (1983). The rough green snake (*Opheodrys aestivus*) in nature and in captivity. *Litteratura Serpentium* 3: 186–192.

Steehouder, A. M. (1984a). Repeated successful breeding of the red striped sand snake *Psammophis subtaeniatus sudanensis*, and some remarks on the 'polishing behaviour' of this species. *Litteratura Serpentium* 4: 90–103.

Steehouder, A. M. (1984b). Experiences with *Coluber viridiflavus carbonarius. Litteratura Serpentium* 4: 104–105.

Steehouder, T. (1985). Successful breeding of *Lampropeltis getulus floridana* (the Florida Kingsnake). *Litteratura Serpentium* 5: 110–113.

Stephenson, G. (1977). Notes on *Tiliqua gerrardii* in captivity. *Herpetofauna* 9(1): 4–5.

Stevens, T. P. (1980). Notes on thermoregulation and reproduction in *Cnemidophorus flagellicaudus. Journal of Herpetology* 14: 418–420.

Steward, J. W. (1958). The dice snake (*Natrix tessellata*) in captivity. *British Journal of Herpetology* 2: 122–126.

Stewart, G. R. (1965). Thermal ecology of the garter snakes *Thamnophis sirtalis concinnus* (Hallowell) and *Thamnophis ordinoides* (Baird and Girard). *Herpetologica* 21: 81–102.

Stewart, G. R. (1968). Some observations on the natural history of two Oregon garter snakes (genus *Thamnophis*). *Journal of Herpetology* 2: 71–86.

Stoel, P. B. (1981). Dwangvoederen: een reddende handeling? *Litteratura Serpentium* 1: 189–197.

Stoel, P. B. (1982). *Epicrates striatus striatus* catches live fish. *Litteratura Serpentium* 2: 157.

Stoffels, H. (1981). Breeding results: *Thamnophis sirtalis parietalis. Litteratura Serpentium* 1: 250.

Storer, T. I. and Wilson, B. M. (1932). Feeding habits and molt of *Crotalus confluentus oreganus* in captivity. *Copeia*: 169–173.

Stoskopf, M. K. and Hudson, R. (1982). Commercial feed frogs as a source of Trematode infection in reptile collections. *Herpetological Review* 13: 125.

Street, D. J. (1973). Notes on the reproduction of the Southern smooth snake (*Coronella girondica*). *British Journal of Herpetology* 4: 335–337.

Subba Rao, M. V. (1983). Reproduction in a fan throated lizard *Sitana ponticeriana. Herpetological Review* 14: 39.

Sugerman, R. A. and Applegarth, J. S. (1980). An instance of natural cannibalism by *Uma n. notata* Baird. *Herpetological Review* 11: 90.

Sura, P. (1981). Captive breeding of *Elaphe rufodorsata* and *Rhabdophis tigrinus* from the

Korean People's Democratic Republic. *British Herpetological Society Bulletin* 3: 20–24.

Sura, P. (1983). The second generation of captive-bred *Rhabdophis tigrinus*. *British Herpetological Society Bulletin* 7: 66–67.

Swain, T. A., Arp, F. and Younkin, R. D. (1980). A preliminary report on the ecology of a tropical, high altitude lizard, *Anadia brevifrontalis*. *Journal of Herpetology* 14: 321–326.

Switak, K. H. (1966). Notes on the nutrition and care of the Madagascar day gecko, *Phelsuma madagascariensis*, at Steinhart Aquarium. *International Zoo Yearbook* 6: 107.

Switak, K. H. (1969). First captive hatching of bushmasters, *Lachesis muta*. *International Zoo Yearbook* 9: 56–57.

Sylber, C. K. (1985). Eggs and hatchlings of the yellow giant chuckwalla and the black giant chuckwalla in captivity. *Herpetological Review* 16: 18–21.

Takenaka, S. (1980). Growth of the Japanese grass lizard *Takydromus tachydromoides* in relation to reproduction. *Herpetologica* 36: 305–310.

Tanner, W. W. and Cox, D. C. (1981). Reproduction in the snake *Lampropeltis pyromelana*. *Great Basin Naturalist* 41: 314–316.

Taub, A. M. (1967). Comparative histological studies on Duvernoy's gland of colubrid snakes. *Bulletin of the American Museum of natural history* 138: 1–50.

Teichner, O. (1978). Breeding the west African dwarf crocodile, *Osteolaemus tetraspis tetraspis*, at Metro Toronto Zoo. *International Zoo Yearbook* 18: 88–89.

Telford, S. R. (1969). The ovarian cycle, reproductive potential, and structure in a population of the Japanese lacertid *Takydromus tachydromoides*. *Copeia*: 548–567.

Tho, Y. P. and Ho, S. Y. (1979). Observations on a batch of *Gekko stentor* eggs. *Malay Nature Journal* 32: 265–269.

Thornhill, G. M. (1982). Comparative reproduction of the turtle *Chrysemys scripta elegans* in heated and natural lakes. *Journal of Herpetology* 16: 347–353.

Thorogood, J. and Whimster, I. W. (1979). The maintenance and breeding of the leopard gecko. (*Eublepharis macularius*) as a laboratory animal. *International Zoo Yearbook* 19: 74–78.

Throp, J. L. (1969). Notes on breeding the Galapagos tortoise, *Testudo elephantopus*, at Honolulu Zoo. *International Zoo Yearbook* 9: 30–31.

Tielemans, H. (1981). Kweekresultaten: *Boa constrictor constrictor*. *Litteratura Serpentium* 1: 72.

Tielemans, H. (1982a). Breeding results: *Boa constrictor constrictor*. *Litteratura Serpentium* 2: 44.

Tielemans, H. (1982b). Breeding results: *Boa constrictor constrictor*. *Litteratura Serpentium* 2: 44–45.

Tinkle, D. W. (1957). Ecology, maturation and reproduction of *Thamnophis sauritus proximus*. *Ecology* 38: 69–77.

Tinkle, D. W. (1962). Reproductive potential and cycles in female *Crotalus atrox* from northwestern Texas. *Copeia*: 306–313.

Tinkle, D. W. (1967). The life and demography of the side-blotched lizard, *Uta s. stanaburiana*. *Miscellaneous Publications, Museum of Zoology, University of Michigan* 132: 1–182.

Tinkle, D. W. (1973). A population analysis of the sagebrush lizard, *Sceloporus graciosus* in southern Utah. *Copeia*: 284–296.

Tinkle, D. W. and Hadley, N. F. (1973). Reproductive effort and winter activity in the viviparous montane lizard *Sceloporus jarrovi*. *Copeia*: 272–277.

Tiser, J. (1980). Die Vermehrung von *Elaphe dione* (Pallas 1773) im Terrarium. *Elaphe*: 38–40.

Tiwari, K. K. (1961). The eggs and flight of the gecko *Ptychozoon kuhli* Stejneger from Car Nicobar. *Journal of the Bombay Natural History Society* 58: 523–527.

Tokarz, R. R. and Jones, R. E. (1979). A study of egg-related maternal behavior in

*Anolis carolinensis* (Reptilia, Lacertilia, Iguanidae). *Journal of Herpetology* 13: 283–288.

Tonge, S. (1985). The management of juvenile Telfair's skinks *Leiolopisma telfairii* with particular reference to the role of ultra violet light. In Townson and Lawrence (editors): 61–72.

Townson, S. (1978). Notes on the Haitian boa, *Epicrates striatus striatus*. *British Herpetological Society Newsletter* 18: 11–14.

Townson, S. (1985). The captive reproduction and growth of the yellow anaconda (*Eunectes notaeus*). In Townson and Lawrence (editors): 33–43.

Townson, S. and Lawrence, K. (1985) (editors). *Reptiles breeding, behaviour and veterinary aspects*. British Herpetological Society, 124 pp.

Townson, S., Millichamp, N. J., Lucas, D. G. D. and Milwood, A. J. (1980) (editors). *The care and breeding of captive reptiles*. British Herpetological Society, 98 pp.

Trautwein, S. N. (1983). Hatching in captivity of a clutch of *Sceloporus undulatus hyacinthinus* eggs. *Herpetological Review* 14: 15–16.

Tremper, R. L. (1978). The captive care of hatchling tortoises. *Herpetological Review* 9: 14–15.

Tremper, R. L. (1982). A note on the use of black light fluorescent tubes for reptiles. *Herptile* 7(1): 19–20.

Trutnau, L. (1984). *Liasis albertisii*—ein seltener Terrariengast. *Herpetofauna (Ludwigsburg)* 6(28): 17–21.

Tryon, B. W. (1975). How to incubate reptile eggs: a proven technique. *Bulletin of the New York Herpetological Society* 11: 33–37.

Tryon, B. W. (1978a). Some aspects of breeding and raising aquatic chelonians: Part I. *Herpetological Review* 9: 15–19.

Tryon, B. W. (1978b). Some aspects of breeding and raising aquatic chelonians: Part II. *Herpetological Review* 9: 58–61.

Tryon, B. W. (1978c). Reproduction in a pair of captive Arizona ridge-nosed rattlesnakes, *Crotalus willardi willardi* (Reptilia, Serpentes, Crotalidae). *Bulletin of the Maryland Herpetological Society* 14: 83–88.

Tryon, B. W. (1979). Reproduction in captive forest cobras, *Naja melanoleuca* (Serpentes: Elapidae). *Journal of Herpetology* 13: 499–504.

Tryon, B. W. (1980). Observations on reproduction in the West African dwarf crocodile with a description of parental behavior. In Murphy and Collins (editors): 167–185.

Tryon, B. W. (1985). Snake hibernation and breeding: in and out of the zoon. In Townson and Lawrence (editors): 19–31.

Tryon, B. W. and Carl, G. (1980). Reproduction in the mole kingsnake, *Lampropeltis calligaster rhombomaculata* (Serpentes, Colubridae). *Transactions of the Kansas Academy of Science* 83: 66–73.

Tryon, B. W. and Hulsey, T. G. (1977). Breeding and rearing the bog turtle, *Clemmys muhlenbergii*, at the Fort Worth Zoo. *International Zoo Yearbook* 17: 125–130.

Tryon, B. W. and Radcliffe, C. W. (1977). Reproduction in captive lower California rattlesnakes, *Crotalus enyo enyo* (Cope). *Herpetological Review* 8: 34–36.

Tucker, J. K. (1976). Observations on the birth of a brook of Kirtland's water snake, *Clonophis kirtlandi* (Kennicott) (Reptilia, Serpentes, Colubridae). *Journal of Herpetology* 10: 53–54.

Tucker, J. K. (1977). Notes on the food habits of Kirtland's water snake, *Clonophis kirtlandi*. *Bulletin of the Maryland Herpetological Society* 13: 193–195.

Van Aperen, W. (1969a). Notes on the artificial hatching of iguana eggs, *Iguana iguana*, at Melbourne Zoo. *International Zoo Yearbook* 9: 44–45.

Van Aperen, W. (1969b). Notes on the breeding of bearded dragons, *Amphibolurus barbatus* at Melbourne Zoo. *International Zoo Yearbook* 9: 51–52.

Vandeventer, T. L. and Schmidt, M. (1977). Caesarean section on a western gaboon viper, *Bitis gabonica rhinoceros*. *International Zoo Yearbook* 17: 140–142.

Vanhoof, L. (1985). Breeding results: *Thamnophis sirtalis similis*. *Litteratura Serpentium* 5: 79.

Van Mierop, L. H. S. and Barnard, S. M. (1976). Observations on the reproduction of *Python molurus bivittatus* (Reptilia, Serpentes, Boidae). *Journal of Herpetology* 10: 333–340.

Van Mierop, L. H. S. and Barnard, S. M. (1978). Further observations on thermoregulation in the brooding female *Python molurus bivittatus* (Serpentes: Boidae). *Copeia*: 615–621.

Van Mierop, L. H. S. and Bessette, E. L. (1981). Reproduction of the ball python, *Python regius*, in captivity. *Herpetological Review* 12: 20–22.

Vanzolini, P. R. (1953). Sobre a diferenciacao geografica de *Gymnodactylus geckoides* (Sauria, Gekkonidae). *Pap. avulsos do dep. de Zool.* 9: 263–270.

Vejerslev, L. O. (1985). Breeding results: *Pituophis melanoleucus catenifer*. *Litteratura Serpentium* 5: 77.

Vernet, R. (1978). Recherches sur l'ecologie de *Varanus griseus* Daudin (Reptilia, Sauria, Varanidae) dans les écosystèmes sableux du Sahara nord-occidental (Algérie). *Bulletin de la Société Herpetologique de France* 5: 30.

Vernet, R. (1982). Étude écologique de *Varanus griseus* Daud. au Sahara nord-occidental. *Bulletin de la Société Herpetologique de France* 23: 33.

Veron, J. E. N. (1969a). The reproductive cycle of the water skink, *Sphenomorphus quoyi*. *Journal of Herpetology* 3: 55–63.

Veron, J. E. N. (1969b). An analysis of stomach contents of the water skink, *Sphenomorphus quoyi*. *Journal of Herpetology* 3: 187–189.

Veron, J. E. N. and Heatwole, H. (1970). Temperature relations of the water skink, *Sphenomorphus quoyi*. *Journal of Herpetology* 4: 141–153.

Verstappen, F. (1981). Breeding results: *Corallus enhydris cookii*. *Litteratura Serpentium* 1: 247–248.

Verstappen, F. (1982). An idea to make young *Epicrates striatus striatus* eat. *Litteratura Serpentium* 2: 155.

Vest, D. K. (1981). Envenomation following the bite of a wandering garter snake (*Thamnophis elegans vagrans*). *Clinical Toxicology* 18: 573.

Vinegar, A. (1973). The effects of temperature on the growth and development of embryos of the Indian python, *Python molurus* (Reptilia: Serpentes: Boidae). *Copeia*: 171–173.

Visch, A. (1985). Breeding results: *Boa constrictor*. *Litteratura Serpentium* 5: 77–78.

Visser, D. (1972). Het bouwen en inrichten van een kas voor het houden van Terrariumdieren. *Lacerta* 30: 67–71.

Vitt, L. J. (1982a). Reproductive tactics of *Ameiva ameiva* (Lacertilia: Teiidae) in a seasonally fluctuating tropical habitat. *Canadian Journal of Zoology* 60: 3113–3120.

Vitt, L. J. (1982b). Sexual dimorphism and reproduction in the microteiid lizard, *Gymnophthalmus multiscutatus*. *Journal of Herpetology* 16: 325–329.

Vitt, L. J. (1983). Reproduction and sexual dimorphism in the tropical teiid lizard, *Cnemidophorus ocellifer*. *Copeia*: 359–366.

Vitt, L. J. and Goldberg, S. R. (1983). Reproductive ecology of two tropical iguanid lizards: *Tropidurus torquatus* and *Platynotus semitaeniatus*. *Copeia*: 131–141.

Vitt, L. J. and Lacher, T. E. (1981). Behavior, habitat, diet and reproduction of the iguanid lizard *Polychrus acutirostris* in the Castinga of northeastern Brazil. *Herpetologica* 37: 53–63.

Vitt, L. J. and Ohmart, R. D. (1977a). Ecology and reproduction of lower Colorado River lizards: I. *Callisaurus draconoides* (Iguanidae). *Herpetologica* 33: 214–222.

Vitt, L. J. and Ohmart, R. D. (1977b). Ecology and reproduction of lower Colorado River lizards: II. *Cnemidophorus tigris* (Teiidae). *Herpetologica* 33: 223–234.

Vogel, Z. (1964). *Reptiles and amphibians their care and behaviour*. Studio Vista 228 pp.

Vokins, M. (1981). Kweekresultaten: *Elaphe obsoleta rossalleni*. *Litteratura Serpentium* 1: 157.

Voris, H. K. and Glodek, G. S. (1980). Habitat, diet and reproduction of the file snake, *Acrochordus granulatus*, in the Straits of Malacca. *Journal of Herpetology* 14: 108–111.

Voris, H. K. and Jayne, B. C. (1979). Growth, reproduction and population structure of a marine snake, *Enhydrina schistosa* (Hydrophiidae). *Copeia*: 307–318.

Voris, H. K., Voris, H. H. and Liat, L. B. (1978). The food and feeding behavior of a marine snake, *Enhydrina schistosa* (Hydrophiidae). *Copeia*: 134–146.

Vosjoli, P. de (1978). Notes on the captive care and maintenance of day geckos *Phelsuma lineata* and *Phelsuma quadriocellata*. *National Association Sound Wild. Prog. Newsletter* 2(1): 67–69.

Vries, S. de (1983). Reproduction of *Boa constrictor ortonii* (Cope) in captivity. *Litteratura Serpentium* 3: 157–161.

Wagemaker, J. A. (1972). Richtlijnen voor het houden van kameleons met enkele notities over een vijftal soorten. *Lacerta* 30: 99–106.

Wagner, E. (1974). Breeding the leopard gecko, *Eublepharis macularius*, at Seattle Zoo. *International Zoo Yearbook* 14: 84–86.

Wagner, E. (1976). Breeding the Burmese python, *Python molurus bivittatus*, at Seattle Zoo. *International Zoo Yearbook* 16: 83–85.

Wagner, E. (1980). Gecko husbandry and reproduction. In Murphy and Collins (editors): 115–117.

Wagner, E., Smith, R. and Slavens, F. (1976). Breeding the gila monster, *Heloderma suspectum*, in captivity. *International Zoo Yearbook* 16: 74–78.

Wales, W. (1982). A versatile vivarium design for snakes and a cautionary tale. *Herptile* 7(4): 19–22.

Walker, J. M. (1966). Morphology, habitat and behavior of the teiid lizard, *Cnemidophorus labialis*. *Copeia*: 644–650.

Walker, J. M. (1980). Reproductive characteristics of the San Pedro Martir whiptail *Cnemidophorus martyris*. *Journal of Herpetology* 14: 431–432.

Walker, J. M. (1982). Reproductive characteristics of the Colima giant whiptail *Cnemidophorus communis communis* Cope. *Southwest Naturalist* 27: 241–243.

Wallace, I. (1978). Observations on captive lizards of the genera *Acanthosaura* and *Calotes*. *South Western Herpetological Society Bulletin* 1: 10–12.

Wallach, J. D. (1970). Nutritional diseases of exotic animals. *Journal of the American Veterinary Medicine Association* 157: 583–599.

Wallach, J. D. (1971). Environmental and nutritional diseases of captive reptiles. *Journal of the American Veterinary Medicine Association* 159: 1632–1643.

Wallach, V. (1980). Interspecific and intraspecific predation in captive bush vipers, (*Atheris squamiger* Hallowell, 1854), with notes on different colour phases. *Journal of the Herpetological Association of Africa* 24: 2–3.

Walsh, R. (1980). Egg-laying and rearing of *Testudo marginata*. *Testudo* 1: 48–50.

Walsh, T. (1977). Husbandry and breeding of *Chondropython viridis*. *National Association Sound Wildl. Prog. Newsletter* 1(2): 10–22.

Walsh, T. and Davis, S. (1978). Observations on the husbandry and breeding of the rufous-beaked snake, *Rhamphiophis oxyrhynchus rostratus*, at the National Zoological Park. *Bulletin of the Maryland Herpetological Society* 14: 75–78.

Ward, R. and Harrell, E. H. (1978). A restraining apparatus for unanesthetized snakes. *Herpetological Review* 9: 139–140.

Warner, S. (1979). Observations on captive snakes: Asiatic Rock Pythons. *South Western Herpetological Society Bulletin* 2: 17–18.

Warrell, D. A., Ormerod, L. D. and Davidson, N. McD. (1976). Bites by the night adder (*Causus maculatus*) and burrowing vipers (genus *Atractaspis*) in Nigeria. *The American Journal of Tropical Medicine and Hygiene* 25: 517–524.

Warren, J. W. (1953). Notes on the behavior of *Chionactis occipitalis*. *Herpetologica* 9: 121–124.

Watchman, G. (1979). A captive breeding record of the skink *Leiolopisma otagense*. *Herpetofauna* 10(2): 15–16.

Watson, G. (1969). Notes on the care of Mastigure lizards, *Uromastix acanthinurus*, at Jersey Zoo. *International Zoo Yearbook* 9: 49–50.

Weaver, W. G. (1970). Courtship and combat behavior in *Gopherus berlandieri*. *Bulletin of the Florida State Museum* 15: 1–43.

Webb, G. J. W., Messel, H. and Magnusson, W. (1977). The nesting of *Crocodylus porosus* in Arnhem Land, Northern Australia. *Copeia*: 238–249.

Weber-Semenoff, D. (1977). Mating behaviour of *Eirenis collaris* (Menetries) in captivity. *Academy of Science U.S.S.R., Proceedings of the Zoological Institute* 74: 36–38 (in Russian; English summary).

Welch, K. R. G. (1978a). Observations on captive snakes: courtship and mating in the colubrid *Drymarchon corais couperi*. *South Western Herpetological Society Bulletin* 1: 2–3.

Welch, K. R. G. (1978b). Notes on the pit viper *Trimeresurus albolabris* in captivity, with a special note on newborn young. *South Western Herpetological Society Bulletin* 1: 8–9.

Welch, K. R. G. (1982a). Observations on some Moroccan reptiles with a specific note on newborn *Haemorrhois hippocrepis hippocrepis* (Linnaeus). *South Western Herpetological Society Bulletin* 4: 21–22.

Welch, K. R. G. (1982b). *Herpetology of Africa: A Checklist and Bibliography of the Orders Amphisbaenia, Sauria and Serpentes*. R. Krieger, Florida, 293 pp.

Welch, K. R. G. (1983). *Herpetology of Europe and Southwest Asia: A Checklist and Bibliography of the Orders Amphisbaenia, Sauria and Serpentes*. R. Krieger, Florida, 135 pp.

Wells, E. (1980). Husbandry of the eastern mud snake (*Farancia abacura abacura*). *Northern Ohio Association of Herpetology Notes* 7(9): 9–12.

Wells, R. (1980). Eggs and young of *Pseudonaja textilis textilis*. *Herpetofauna* 12(1): 30–32.

Wells, R. (1981). Remarks on the prey preferences of *Hoplocephalus bungaroides*. *Herpetofauna* 12(2): 25–28.

Welzel, A. (1981). Die Nachzucht von *Anolis oculatus montanus* im Terrarium. *Herpetofauna (Ludwigsburg)* 3(13): 22–24.

Werb, K. (1979). Artificial incubation of the eggs of the Aesculapian snake (*Elaphe longissima*). *Herptile* 4(1): 31–32.

Werb, K. (1980a). Notes on the leopard snake, *Elaphe situla*, with comments on the maintenance of this species in captivity. *British Herpetological Society Bulletin* 2: 29–30.

Werb, K. (1980b). Notes on breeding the leopard gecko in captivity, *Eublepharis macularius*. *Herptile* 5(4): 9–10.

Werner, D. I. and Miller, T. J. (1984). Artificial nests for female green iguanas. *Herpetological Review* 15: 57–58.

Werner, Y. L. and Goldblatt, A. (1978). Body temperature in a basking gekkonid lizard, *Ptyodactylus hasselquistii* (Reptilia, Lacertilia, Gekkonidae). *Journal of Herpetology* 12: 408–411.

West, L. W. (1981). Notes on captive reproduction and behavior in the Mexican Cantil (*Agkistrodon bilineatus*). *Herpetological Review* 12: 86–87.

Wharton, C. H. (1966). Reproduction and growth in the cottonmouth, *Agkistrodon piscivorus*. Lacepede, of Cedar Keys, Florida. *Copeia*: 149–161.

Wijk, B. van (1985). Breeding results: *Diadophis punctatus*. *Litteratura Serpentium* 5: 32.

Wilhoft, D. C. (1963). Reproduction in the tropical Australian skink, *Leiolopisma rhomboidalis*. *American Midland Naturalist* 70: 442–461.

Willemsens, N. M. C. (1971). Enkele ideeên voor de bouw van eenvoudige terraria. *Lacerta* 30: 14–16.

Williams, K. L. (1978). Systematics and natural history of the American milk snake, *Lampropeltis triangulum*. *Milwaukee Public Museum Publications, Biology and Geology* 2: 1–258.

Wilson, D. (1959). The hatching and rearing of the cobra *Naja melanoleuca*. *British Journal of Herpetology* 2: 159–162.

Woerkom, A. B. van (1981). Het voederen van *Eryx colubrinus loveridgei*. *Litteratura Serpentium* 1: 181–182.

Woerkom, A. B. van (1984). Breeding results: *Elaphe obsoleta rossalleni*. *Litteratura Serpentium* 4: 28–29.

Wolf, J. (1985). Successful breeding of *Epicrates cenchria* (Linnaeus 1758). *Litteratura Serpentium* 5: 58–63.

Wolk, L. P. (1985). Beobachtungen zur Nachzucht von Würfelnattern (*Natrix tessellata*) im Zimmerterrarium. *Elaphe*: 44–45.

Wolverkamp, J. (1985). Breeding results: *Thamnophis radix haydeni*. *Litteratura Serpentium* 5: 76.

Wright, A. H. and Wright, A. A. (1957). *The handbook of snakes of the United States and Canada*. Cornell University Press, Vol. 1.

Wright, A. S. (1986). Notes on breeding the Florida kingsnake, *Lampropeltis getulus* floridana Blanchard, in captivity. *Journal of the Association for the study of Reptilia and Amphibia* 3: at press.

Wright, D. (1982). The maintenance of *Vipera berus* in captivity. *Herptile* 7(3): 2–4.

Yadav, R. N. (1967). A note on the breeding of pythons, *Python molurus*, at Jaipur Zoo. *International Zoo Yearbook* 7: 182–183.

Yadav, R. N. (1969). Breeding the mugger crocodile, *Crocodylus palustris*, at Jaipur Zoo. *International Zoo Yearbook* 9: 33.

Yamamoto, K. (1975). An observation on copulation of the lizard *Takydromus tachydromoides*. *Japanese Journal of Herpetology* 6: 52.

Yntema, C. L. (1976). Effects of incubation temperatures on sexual differentiation in the turtle, *Chelydra serpentina*. *Journal of Morphology* 150: 453–462.

Yntema, C. L. (1978). Incubation times for eggs of the turtle *Chelydra serpentina* (Testudines: Chelydridae) at various temperatures. *Herpetologica* 34: 274–277.

Zehr, D. R. (1969). Mating, ejaculate, egg laying and hatching of the fox snake, *Elaphe vulpina vulpina*. *Journal of Herpetology* 3: 180–181.

Zeiller, W. (1969). Maintenance of the yellowbellied seasnake, *Pelamis platurus*, in captivity. *Copeia*: 407–408.

Zovichian, W. H. (1971a). Captive nesting of bog turtles. *Bulletin of the Maryland Herpetological Society* 7: 43–45.

Zovichian, W. H. (1971b). Humidity as a growth factor in hatchlings of *Clemmys muhlenbergi*. *Bulletin of the Maryland Herpetological Society* 7: 93–95.

Zwart, P. and Van Ham, B. (1980). Keeping, breeding and raising garter snakes (*Thamnophis radix*). In Townson and others (editors): 81–85.

Zweifel, R. G. (1962). Notes on the distribution and reproduction of the lizard *Eumeces callicephalus*. *Herpetologica* 18: 63–65.

Zweifel, R. G. (1980). Aspects of the biology of a laboratory population of kingsnakes. In Murphy and Collins (editors): 141–152.

Zweifel, R. G. and Lowe, C. H. (1966). The ecology of a population of *Xantusia vigilis*, the desert night lizard. *American Museum Novitates* 2247: 1–57.

Zwinenberg, A. (1976a). De boomsnuffelaar (*Dryophis nasuta*). *Aquariumwereld* 29: 8–10.

Zwinenberg, A. (1976b). *Leptophis ahaetulla* een onbekende boomslang uit tropisch Afrika. *Aquariumwereld* 29: 78–83.

Zwinenberg, A. (1977). *Leptophis ahaetulla*. *Dt. Aquar. Terr. Z.* 30: 64–68.

# Index to scientific names